FLORIDA STATE
UNIVERSITY LIBRARIES

FEB 2 1994

TALLAHASSEE, FLORIDA

WINSTON CHURCHILL
Architect of Peace

**Recent Titles in
Contributions in Political Science**

Professional Developments in Policy Studies
Stuart Nagel

County Governments in an Era of Change
David R. Berman, editor

First World Interest Groups: A Comparative Perspective
Clive S. Thomas

Cold War Patriot and Statesman: Richard M. Nixon
Leon Friedman and William F. Levantrosser, editors

Legislators, Law and Public Policy: Political Change in Mississippi and the South
Mary DeLorse Coleman

Provisional Irish Republicans: An Oral and Interpretive History
Robert W. White

The Political World of a Small Town: A Mirror Image of American Politics
Nelson Wikstrom

Ownership, Control, and the Future of Housing Policy
R. Allen Hays, editor

The Presidency in an Age of Limits
Michael A. Genovese

Leftward Ho! V. F. Calverton and American Radicalism
Philip Abbott

Public Administration in China
Miriam K. Mills and Stuart S. Nagel, editors

Public Policy in China
Stuart S. Nagel and Miriam K. Mills, editors

Minority Group Influence: Agenda Setting, Formulation, and Public Policy
Paula D. McClain, editor

WINSTON CHURCHILL
Architect of Peace

*A Study of Statesmanship
and the Cold War*

STEVEN JAMES LAMBAKIS

Contributions in Political Science, Number 322
Colin Gray, Series Editor

GREENWOOD PRESS
Westport, Connecticut • London

Library of Congress Cataloging-in-Publication Data

Lambakis, Steven James.
   Winston Churchill, architect of peace : a study of statesmanship and the Cold War / Steven James Lambakis.
     p. cm.—(Contributions in political science, ISSN 0147-1066 ; no. 322)
   Includes bibliographical references and index.
   ISBN 0-313-28823-2 (alk. paper)
   1. Great Britain—Foreign relations—1945- 2. Churchill, Winston, Sir, 1874-1965. 3. United States—Foreign relations—1945-1953.
4. World politics—1945-1955. 5. Cold War. I. Title. II. Series.
DA588.L34   1993
941.084'092—dc20   92-42674

British Library Cataloguing in Publication Data is available.

Copyright © 1993 by Steven James Lambakis

All rights reserved. No portion of this book may be reproduced, by any process or technique, without the express written consent of the publisher.

Library of Congress Catalog Card Number: 92-42674
ISBN: 0-313-28823-2
ISSN: 0147-1066

First published in 1993

Greenwood Press, 88 Post Road West, Westport, CT 06881
An imprint of Greenwood Publishing Group, Inc.

Printed in the United States of America

The paper used in this book complies with the Permanent Paper Standard issued by the National Information Standards Organization (Z39.48-1984).

10 9 8 7 6 5 4 3 2 1

Copyright Acknowledgments

The author and publisher gratefully acknowledge permission to reprint the following copyrighted material:

Excerpts from *Winston S. Churchill: His Complete Speeches.* Edited by Robert Rhodes James. New York: Chelsea House Publishers, 1974.

Excerpts from *Never Despair: Winston S. Churchill 1945-1965* by Martin Gilbert. Boston: Houghton Mifflin Company, 1988. British Commonwealth rights granted by Curtis Brown Group Ltd, London on behalf of the Estate. Copyright The Estate of Sir Winston S. Churchill.

To my Dad,

James M. Lambakis,

in Memory

Contents

Foreword ix

Preface xi

1. Introduction 1

2. Some Elements of Churchill's Political Understanding 7

3. The Grand Alliance: Grand Forces, Great Men, and a Grave New World 33

4. Churchill at Fulton: The Precarious Peace 85

5. Churchill's Postwar Statesmanship
   Part I: Force and International Politics 109

6. Churchill's Postwar Statesmanship
   Part II: Negotiation and Persuasion 131

7. Conclusion 163

Bibliography 175

Index 181

Foreword

In this splendid book Steven Lambakis both explains Winston Churchill the statesman and allows that explanation to raise themes and questions central to the quality of international life. *Winston Churchill—Architect of Peace* is an essay on statesmanship using as its vehicle the person who is all but synonymous with the concept in the twentieth century. The contrast could scarcely be greater between Lambakis' book, which is anchored in history, philosophy, and personality, and much of the arid theorizing that passes for scholarship today in the field of international relations.

The story told in these pages is fraught with paradox, at the least with apparent oppositions. For example, the relationship between the theory and the practice of statecraft is a constant theme. In a felicitous judgment the author advises that "the sword and the soapbox gave life to the pen." I wonder how many of the leading contemporary contributors to international relations theory have either wielded the sword or stood upon the soapbox. Personal experience at "the sharp end" of statecraft certainly is not everything, indeed it can be overvalued, but at least such a credential helps remind one that statecraft is a practical matter and not a thing of beauty apart, a fine art.

Other dualisms, or nexi, developed well in this book include those between peace and justice, between arming and parleying, between realism in statecraft and ethical principles, and between great men and their times. *Winston Churchill—Architect of Peace* is about a principled realist who understood that although statecraft is the art of the possible, it is an art that needs to be guided by the shining light of a clear vision of the desirable. A thought triggered by reading this book is that many statesmen and would-be statesmen can be identified as big—as contrasted with small—people. By that simplistic, roughcut distinction, I mean that there are political leaders who think on a broad canvas that includes a significant temporal element and there are those who do not. Also, I must add, there are those who think big, but who happen to think wrong! Great men and women are not necessarily good men and women.

Such qualities as scope and temporal range of vision and a sense of moral purpose are as rare among political leaders and high officials as they are slighted in the scholarly literature. It is a hallmark of statesmanship that "the vision thing," as former President George Bush once observed self-revealingly, is all but second nature. Moreover, as Churchill exemplified by his action and extolled in his spoken and written words, a lasting peace can be fashioned only on the basis of a tolerably just international order. True statesmen answer the large questions correctly. Churchill was emphatically right about the nature of the U.S.S.R., as, in their turns, were Ronald Reagan and Margaret Thatcher. The practice of statecraft without a principle and vision readily degenerates into an opportunistic drift from one tactical expedient to another. In the words of the old adage: if you don't know where you are going, any road will take you there.

Winston Churchill—Architect of Peace is a book about the largest questions of international peace and security and is rooted concretely in the inspiring life and times of a man who virtually defines what we mean by a statesman.

Colin S. Gray,
Chairman,
The National Institute for Public Policy

Preface

The aim of this book is twofold—to explain a rather complex and little-examined period in the career of Winston S. Churchill, and to expand the reader's understanding of statesmanship. Statesmanship, understood in the classic sense (the sense taken here), means purposeful political action—action that is directed toward the improvement of the political community.[1] It combines the contemplation of political ends and an understanding of enduring, universal principles with activity in the political realm. Action without guidance from higher principle is foolish, while philosophic reflection on political things without any attempt to use it is idle. To study Churchill is to study this art of combining, and balancing, thought with action.

Understanding Churchill's statesmanship during World War II and the early Cold War period can be rather challenging. He appeared sometimes to have abandoned his principled stand against communism, even willing to sacrifice western security interests to further his rather ambitious and controversial diplomatic initiatives. He also has been accused of seeking confrontation with the Soviet Union and pursuing policies that began the Cold War between East and West. What are we to make of all this? By way of exploring some of the issues of his day, examining in detail his written and spoken words, studying his political consistency, and outlining a few of the principles he cherished, this book is intended to bring some order to existing scholarship regarding this period of Churchill's life.

Winston Churchill—Architect of Peace reflects Churchill's long-held belief that peace "is to be labored after." It is a tribute to the important contributions he made to those postwar policies that, in fact, had granted the West nearly a half century of relative peace in the face of a very dynamic and dangerous threat. The title of this work reflects his postwar goal of constructing in the world, hand in hand with the United States and other freedom-loving states, a "temple of peace," an arrangement among the democracies that would help them to secure their safety and their liberties.

Peace, of course, cannot be "designed" and "built" according to some blueprint; for the art of politics cannot be practiced to such rigorous standards. It also is not true that peace is beyond our grasp; we do not have to accept our fate. In the pursuit of peace, then, there is a role for political action or statesmanship. To be sure, it is an inexact science; statesmen cannot take refuge in mathematical certainties. They must deal comprehensively with all of life's frictions and humanity's caprice. The theme of this work is: statesmanship that incorporates the necessary political and practical wisdom reflected in Churchill's activities has been, and can be, our earthly salvation.

I was a student at the Catholic University of America in Washington, D.C. when the major share of the writing for this book was completed. I am grateful, therefore, to the university for its support and the individuals who provided some very welcome and important criticisms, especially Drs. James P. O'Leary, Christopher Kelly, and Joan Barth Urban. In addition, I would like to thank Dr. Colin Gray of the National Institute for Public Policy for his guidance and Dr. Larry Arnn and Matt Spalding of the Claremont Institute in Montclair, California for their helpful comments leading up to the final preparation of this book. I am, of course, solely responsible for any and all errors found in this work.

I would like to give special acknowledgement and thanks to Chelsea House Publishers for permission to reprint excerpts from *Winston S. Churchill: His Complete Speeches*, edited by Robert Rhodes James, and to Houghton Mifflin Company and Curtis Brown for permission to reprint portions of the final volume of Martin Gilbert's masterful biography, *Winston S. Churchill: Never Despair*.

I have dedicated this book to my father, James M. Lambakis, whose example in life and undying love for his family always will be my inspiration.

And for providing the necessary sustenance for my living and happiness, I am grateful for the love and moral support I receive without fail from my wife Tracie and my son Matthew.

NOTE

1. See, for example, the explanation of Aristotle: If the goal is to understand politics, "must we not rather abide by the maxim that in matters of action the end is not to study and attain knowledge of the particular things to be done, but rather to do them? Surely, *knowing* about excellence or virtue is not enough: we must try to possess it and *use it*" (emphasis added). Aristotle, *Nicomachean Ethics*, trans. Martin Oswald (Indianapolis: Bobbs-Merrill, 1979), p. 295 or 1179b1-4.

And wherever men are fighting against barbarism, tyranny, and massacre, for freedom, law, and honour, let them remember that the fame of their deeds, even though they themselves be exterminated, may perhaps be celebrated as long as the world rolls round.

—Winston Churchill

WINSTON CHURCHILL
Architect of Peace

Chapter 1

Introduction

The movement in Eastern Europe and the former Soviet Union toward political and economic reform near the close of the present century gives warrant for millions to hope that a long and terrifying chapter in world history on twentieth century totalitarianism finally has reached its conclusion. The infamy of these decades, together with the new terrors of the nuclear age, lent a novel and frightening character to international politics. The Soviet Union's Lenin and Stalin, Germany's Hitler, Cuba's Castro, and North Korea's Kim Il-Sung all had exhibited a feverish ideological agenda that suffocated the traditions and belittled the more temporal ambitions of their past rulers. Indeed, the international system in this century came to be recognized as one composed of states that varied as much in principle as in culture and geography. Additionally, discoveries in the physical sciences introduced a weapon capable of taking wars to the very extreme and jeopardizing the existence of whole nations. As Leon Trotsky once noted, and his observation rings true even today, "[a]nyone desiring a quiet life has done badly to be born in the twentieth century."[1]

While the twentieth century cast this pall of radicalism over the world, the case also can be made that modernity has changed very little. Despite indications that mankind has embarked on a new political journey, the nature of peace and war, state goals, the permanency and universality of human ambitions, vices, and virtues fundamentally have not been altered by history. Happily, there is still room for great men, men of grand visions, men capable of defying "fate" and leaving their mark on the world. The evidence of our age is that history has not abolished or diminished statesmanship. The revolutions of 1990 and 1991 have demonstrated that communism is not irreversible, and that ideology and regimes driven by the ideological impulse do have limits. Even in an age when events are "driven" by the relentless march of History, a man still can turn the political tides with the force of his ideas and the energy of his own relentless ambition and action.

If one had to choose one man from this century who best embodied this spirit of confident statesmanship, one would have to consider, most notably, Winston S. Churchill.[2] Churchill wrote of his famous ancestor, John Churchill, the great strategist and statesman the Duke of Marlborough, that "in a portrait or impression the human figure is best shown by its true relation to the objects and scenes against which it is thrown, and by which it is defined."[3] And this is how we shall view Churchill.

Born in the Victorian age, Winston Churchill lived to witness and actively participate in two very different and remarkable eras of human history. He saw the world in the most glorious of times, and he looked on in times when it was filled with ignominy and hatred. The writings and speeches of Churchill arguably may be considered the foremost resource for understanding war and peace in this current age. Churchill himself fought in numerous wars in Asia and Africa. A renowned journalist, he chronicled many of the confrontations that he either participated in or simply witnessed. By the turn of the century his occupation had become that of the consummate politician, though, much to the joy and benefit of future generations, he never ceased to write for the public prints. For more than half a century thereafter, in one capacity or another, he would provide controversial and inspirational leadership for Great Britain. Indeed, many of his later years were consumed in leading the entire free world.

As a source of inspiration and a font of political wisdom, the brilliancy of Winston Churchill's statesmanship before and during the second world war is difficult to deny. However, his statesmanship after that war has not received the attention or the praise to match, despite the acclaim he received for the speech delivered at Fulton, Missouri in 1946. The assessments of his postwar activities have been far from unanimous in assent or dissent. Despite his unblemished record of bitter opposition to the political systems and doctrines of the Communists, Churchill's postwar initiatives to reach an accommodation with the Soviet leaders caused consternation among many in his Conservative Party (even in his own cabinet) and among Britain's allies. One purpose of this book is to examine the apparent contradiction in Churchill's policies during the immediate postwar years, to look at the question and the nature of political consistency, and to deepen our understanding of the nature of peace in the nuclear age. Because of the timeless character of Churchill's political understanding, the discussion here has relevancy even in the post-Cold War era.

One of the least mutable factors in the international system is the persistence of disagreement, sometimes violent disagreement, among the states that compose it. In Chapter two, we will begin with Churchill's assessments of war; for by understanding war and its causes, we can begin to understand the sources of stability and peace. Churchill believed that peace was but an interval between two wars. Often the seeds of war are sown at the conclusion of the last one. How men managed the peace after the victory, he thought, would determine the fates of many nations. Wars were nearly always avoidable. Familiarity with man's past (including those moments of political folly and brilliance), adequate forethought, and decisive action, action compelled along a rational course, are all

Introduction

elements of statesmanship critical to this task. To avoid war, Churchill reminded his readers in June 1936, "that effort must be practical. Sentiment by itself is no good; fine speeches are worse than useless; shortsighted optimism is a mischief; smooth, soothing platitudes are a crime."[4] Churchill stood by this assessment throughout his career.

Churchill recognized that the radically heterogeneous nature of the international system was a critical factor in the life of states. There are, in other words, regimes that are more peaceably inclined than others, and these generally took the form of liberal democracy. The collective interests of these states, he believed, mandated their continuous association with one another on issues involving common security. In Chapter two, the genesis of Churchill's aspiration to achieve strength with the unity of all states that base their political order on principles of freedom unfolds and shall be developed further in subsequent chapters. Unity is vital, Churchill believed, especially in light of the new threats posed to the liberal polities. Chief among those new threats very early on was Bolshevism. Churchill initially campaigned vigorously for the destruction of what he saw as a state run by criminals and barbarians. His initial opposition to this form of tyranny was unbending, even to the point of withholding diplomatic recognition from the fledgling Soviet government.

The imperative of survival eventually brought the totalitarian East and free West together in a most unnatural marriage so that their combined forces could be welded together to defeat Nazi German aggression on the Continent. The formation of the Grand Alliance was viewed as a momentous event not only for the victory it was almost assured of delivering, but also for the hope it generated that a lasting peace could be founded in the immediate aftermath of the war. Churchill was among those who nurtured this optimism. The American political commentator Walter Lippmann similarly believed that the postwar foreign policy of the United States ought to be dedicated to continuing the wartime alliance with the Soviet Union after the victory. Such an alliance would be essential to the "general order of the nations," and it would permit the United States to meet her manifold commitments abroad. He wrote the following in his *U.S. Foreign Policy: Shield of the Republic*:

Combined action by America, Britain, and Russia is the irreducible minimum guarantee of the security of each of them, and the condition under which it is possible even to begin to establish any wider order of security.

The formation of this nuclear alliance must in our thinking and in our action take precedence over all other considerations.[5]

The marriage of convenience among Great Britain, the United States, and the Soviet Union, Churchill believed, if acted upon rightly, could be transformed into a more solid international union. The stakes, after all, were enormous. The vital interests of all the great states would be affected. New precautions had to be taken to better ensure that these same states would not stumble once again into war. "Great quarrels," he maintained, "arise from small occasions but seldom from small causes."[6]

The conclusion of the second world war, in Churchill's own words, had been marked by triumph and tragedy. The establishment of a bloc of despotic political orders across Eastern Europe marred the triumph of the Grand Alliance over Hitler's totalitarianism and arrogant aggression. The seeds of future international confrontation once again had been sown. Once again the sower came and labored uninvited and almost unnoticed. These issues will be reviewed in Chapter three.

The onset of the nuclear age did not alter the validity of Churchill's insights into the causes of war. The violation and nonfulfillment of the Yalta accords by Stalin and the perceived aggressive intentions of his communist state worried Churchill sufficiently to supplement his pleadings for a lasting settlement with calls for military vigilance and unity among the western democracies. At Fulton, Churchill laid before his American audience a grand strategy for dealing with the new threats to Europe and the world. Chapter four will consider this speech in some detail. The "Sinews of Peace," after all, laid the groundwork for Churchill's postwar foreign policy, which he implemented to satisfy the needs of security with both diplomatic and military measures. Strength must precede negotiation, he warned, but a final settlement with the Soviet Union, if it could be realized, was the greater objective of his strategy.

The need for military strength will be examined more closely in chapter five, while Chapter six will concentrate on Churchill's diplomatic initiative to reach a lasting accommodation with the Soviet leaders. In order to understand Churchill's political consistency, one needs to examine its complexity. His was a two-fisted approach, both in the sense that force was necessary to support negotiations and in the sense that Churchill was aiming to secure a stable peace from two different directions (pounding the enemy with "containment" type policies on the one hand and bold diplomatic overtures on the other).

The emphasis on appeasement or accommodation did not mean Churchill had "sold out" to the Communists or abandoned his convictions. Similarly, talk of an "iron curtain" or the need to build thermonuclear weapons did not translate well into jingoism, McCarthyism, or a lust for war and confrontation. Consistency, it will be shown, could be found in his commitment to the principles of liberal democracy, his grand regard for the virtues of military preparedness, and his aspiration to fashion within the world the alliances, organizations, and proper attitudes among the most prominent statesmen to secure a true and firmly grounded peace.

Churchill's aspirations for peace went further than most people may have liked, for his objectives extended well beyond containment and a formal settlement treaty. He believed that true international harmony would come only once communism had been deposed as the single largest threat to the free world. This would have meant, of course, that the Soviet Union (or its successor state) would have had to cease its revolutionary activities and engage in more normal diplomatic behavior. To effect such a transformation within the main fortress of communism by welcoming the Soviet leaders into the "community of nations" was the final objective of Churchill's postwar statesmanship. He believed that the future peace and prosperity of the world hinged upon the closer cooperation of all the major powers in matters of security, economy, and diplomacy. The key to this achievement lay in the discovery of national interest and recognition that it is the desire of all or most peoples to prosper and live well in conditions of freedom.

While Churchill never was entirely candid with Stalin about these objectives—for how could he have approached the Soviet leader as a subversive?—he fixed his sights upon them nonetheless and hoped that greater ties between East and West would subtly effect a political transformation. Churchill prudently hedged his initiative by pressing simultaneously for greater military strength, including the development of nuclear weapons. Again, it is important to keep in mind the complexity of Churchill's statesmanship, that he never intended to go to the negotiating table without coercive measures in hand. Neither did he trumpet his call to arms without leaving an avenue open to peaceful negotiation.

Winston Churchill, were he alive today, no doubt would be smiling. For what he had striven for seems to be within reach. The postwar objective that consumed him was total reconciliation between East and West; and if not a satisfactory reconciliation, then he would have settled for the diminution of the threat posed by the East and the mitigation of communist revolutionary influence worldwide. What statesmanship by western leaders could not accomplish in the East-West relationship (other than by the founding of a very effective western collective security arrangement—NATO), time apparently has managed to achieve. Over the years, communism as an ideology has faded, the economies of the Soviet-styled political orders have deteriorated, and many former communist leaders are ironically looking to the West for answers. It was Churchill who, perhaps slightly ahead of his time, repeatedly expressed his belief that within the political and economic structures of the West, Soviet leaders would find hope for the future well-being of their people.

NOTES

1. Cited by Isaiah Berlin, "Political Ideas in the Twentieth Century," *Foreign Affairs* (April 1950), p. 351.

2. Churchill sometimes expressed his belief that there was a process of natural selection at work in the world and that some men were destined or inclined toward greatness. See Winston S. Churchill, *Marlborough: His Life and Times*, bk. 1 vol. 1 (London: George G. Harrap & Co., Ltd., 1958), p. 136.

3. Churchill, *Marlborough*, bk. 1, vol. 1, p. 19.

4. Winston S. Churchill, *Step By Step: 1936-1939* (New York: G.P. Putnam's Sons, 1939), p. 26.

5. Walter Lippmann, *U.S. Foreign Policy: Shield of the Republic* (Boston: Little, Brown and Company, 1943), p. 164.

6. Winston S. Churchill, *The Second World War*, vol. *1*, *The Gathering Storm*, (Boston: Houghton Mifflin Company, 1948), p. 266.

Chapter 2

Some Elements of Churchill's Political Understanding

> There is no high explosive so powerful as the soul of a free people.
> —Winston Churchill[1]

Before we can understand Churchill's statesmanship following the second world war, we must first come to terms with his understanding of the nature of interstate politics. Since Churchill never published a systematic treatise on government, there is some danger in assuming that he even had a rigorous scheme of theories or a bedrock of first principles. Churchill, like Edmund Burke, was leery of the theoretician, the purveyor of abstractions. Said Burke, in the opening pages of his *Reflections On The Revolution In France*:

But I cannot stand forward, and give praise or blame to any thing which relates to human actions, and human concerns, on a simple view of the object, as it stands stripped of every relation, in all the nakedness and solitude of metaphysical abstraction. Circumstances (which with some gentlemen pass for nothing) give in reality to every political principle its distinguishing colour, and discriminating effect.[2]

A statesman, rather, is best advised to pay strict attention to facts, historical events, and traditions.

Churchill lived to act, not to theorize, to participate on the world stage, not to publish academic treatises. This, though, is an insufficient account of this man's life. For in fact he wrote great books. Churchill's writings are enlivened throughout, and reliably so, with great ideas and penetrating insights. Despite his belief early in life that "a man's Life must be nailed to a cross of either Thought or Action," thought and action came together in the story of Sir Winston Spencer Churchill.[3] Indeed, a mark of his greatness is that he so successfully combined action with thought.

Great political, ethical, and historical questions never interested Churchill until he completed his formal schooling and entered into the service of His Majesty's Government in The Fourth Hussars in Bangalore, India.[4] Inspiration to delve into the riches of history and learn the words and deeds of the great men escaped his impressive mental gaze until that time when he decided to make his mark on the world in the military and, later, political arenas. Then did the words and ideas flow; then did the encapsulated social, political, and military theories take their form. The sword and the soapbox gave life to the pen and inspired this century's most famous and learned orator, author, and statesman.

This chapter will outline broadly Churchill's understanding of certain attributes of international politics, which, by his own account, are permanent in character. Even a sketchy picture should offer a sufficient understanding of his thoughts on government and international relations and assist our efforts to define his post-World War II policies toward the Soviet Union. By establishing a "Churchillian" world view, it is hoped that consistent patterns in his thoughts and actions can be established.

This chapter also will introduce us to the limits of statesmanship and politics, limits that even Churchill attempted to expand by his post-World War II diplomacy—to no tragic end. There was perhaps no man more well-versed on the nature of modern politics. However, even Churchill fell short, but not by much, in his understanding of the rigidity of Soviet politics and ideology and the possibilities open to men to structure lasting peace or to avoid war.

WAR

Churchill believed war to be one of the rare constants in international politics. War was, by his own definition, a most natural phenomenon among states. As it has for centuries, contests over competing interests and ideas take place in an essentially lawless world order. The keenest expressions of this phenomenon is the military battle and the defensive preparations nations undertake in order to offset the disposition of other nations to make war. War is ever present and influences every level of foreign policymaking, regardless of the point in history and the character of the states that compose the international system.

On the eve of the conflict with Nazi Germany, Churchill reiterated this one undeniable fact about the international system: "the history of the human race is a history of war, and the records of thousands of years show only a few uneasy intervals of peace."[5] In other words, the natural flow of state relations will bring forth conflict as long as this flow remains uninterrupted. If peace is to be won, it must be labored after. Men must work to create those "intervals" if their lives are not to be consumed by attention to survival.

The war against Hitler could have been avoided almost up to its very inception. In his first volume of *The Second World War*, entitled *The Gathering Storm*, Churchill exhorted his readers to understand just how it was that the peaceful nations let peace slip through their fingers and permitted "The

Unnecessary War." Indeed, as if to point out the degree to which statesmen influence the prospects for peace and war, the theme of *The Gathering Storm*, boldly announced at the outset, is "How the English-speaking peoples through their unwisdom, carelessness, and good nature allowed the wicked to rearm."

His thoughts on the fundamental proclivities of states remained unchanged even after this mighty conflict. In a speech delivered to the people of Norway on May 13, 1948, Churchill urged his audience never to forget that life is a continuous struggle. Hold high the banner of freedom, he exhorted them, for which so many had so nobly sacrificed their lives. A state's security primarily rests on this foundation.[6] A state is "safe" to the extent it is prepared to uphold its sacred principles and secure its survival, since the reality of the international struggle and the inherent nastiness of the world always will preside over the scene whether a nation holds high its banner or cowers behind fortress walls. Disarmament initiatives, to further the explanation, always are to be held suspect, for they are many times the product of political ideas that deny this fundamental reality.[7]

It would be wrong to presume that Churchill relished the prospect of war or revelled in its glory. The battlefield revolted him, so he recorded in his history of the first world war, for the vile acts of "utter folly and barbarism" that were often perpetrated upon them.[8] He recognized that wars brought out the truly wicked in men, who then preyed upon the innocent. Martin Gilbert, Winston Churchill's official biographer, relates that "with each successive [warring] experience [in his youth]—in India, in Africa, and in Europe—he was to remain emphatic that, however just he, or society, might regard a war, it could only lead to suffering and misery."[9]

Although war is a prominent feature in world politics, its inevitability in almost any particular instance does not follow. If Churchill's tenet of international relations is that wars will happen, it would be superseded by one more pure and accurate: "There are no certainties in human life or in the life of states."[10] This is not to say that general laws of nature escape the human intellect, nor that statesmanship is impossible. Churchill meant to convey, rather, that human activity is filled with variables that make accurate prediction of a state's actions tenuous at best. It is the statesman's task to utilize what can be known in conjunction with his sense of what is probable.

Statesmen act upon compulsions of interest or power (national and personal), glory, and ideas, embracing historical and eternal objectives, all of which defy rigorous empirical science. One critical observer noted that one cannot even assume that a statesman will choose life or survival above all else. Political theorist Raymond Aron understood that "there are goals for which the individual accepts a risk of death. The same is true of collective units. . . . Security can be a final goal: to be without fear is a fate worthy of envy; but power, too, can be a final goal: what does danger matter once one has known the intoxication of ruling."[11]

Churchill reminded his readers of this in his tale of the second world war that it is easy for historians and others who do not have to live and act from day to day to say that Hitler would have conquered the world if he had been left alone for another two or three years before attacking Poland. However, this made little sense, he noted. Hitler was resolved to hurry and make war while he was in his prime.[12] By living and acting day to day, a man has the opportunity to experience the frictions of life and the capricious natures of other men, especially in politics. A good statesman, therefore, is one who understands the human things, who is a decent judge of character and a learned appraiser of men and regimes. Aristotle argued this point in his *Nichomachean Ethics*:

Each man can judge competently the things he knows, and of these he is a good judge. Accordingly, a good judge in each particular field is one who has been trained in it, and a good judge in general, a man who has received an all-round schooling. For that reason, a young man is not equipped to be a student of politics; for he has not experience in the actions which life demands of him, and these actions form the basis and subject matter of the discussion [politics].[13]

Churchill's success stemmed from his own experience and his understanding of the experience of others, which requires a thorough education about the past.[14]

Political knowledge must accompany the desire to prevent war. Nothing is inevitable in politics for the very reasons that life is made up of so many intangibles and that men can change the course of events through statesmanship. Churchill possessed a powerful faith in his own ability to direct and influence political activities. He sought with persistence throughout his career to reconcile nations hostile to one another; for international hatreds disposed men to military battle. However, sometimes war cannot be avoided when the safety, lives, and freedoms of ordinary people are at stake. "War is horrible, but slavery is worse."[15]

Sometimes war can be avoided only if the targeted or victimized countries prepare to make war. Angered by the lethargy and inaction of the democracies, Churchill commented on the rueful beginnings of the second world war. He insisted that there hardly ever could have been a war more easy to prevent than this one.

I have always been ready to use force in order to defy tyranny or ward off ruin. . . . In their loss of purpose, in their abandonment even of the themes they most sincerely espoused, Britain, France, and most of all, because of their immense power and impartiality, the United States, allowed conditions to be gradually built up which led to the very climax they dreaded most.[16]

The preservation of order relies upon the abilities of nations to maintain armaments and alliances. Indeed, he believed that "the lucid intervals of peace and order only occur in human history after armaments in the hands of strong governments have come into being."[17] In Churchill's eyes, both moral and physical forces must be brought together to support the reign of law in the world. Put an end to the quarrels, in other words enact "moral disarmament,"[18] if a weapons disarmament is desired. On several occasions after the war against the

Axis Powers, Churchill reaffirmed his earlier conclusions. On one occasion in May 1947, he argued that war was not inevitable, but it would be if western leaders, the United States and Great Britain, were to follow the policy of appeasement and unilateral disarmament.[19]

An important tool for the preservation of peace for Churchill was an international alliance based upon the principle of collective security. This shall be discussed in more detail in Chapter four, but for now let it be established that Churchill looked upon these collective political assemblies with great faith. Following the second world war he was to look to the United Nations Organization as one of the vital workhorses for peace. Before that conflict, he gave his all to defend and secure the survival of the League of Nations, which represented "the noblest and most coherent endeavor of the peoples of the world to escape from the horrors of war by confronting aggression collectively with serious deterrents."[20] Alliances, regional pacts, and international conferences and organizations could work to tip the precarious balance between peace and war in favor of establishing a community of interests in the world, or in a particular region of the world, as far as it was possible.

All this said, it would be grossly inaccurate to conclude that some wars were not more apt to occur than others. At times, the flow of events are too conclusive, too grand, to be diverted. Consider the first great war of this century. "I do not think," wrote Churchill,

that any movements on the European chessboard could have prevented the challenge to world peace sooner or later of the ever-growing overweening military power and temper of Germany. . . . [G]iven the world as it was at the beginning of the Twentieth Century, I doubt if anything could have averted the hideous collision.[21]

Despite the most noble exertions to find alternatives to direct conflict, certain international arrangements and regimes are more inclined to foster the conditions of war. As the 1930s progressed and Hitler prepared for conquest, the probability that statesmanship could call a halt to the madness decreased with the passage of time. Here was a case where opportunities and hope were lost over time through shortsightedness and imprudent policies and action.

Some wars have their origins in events that stem from a conflict of principles, and hence, may be beneficial, if this term can be used, to mankind. Churchill considered that the "great American Civil War . . . must upon the whole be considered the noblest and least avoidable of all the great mass-conflicts of which till then there was record."[22] This war was fought not only to rid a nation of the vile institution of slavery, but also to reunite a union and the national trust in the Declaration of Independence. Democratic men like Churchill incline themselves to civilized rule, lawful order, and a decent respect for the rights of man. When these liberal principles are jeopardized or besieged, the avoidance of war is not necessarily the preferred alternative. He understood that there was no equality between right and wrong. "The great causes and principles for which Britain and the United States have suffered and triumphed are not mere matters of the balance of power."[23]

As we shall see, Churchill evinced a remarkable sensitivity for the tragic nature of politics. He reflected upon the unfortunate and tragic outcome of the second world war and unhappily concluded that "from every version of success, however great, comes forward something to make a greater struggle necessary."[24] Part of the tragedy of politics is that peace is often elusive, and it is so despite the strength of all who will it. Of the tragic 1930s Churchill wrote that "[n]early all European States are anxious for a quiet life . . . although this may involve them in much greater troubles later on."[25] No finer tale is told of man's accursed situation than when Churchill related the trials and tribulations experienced by his great ancestor, the Duke of Marlborough, in his quest to restrain the tyrant Louis XIV from dominating Europe. Peace was within reach at many stages of that long conflict, which marred the beginning of the eighteenth century. "All sought peace," he wrote, "and all failed to find it."[26]

In 1936, Churchill wrote that "the vast central mass of mankind, including no doubt a majority of the populations of communist and Nazi countries, would like to be let alone to live in peace."[27] The violation and destruction of our private lives and property is the proper definition of both war and tyranny, and are clear-cut evils within Churchill's political understanding. Certainly men and nations always are poised for survival, and war is a constant feature of world politics. Reason can help mitigate some of the harsh circumstances in which men find themselves. Through the practice of statesmanship, most notably, men can reduce the extent to which the anarchy of the international system threatens their political order.

On the one hand, wars can be avoided through artful manipulation and forethought. On the other hand, despite the passion men have for peace, harmonious relations often are elusive for the reasons that some rulers have objectives beyond mere survival and some events have an inexorable quality about them. Nations hold certain ideals and principles high enough to warrant the mobilization of the citizenry to fight an inspired and vigorous battle in their defense. War is not always the worst evil, nor is it the worst alternative.

LIBERAL AND DESPOTIC POLITICAL ORDERS

Another attribute of the international system that demands recognition by all who lay claim to understanding state relations is the existence of a variety of regimes, or forms of government. Churchill excelled in his understanding of politics because he perceived that different states pursued different goals, and that the governments of these states possessed corresponding institutions, moral qualities, and characteristic methods for achieving those goals.[28] Again we can turn to Aristotle to further our own understanding of teleology and political things. He wrote in his *Rhetoric* that one could understand the qualities of governments in the same way as one learns the qualities of individuals, "since they are revealed in their deliberate acts of choice; and these are determined by the end that inspires them."[29] As Churchill said of the threatening and aggressive powers of the 1930s: "These are the heaving, thrusting, pulsating organisms which think and act with purpose."[30] States are creations of nature; they possess dynamic life, and only with extreme difficulty are they likened to the deadness of "billiard balls," units that function by cause and effect in the service of "stability."[31] To abstract from the existing complex teleology in the formulation of a theory of international relations is to depict a soulless international order, a system of states that are devoid of purpose and found lacking in the very spring that lends vibrancy and drama to state relations.

For Churchill, the regimes of this century essentially are either liberal or despotic in nature. The international system is composed of an entire spectrum of variations between these two poles. In its essence, this scheme retains Aristotle's own categories of states discussed in *The Politics*, which places the different governments, to simplify his treatment somewhat, as either working for justice or injustice, for or against the common good.[32] Let us explore in some detail the composition of these two different orders.

Political democracy was the archetypical liberal order in Churchill's scheme. In a speech in Brussels, November 1945, Churchill spoke about the future of Europe and the roles that the themes of democracy and liberty would play in the physical and moral restoration of that war-torn continent. As he had done on many prior occasions, Sir Winston took the time to describe the "practical tests" by which the virtue and reality of political democracy could be measured:

Does the Government in any country rest upon a free, constitutional basis. . . ? Is there the right of free expression of opinion, free support, free opposition, free advocacy, and free criticism of the Government of the day? Are there Courts of Justice free from interference by the Executive or from threats of mob violence, and free from all association with particular political parties? . . . . Will the rights of the individual, subject to his duties to the State, be maintained, asserted, and exalted? In short, do the Government own the people, or do the people own the Government? Here are some of the more obvious tests by which the political health and soundness of *any* community may be ascertained.[33]

Above all, he insisted, there must be tolerance and respect for minority rights.

There is no question that freedom for Churchill meant political freedom, and that political freedom was prior to all other freedoms. Law is the basis of the liberal order and the best guarantor of freedom for the citizens. Churchill pointed out that we must reach all the way back to Alfred The Great in the ninth century to discover what he referred to as the founding of English common law, ultimately the source of all the lawful orders as we know them today.[34] These English precepts, virtually a "blend of the Mosaic code with Christian principles and old Germanic customs," were continually amplified over the centuries and became part of an established body of jurisprudence that eventually would secure the liberties of millions of people.

The Magna Carta, or the Great Charter of Liberties, was the first instrument that broadly affirmed the principle that properly orders the Crown under the force of law. *Rex non debet esse sub homine, sed sub Deo et lege.*[35] This document constituted one of the first checks upon personal government "with all its latent possibilities of oppression and caprice. . . ." In a 1943 speech at Harvard, in the midst of a grueling struggle against the tides of oppressive rule, Churchill reiterated his position on the nature of good government:

Law, language, literature—these are considerable factors. Common conceptions of what is right and decent, a marked regard for fair play, especially to the weak and poor, a stern sentiment of impartial justice, and above all the love of personal freedom, or, as Kipling put it, 'Leave to live by no man's leave underneath the law'— these are common conceptions on both sides of the ocean among the English-speaking peoples.[36]

The people, as we read in the lengthy passage quoted above, are to be the rulers to the extent that their opinions should guide and control the actions of those elected or appointed to hold public office. Men who hold the public trust are not to set their own agendas upon taking their official seats. Rather, a constant relationship between the people and the rulers should be established so that government remains, recalling the words of Abraham Lincoln, "of the people, by the people, and for the people."

In a 1947 speech to the House of Commons, Churchill repeated his belief that "democracy is the worst form of Government except all those other forms that have been tried from time to time." He concluded that despite this sometimes very inefficient form of governance, "there is the broad feeling in our country that the people should rule" since their liberties are at stake.[37] Here it becomes apparent that certain regime types are more contributory to a quiet existence for its citizenry.

In the tradition of Montesquieu, John Locke, and *The Federalist*, Churchill strongly favored the division of power in the Constitution. In other words, "societies in quiet years should be constructed [with] overwhelming force on the side of the rulers [and] innumerable objections to the use of any part of it."[38] Democratic leaders ought to be obliged to work in an upright manner on the problems of the polity. To best ensure this, checks ought to be placed on the powers of the different branches of government in order to disallow their interference in all of the functions of government and to restrict their attention to the powers granted them by the constitution or common law. The idea that circulated in the Nazi and communist orders that a group of "superplanners," with their unlimited powers, could better know the needs of the people is antithetical to good government and democracy, for it violates the basic institutions of liberty.[39]

Churchill never succumbed to the forces of relativism and the arguments of ethnocentricity, to the extent that these concepts thrived in his time. As a thoroughly liberal man, he did not hesitate to declare that these principles of government were necessary to the political health of any community. He believed that the passion for freedom and democracy was universal. This is not to say that Churchill understood all other forms of government to be thoroughly unfit for man. Through his profound experiences in politics and knowledge of history, however, this learned parliamentarian came to recognize that constitutional democracy was the best form of government for ensuring the welfare of the ordinary citizen. Liberal democracy generally worked to instill a greater degree of moderation and toleration of diverse political opinions, religious practices, and social existences. Less tolerant governments wear hard on the human spirit, or else they attempt to deny it completely. Minorities should beware when majority hatreds and suspicions prevail in a polity and the institutions to halt its excesses are non-existent.

The safeguards and forms of the liberal order are so much a product of long-term practice and sober reflection upon the relationship between the elected and the electors, Churchill marvelled, that "the famous phrase 'Government of the people by the people for the people' has in many states proved a mere illusion."[40] And, indeed, in some states the trick of illusion is not even attempted.

With consistent valor, Churchill championed those very political principles and institutions that one day would turn him out of the office of prime minister. His failed bid for reelection came at a time when he was most revered by his countrymen. Not only was this incident welcome testimony to the possibility of just government when the political institutions are properly formed, it also testified to Churchill's unambiguous defense of these political mechanisms even in times when they did not serve well his personal ambitions and provided a shining example of Churchill's own devotion to lawful, peaceful government.

Throughout his career, Churchill did not shy away from illuminating the differences between good and sinister politics. The persistent appearances of illiberal or despotic orders in the history of man provide us with another fact of the international system recognized by Churchill. As one would surmise, the ends of the despotic forms of government are antithetical to those of the liberal order; for they rule in the interest of the rulers or the state, and their interests and ideas have a iron hold on political priorities. Nazi Germany was one example of "a nation which ha[d] abandoned all its liberties in order to augment its collective might," the despotic unity of the state smothering life's natural diversities. "There is a nation," he continued, "which with all its strengths and virtues is in the grip of intolerance and racial pride unrestrained by law."[41] In such a manner are the virtues of a nation allowed to spoil.

A tyranny, wrote Churchill,

may be defined for practical purposes as the arbitrary rule of one man without regard to the wishes of millions. A tyrant is one who allows the fancies of his mind to count for more in deciding action than the needs, feeling, hopes, lives and physical well-being of the people over whom he has obtained control. A tyrant is one who wrecks the lives of millions for the satisfaction of his own conceptions. So far as possible in this world, no man should have such power, whether under an imperialist, republican, militarist, socialist or soviet form of Government.[42]

Following World War I, a feeble Weimar Germany allowed a tyrant to rise up in its midst in part because the powers of nationalism and emotionalism weakened the shaky foundation of the new law in Germany and tore apart the young institutional structures. Hitler was able to wield the power of Khan with a suspect electoral mandate of barely a majority of voters. In a healthy democratic polity, the Nazi's national support would have had great influence in the state. But under Hitler's regime, minorities soon learned that they had no rights.[43] The tyrant is, by definition, the law—his is a personal rule. As we shall see below, the disrespect displayed by the tyrant for legitimate order at home bleeds over to his foreign policy and emerges in his contempt for legitimate international orders.

One of the aims of civil law in liberal democracies is to enforce a sphere of privacy so long as the activities within that sphere do not do injury to the rest of the commonwealth. Despotisms invade the private lives of the citizens to enhance their already overgrown powers in order to maximize the security of the ruling class and to enforce their decrees upon the populace. Such political conditions naturally create timid men, and timid men rarely will challenge the dubious prerogatives of the tyrant. These facts prompted Churchill to ask Parisians in September 1936; how democratic men could bear "to be gagged and muzzled; to have spies, eavesdroppers and delators at every corner; to have even private conversation caught up and used against us by the Secret Police and all their agents and creatures; or to be tried by political or Party court for crimes hitherto unknown to civil law?"[44]

Churchill's remarks were reminiscent of Aristotle's, who wrote that to preserve their rule, tyrants have resorted to "lopping off the preeminent and eliminating those with high thoughts—and also not permitting common messes, clubs, education.... Leisured discussions are not allowed.... Residents are made to always be in evidence...; in this way their activities would escape notice least of all.... [There are] spies ... and eavesdroppers." Friends would be set against friends.[45]

Churchill accused both the Nazi and communist orders of ruthlessly upholding the interest of the ruling Party, even to the degree that truth is blurred with the untruth.[46] Churchill, using the master-slave distinction discussed by Aristotle in book one of *The Politics*, said of one of his many meetings with the other two members of the Grand Alliance: "On my right sat the President of the United States, on my left the master of Russia."[47] It is no accident that Roosevelt is referred to here as a First Citizen of a republic that enshrines the principle that all sectors of the citizenry are eligible to rule, while Stalin Churchill refers to as a "master," or the sole font of reason and political genius in all the Russian Empire, with the ability to rule over the slavish masses.[48]

The inefficiencies of liberal democratic politics alluded to above leave those regimes inferior in organizational skills and effectiveness when compared to the more despotic governments. Churchill, in a detached manner, admired the ruthless persistence with which dictators like Lenin pursued their ends as well as their abilities for rigid organization and painstaking planning. When it came to ruling, Soviet Russia had the most efficient form of despotism in the long history of politics.[49] However, the top priorities of governments ought not to begin by looking to the rigor of the means. Rather, the political ends ought to be the first points of departure. What are the ends that are being so "effectively" pursued? Good government begins with the pursuit of the common interest, and the question of effectiveness and organization in the interest of efficiency rightly follows.

With this we return to the subject of war. The existence of regimes antithetical in principle and interest lends further tension to international life. Political theorist-sociologist Raymond Aron referred to this reality as the "heterogeneity of the global system," and defines such a system as one in which the states are organized according to different principles. According to Aron,

A diplomatic circumstance is not completely understood so long as we limit ourselves to describing the geographical and military structures of the alliances and hostilities, to situating on the map the points of strength, the lasting or occasional coalitions, the neutral powers. We must also grasp the determinants of the behavior of the principal actors—in other words, the nature of the states and the objectives sought by those in power. *Thus the distinction between homogeneous systems and heterogeneous systems seems to me fundamental.*[50]

Liberal governments are, by and large, status quo powers, desirous of peace and a working cooperation with other nations. Lawless regimes, however, usually do not aspire to maintain the peace, especially when war appears to offer large rewards or greater security for their rulers. Churchill remarked of the German and Italian dictators: "They mock at all ideas of morality or international law.... They do not hesitate to tell the grossest falsehoods to the ambassadors of Powers with whom they profess to live in friendly relations.... They extol and glorify force and fraud, and they are prepared to use them both to the utmost limit."[51] The Communists "pay lip-service to the doctrine of peace, but by peace they mean submission to their will and system."[52]

A state of war does exist in the twentieth century even without the occurrence of military battle. Some men have referred to this phenomenon as the "Cold War." The totalitarian impulse (state-organized barbarism) does not limit itself to any one particular region of the world. As Churchill knew, it could infect any political order either from within or by invasion from without. The empowerment of ideology in the twentieth century imposed a most tragic circumstance upon millions of ordinary people that rivals the hideous consequences of war. Confronted as some men and women are by inhuman ideologies in their homelands, they try to behave as gentlemen and women. Nevertheless, these same people are driven against one another by forces and doctrines "as wantonly and as remorselessly as they ever were in the ages of absolute Emperors and Kings."[53]

The Bolsheviks came out belligerently against the comity of nations. Churchill understood that Bolshevism could only be propagated and maintained by violence.[54] What, then, should be the foreign policy of basically peaceful states toward governments that must resort to violent politics to sustain themselves and that scoff at the international institutions that give at least a semblance of order to state relations? What should be the policy of the liberal democracies? Churchill was unwavering on this point of policy: it was the duty of all men and women to offer "resistance to tyranny in all its forms."[55]

There was no hint of an apologetic tone in Churchill's remarks on democracy's behalf. There was, rather, an awareness that democracies need inspiration to maintain their defenses based on a passion for those very principles that are contrary to the more despotic orders. Again, Churchill's reasoning:

I regard these parliamentary institutions as precious to us almost beyond compare. They seem to give by far the closest association yet achieved between the life of the people and the action of the State. . . . It should be the duty of faithful subjects to preserve these institutions in their healthy vigour, to guard them against the encroachment of external forces, and to revivify them from one generation to another from the springs of national talent, interest, and esteem.[56]

Democracies must coexist, after all, with less tolerant, more aggressive forms of government. War is never certain to come about, but it is always a prospect. But by remaining strong, the more confident liberal nations can give protection and inspiration to the weaker ones so that the risk of experiencing the trauma of either war or tyranny can be diminished.[57]

The challenge posed to the statesman of a nation where "by far the closest association yet achieved [exists] between the life of the people and the action of the State," i.e., democracy, is one of educating a varied populace in the facts of the international system and the soul of the nation. His chief tool is that of persuasion; for, the statesman is not a ruler over his subjects, but a leader who has assumed the first position in the polity, a position that demands sensitivity to the opinions of the other citizens. He is not a master, but a servant. In Churchill's view, to act outside these bounds would be shameless. The promise of good government relies upon the attention political men pay to the particular concerns of a society, the family, the local communities, and the multiple private associations.

> To make a happy fire-side clime
> For weans and wife
> There's the true pathos and sublime
> Of human life.[58]

CHURCHILL ON COMMUNISM

The preceding remarks have furnished us with a few introductory ideas concerning Winston Churchill's conception of the decent forms of government and their impact on international politics. The remainder of this chapter is devoted to rooting out his understanding of the nature of communism and its relationship to the rest of the international community.

"History is politics applied to the past," remarked Soviet Marxist historian Mikhail Pokrovsky.[59] While Soviet political leaders may not think twice about forcing a psuedo-reality upon their past, such falsification was one communist characteristic that revolted Churchill. Absent a relatively accurate account of history, final judgments on present political and military dramas would be well nigh impossible. The business of political science and statesmanship involves at its core knowledge of other regimes, the different constitutions, military strengths, and their economic-social systems. History, as Churchill understood it, was vitally important for the benefit of knowledge based on experience. "Efforts should be made to maintain the actual facts that occurred . . . [to] understand how it is we are all here in the world."[60]

Churchill's political approach embraced live notions of right and wrong and relied heavily upon a belief in the permanency of human nature. "Scientists should never underrate the deep-seated qualities of human nature and how, repressed in one direction, they will certainly break out in another."[61] What moral cognition lacked, though, was a solid base from which to draw solid conclusions about day-to-day events and patterns. History could provide that base. "Knowledge of the past is the only foundation we have from which to peer into and try to measure the future."[62] His measured observations about Bolshevism and the founding of the Soviet state, then, are quite relevant to this project. Questions about the consistency of his policy toward the Soviet Union, therefore, may begin here.

Bolshevism meant suffering for the great Russian masses; it meant a ruthless political mastery by criminals, malcontents, and intellectual misfits; and it meant an invitation for an entire nation to experience the horrors of tyranny, pestilence, and famine. The newly established Soviet Union represented man's worst efforts at governance and received from the outset Churchill's belligerent opposition.[63]

While calling for peace and reconciliation with the German people back in the summer of 1919, Churchill also tried to direct British foreign policy to encourage all those forces in Russia that were striving for the destruction of the Bolshevik tyranny and the establishment of a genuine democratic order for the Russian people and other nationalities under their control.[64] In Churchill's eyes, the Bolsheviks offered mankind a rare form of revulsion in its rule that set it apart from most of the tyrannies of the past.

To the Russian revolutionary anarchist, Boris Savinkov, a man in whom Churchill took a great interest for his struggle first with, and then against, the Bolsheviks. The new revolutionary order established by Trotsky and Lenin betrayed the true ideals of the Russian people—freedom. Savinkov referred to the new tyranny as possessing the same qualities of despotic rule as under the Czars. This new government was the same tyranny but in different trappings. On the other hand, according to Churchill, Savinkov believed that the Soviet leaders had enslaved Russia more powerfully than ever.[65]

The newness of this form of tyranny was a quality that Churchill consistently stressed. There was in fact a sphere of freedom under Czarist rule. Even the democracy that the revolutionaries carried into Russia was short-lived. Lenin was quick to use his leverage to rid the polity, by force and rhetoric, of all the elements in Russia that posed a challenge to his communist ideals. Lamented Churchill: Gone for ever was the Empire of Peter the Great, and the long-dreamed-of liberal Russia, and the Duma, and the already summoned Constituent Assembly. Cast into outer darkness with the Czarist Ministers were the Liberal and Radical politicians and reformers.[66] Russia fell into a self-imposed dark age; "every gradation of political opinion known to men crumpled up almost simultaneously."

To the famed Russian author Alexander Solzhenitsyn, communism was essentially alien to the Russian tradition, a diseased system of rule imported from the West, the brain child of the German intellectual Karl Marx.[67] Churchill, agreeing in principle with Solzhenitsyn, believed that Bolshevism, instead of reflecting a Russian national interest or position, espoused more vociferously an international position, one advocating worldwide revolution. The Bolsheviks did not represent Russia, nor did they claim to represent her. For this reason, Churchill could not believe that Russia's fundamental ideas ever would "rest durably or recognisedly in those hands."[68]

Indeed, Russia had suffered a great political tragedy. The Bolsheviks took from her in one move both peace and the victory that was within her grasp.[69] The tragedy was in fact compounded by the imposition of a "superhuman tyranny" across the great Russian land mass, a political system supported by a "sub-human doctrine." This despoiled land, after 1917, became "a state without a nation, an army without a country, a religion without a God."[70] The Russian people were the victims of an intellectual fantasy, and, as we shall see, the salvation of that nation would depend upon the courage and persistence of her people. Far from assaulting the Russian people, Churchill relied on Russian nationals to reinstate a civilized form of government.

Communism, "the foul baboonery of Bolshevism," was so hideous in part because of the destruction it wrecked upon civilization and ancient traditions. "[Lenin] repudiated God, King, Country, morals, treaties, debts, rents, interest, the laws and customs of centuries, all contracts written or implied, the whole structure—such as it is—of human society."[71] Lenin had, in fact, replaced God as a source of spiritual inspiration for the oppressed peoples of the world.[72] He was "The Grand Repudiator." Natural political, social, economic, and religious activities and associations suffered torturous disruptions in the radical reorganization of the Russian state on the model of Asiatic despotism. It was a most abject spectacle of "equalitarian squalor," related Churchill in 1920:

[T]he theories of Lenin and Trotsky have fatally, and may be finally, ruptured the means of intercourse between man and man, between workman and peasant, between town and country; . . . They have driven man from civilization to a barbarism worse than the stone age, and have left him the most awful and pitiable spectacle in human experience.[73]

The philosophy of communism sought to begin the recreation of human nature to better fit the tasks of the Communist society and to beat the souls of its subjects to make them less resilient.[74]

The Soviet Union never experienced a shortage of apologists, and it was against the contrived and twisted presentations of communism by dreamers and savants like Sidney and Beatrice Webb and George Bernard Shaw that Churchill had to do rhetorical battle. Churchill detested Bolshevism not so much for its economic system, although he thought it was destructive of prosperity, but rather for its political doctrine of equality, mass life and collectivism (their aim being to reduce men to ants),[75] and its disavowal of Christian ethics and a civilized rationality. How could western men seriously undertake to defend such "baboonery?" Partaking in a bit of sarcasm in an answer to some of the sublime abstractions he found in the writings of Shaw, Churchill explained that

[h]ere we have a state whose subjects are so happy, that they have to be forbidden to quit its bounds under the direst penalties; whose diplomatist and agents sent on foreign missions, have often to leave their wives and children at home as hostages to ensure their eventual return. . . . Here is a land where God is blasphemed, and man, plunged in this world's misery, is denied the hope of mercy on both sides of the grave. . . . Here we have a power actively and ceaselessly engaged in trying to overturn existing civilizations by stealth, by propaganda, and when it dares, by bloody force. . . . Decent, good-hearted British men and women ought not to be so airily detached from realities, that they have no word of honest indignation for such wantonly, callously-inflicted pain.[76]

Winston Churchill despised Bolshevism for many of the same reasons he despised the growth of socialism in his own country through the Labour Party. They both, though to different degrees, were destructive of democracy and fundamental liberties in their radical approaches to politics and their ignorance of the significances of national principles, precedents, and traditions. Restraints, the recognition of the limits of politics, are necessary for a people to have a civilized form of government.

The reimposition of order upon the Russian nation after the Bolshevik piracy of power was seen as vital to the reestablishment of peace in the world, a world which, back in 1918 and 1919, still was reeling from the aftershocks of the great continental war. Churchill wrote in a letter he never sent to Prime Minister Lloyd George in 1919 that "(t)here will be no peace in Europe until Russia is restored. There can be no League of Nations without Russia."[77] Britain could not disinterest herself in the affairs of Russia. Inaction would place vast areas of Central and Eastern Europe in a vice between Bolshevik Russia and Germany and threaten the hard-won peace structured at Versailles. By leaving Germany free to regain her influence over Russia, she would strengthen herself beyond her pre-war capabilities, and Russia herself would be left to sow the seeds of revolution in Europe. Such a situation would leave Britain's interests in the East and in India "perilously affected" and would rain down "humiliation and defeat" upon the victorious nations.

The turmoil in Russia was a direct result of the world war initiated by the Germans who sought to dominate the European continent. The war brought upheaval to the Czarist political order and caused great discontent among the Russian people who were profoundly dissatisfied with the policy of Nicholas II to continue the war as an enemy of the Central Powers. Russia, in a few words, was ripe for domestic insurrection, and the architects of Germany's war effort did not let this fact pass unnoticed. Churchill thought of Lenin as a tool of the Germans, an instrument of German war policy that would hasten the fall of the provisional government and relieve the pressure on the German eastern front.

To use Churchill's metaphors, by permitting Lenin's famed departure from Switzerland by train in a sealed (quarantined) passenger car, Germany quite shrewdly injected a poison, "a phial containing a culture of typhoid or cholera," into the Russian body politic that would spread like a disease through her system and ultimately choke the life out of her.[78] The poison of Bolshevism spread as predicted until the entire command of the White Russian forces was infected.[79] Mutiny, demoralization, and undisciplined behavior soon plagued a good many of the national armies.

The foreign policy implications for the western nations, as Churchill was to remind us after the second great war, were monumental. A heavy price was paid for the failure to strangle Bolshevism at its birth and return Russia into the "community of nations."[80] He viewed the situation in 1919 with great consternation. Eastward of Poland, he explained:

lay the huge mass of Russia—not a wounded Russia only, but a poisoned Russia, an infected Russia, a plague-bearing Russia; a Russia of armed hordes not only smiting with bayonet and with cannon, but accompanied and preceded by swarms of typhus-bearing vermin which slew the bodies of men, and political doctrines which destroyed the health and even the soul of nations.[81]

From his exalted position in Lloyd George's war cabinet, Churchill entrenched himself to do battle against this new Soviet Russia. There was, after all, no possibility of a true accommodation with the Bolsheviks. Bolshevik Russia, because it actively warred against civilized society, never could be a party to the League of Nations. The Communists sought "as the first condition of their being" the destruction of all existing political institutions. With Lenin and the Communists there could be neither truce nor pact.[82] This aim of world revolution, Churchill emphasized, could be pursued equally in peace or war. In fact, he understood a Bolshevist peace to be only another form of war.[83]

There was, then, an unfinished task. The desire of the Allies was to see peace restored in Russia based upon the will of the broad mass of the Russian people.[84] As was discussed in the earlier sections of this chapter, the principle used by Churchill to justify intervention rested on his belief that the eradication of monstrous forms of government is a high duty of all men. All tyrants are the enemies of the human race and should be overthrown.[85] While the question of intervention into the affairs of another country is troublesome, Churchill believed, at both ends of his career, that such a policy was acceptable, and entirely desirable in the case of Soviet Russia, if there were a resultant good and if the intervention were effective.[86] And indeed, the ruin of Lenin and Trotsky, the principal architects of Soviet despotism, seemed to be imperative for world recovery and international peace.

The threat of Bolshevism weighed so heavily upon Churchill, that even before the armistice with Germany in 1918, Churchill spoke of the need to rearm the German forces for fear that Bolshevism may spread further into the European continent.[87] Russians also would have to be assisted with military aid and moral support in their struggle to save their nation. Thus, began Churchill's willingness to work with the likes of White Russian General A.I. Denikin and Admiral A.V. Kolchak, after Kerensky's miserable attempts to sustain the weak provisional government established after the overthrow of Nicholas II, in the hopes that a more just constitutional order would emerge in Russia. Churchill was criticized at times for supporting the erratic and anti-Semitic Denikin, but he believed that a close relationship with the general and the supply of arms from Great Britain would have a modifying influence on his behavior and give a fighting chance to the forces of democratization.[88] In any case, Denikin represented the solitary hope for the victory of the anti-Bolshevik forces over the greater evil of Leninism.

While the scope of this book does not permit us to cover entirely the political drama that took place in Britain between those who favored the destruction of the Bolsheviks, principally Churchill, and those who pressed for recognition of Lenin's government and the resumption of normal relations, a few points should be made here to more clearly define Churchill's position. Churchill started his policy of intervention with the support of many in the government, including Lloyd George. But this advantage soon dissipated as the anti-Bolshevik forces suffered several military defeats, thus dampening any enthusiasm that once existed among the British politicians.[89] Churchill soon found himself very much alone in the pursuit of his interventionist policy.

Churchill did battle with his own government on several pivotal questions. Ought the trade interests of Britain in Russia come before the struggle against a tyranny that threatened to encroach on Britain's interests in the long run? The prime minister's cabinet concluded, after the abandonment of Denikin, that "it was highly important for the British Empire that trade with Russia should be resumed with as little delay as possible."[90] Was it possible, as Lloyd George believed, to persuade the Bolsheviks as to the errors of their ways? Mikhail Heller and Alexander Nekrich wrote that "Lloyd George formulated the principle of a policy that was to become standard for the West vis-á-vis the Soviet Union: to smother bolshevism with generosity."[91] Financial problems also strained Churchill's policy as his opponents found his schemes to be wasteful nonetheless. Lloyd George declared in April 1919 that "he would rather see a Bolshevik Russia than a bankrupt Great Britain."[92]

All of these political outcomes must have appeared ominous to Churchill, who predicted that the states adjacent to Soviet Russia, Poland being of greatest concern to Churchill and Lloyd George, would one day also bear the burden of a Soviet-styled government.[93] Indeed, after the war, there arose a powerful antimilitarist sentiment across the continent, ideal sowing ground for Bolshevik peace slogans and agitation.

Churchill was willing to save through his diplomacy and strategy as much of Russia as he could, to achieve what was at that point achievable. He was to utilize a variation of this diplomacy in his relations with Soviet Russia after World War II; for he recognized that a goal was not always perfectly attainable and that circumstances often modify the policy of the statesman. Churchill was willing to negotiate from the beginning with the Soviet regime when the British negotiating position was strong in order to achieve a modicum of peace, to relieve the oppression of the populations under Bolshevik control, to arrange a cessation of propaganda coming into Western Europe and the interference in the political affairs of her Middle Eastern and Central Asian neighbors, and to obtain a general release of prisoners.[94]

Churchill even supported a comprehensive political agreement with the Soviets proposed by Lord Curzon, but he often was thwarted from attaching his own conditions to such agreements. With the situation in Russia souring with each passing week, Churchill desired Generals Denikin and Wrangel, whose forces were being gradually driven out of central Russia, to open negotiations with the Bolsheviks to fashion a compromise peace. In a letter to Lloyd George in March 1920, Churchill expressed himself as follows:

I sh[oul]d be prepared to make peace with Soviet Russia on the best terms available to appease the general situation, while safeguarding us from being poisoned by them. I do not of course believe that any real harmony is possible between Bolshevism & present civilisation. *But in view of the existing facts a cessation of arms & a promotion of material prosperity are inevitable: & we must trust for better or for worse to peaceful influences to bring about the disappearance of this awful tyranny & peril*. . . .[95]

The preceding is a brilliant example of Churchillian statesmanship. There were limits to what a statesman could accomplish in Russia in 1920. Churchill consistently detested the communist political system; but in the interest of peace he compromised a policy that may have worked earlier on but which had, with the passage of time, become entirely impractical in view of the political situation in Britain and the questionable military viability of the White Russian forces. These ideas in no way contradict an earlier one when he asked the question: "What sort of a Peace(!) shd [sic.] we have, if all Europe & Asia from Warsaw to Vladivostock were under the sway of Lenin?"[96] Such a situation, for all its resulting barbarity, would not constitute a real peace. His opposition to the Soviet form of rule and to the spread of communism (and communism, unlike other forms of tyranny, was impelled to spread itself to other regions of the globe), which threatened to overwhelm the free world, remained steadfast until the end.

Churchill, always one to try a different approach, believed a form of reconciliation and the introduction of a broader base for political participation to be a real possibility if foreign aid were offered the Soviet leadership.[97] However, Churchill, opposing the policy proposals of Lloyd George and Lord Curzon, strongly advocated that the Soviets must compromise their political doctrine if the Soviet Union were to be welcomed into the international community.[98] Short of internal change, Churchill was confident that any bargain would prove meaningless.

Throughout the remainder of his political career, Churchill would work, with varying degrees of success, to arrive at peaceful terms with the Soviet leaders and to warn the world of the dangerous excesses of communism. As he predicted back in 1919, the Soviet Union would emerge upon the world scene as a significant factor in world politics.[99] Only the foolhardy would choose to ignore this development. It is the author's contention that Churchill's activities and thoughts would remain entirely consistent with the preceding points here just made. With a steadfastness rarely to be found in the hearts of other statesmen in this century, Churchill defended the principles and practices of the liberal governments of the West, including those within the British Empire, and alternately condemned tyranny wherever he found it; he railed against movements and ideas that brought disruption and class hatred to the lawful regimes; he sought to reduce international tensions for fear of the horrific and tragic consequences of uncontrollable hatreds and ambitions that usually resulted therefrom; and he endeavored to prepare the peaceful nations to defend themselves against aggressor nations.

To briefly summarize, Churchill understood war to be natural in the international system, arising as it frequently does from intense political disagreements, historical animosities, and the lust for personal glory and power. Statesmanship, the political art of molding one's environment, is but one of the moderating factors in the world. Wars, therefore, are seldom inevitable. Churchill consistently demonstrated his profound understanding of political affairs and had measureless faith in his own abilities to act on the world scene in a manner consistent with peace or justice.

Churchill also recognized that the international system was composed of liberal and despotic political orders. The rule of law and the existence of constitutional limitations on the government characterized the former while the absence of constraints on the rulers characterized the latter. In the interest of security, statesmen and citizens of liberal democracies ought to be made aware of the existence of regimes that operated on unfamiliar or opposite principles. Often, the very heterogeneity of the international system creates tensions among the states that compose it.

Bolshevism, for Churchill, meant injustice and suffering for the great masses of Russian people. Communism was man's worst efforts at governance.

The Bolshevik platform meant increasing instability in the world. Churchill opposed recognition of Lenin's new regime and fought to almost the last (Russian) man to subvert it by force. In the interests of peace, and recognizing in 1920 that his form of opposition was no longer practical, Churchill worked to fashion an acceptable compromise with the Soviet Union. His attempts at reconciliation did not mean, however, that he had bowed down before the new Soviet tyranny.

NOTES

1. Churchill, "Thoughts on the Royal Visit," *Step By Step*, p. 231.
2. Edmund Burke, *Reflections on the Revolution in France and The Rights of Man by Thomas Paine* (Garden City, NY: Doubleday & Company, 1961), p. 19
3. Winston S. Churchill, *The Story of My Early Life: A Roving Commission* (New York: Charles Scribner's Sons, 1941), p. 113.
4. See Churchill, "Education in Bangalore," *The Story of My Early Life*, pp. 109-121.
5. Winston S. Churchill, "Will There Be War In Europe—and When?" *The Collected Essays of Sir Winston Churchill*, vol. 1, *Churchill and War*, ed. Michael Wolff, (Bristol: Library of Imperial History, 1976), p. 436.
6. Winston S. Churchill, *Winston S. Churchill: His Complete Speeches*, ed. Robert Rhodes James (New York: Chelsea House Publishers in association with R.R. Bowker, 1974), p. 7,647.
7. See, for example, Churchill, *Step By Step*, pp. 55 and 57-59.
8. Martin Gilbert, *Winston Churchill: The Wilderness Years* (Boston: Houghton Mifflin Company, 1982), p. 10.
9. Martin Gilbert, *Churchill's Political Philosophy* (Oxford: Oxford University Press, 1981), p. 3. See also pp. 12-13 and 23. See also Winston Churchill, "How To Stop War," *Step By Step*, p. 25, How to stop war "is the supreme question which should engage the thoughts of mankind. . . . [E]xcept for a few handfuls of ferocious romanticists, or sordid would-be profiteers, war spells nothing but toil, waste, sorrow and torment to the vast mass of ordinary folk in every land."
10. Churchill, *The Gathering Storm*, p. 260. See also p. 201.
11. See Raymond Aron, *Peace and War: A Theory of International Relations*, trans. Richard Howard and Annette Baker Fox (Garden City, NY: Doubleday & Company, 1966), pp. 71-93.
12. Churchill, *The Gathering Storm*, p. 260.
13. Aristotle, *Nichomachean Ethics*, pp. 5-6. See also book 6, especially pp. 158-161.
14. See, for example, Churchill, "Will There Be War in Europe—And When?" *Churchill and War*, p. 436.
15. Words spoken by Churchill on January 7, 1939, on the eve of the long struggle with Nazi Germany, found on the title page of Gilbert, *The Wilderness Years*.
16. Churchill, *The Gathering Storm*, p. 41.
17. Quoted in Thomas Sowell, "Visions of War & Peace," *Encounter* (December 1987), pp. 40-49.
18. Churchill, "To End War," *Churchill and War*, vol. 1, p. 351.

19. Martin Gilbert, *Winston S. Churchill*, vol. 8, *Never Despair: 1945-1965* (Boston: Houghton Mifflin Company, 1988), p. 331.

20. Churchill, *Step By Step*, p. 179. See also p. 27.

21. Winston S. Churchill, *Great Contemporaries* (London: Thornton Butterworth Ltd., 1937), p. 27. See also Gilbert, *The Wilderness Years*, p. 55.

22. Winston S. Churchill, *A History of the English Speaking Peoples*, vol. 4, *The Great Democracies,* (New York: Dodd, Mead & Company, 1966), p. 263.

23. Winston S. Churchill, *The Second World War*, vol. 6,*Triumph and Tragedy*, (Boston: Houghton Mifflin Company, 1953), p. 579.

24. He was referring here, of course, to the eventual Soviet domination of Central and Eastern Europe. Cited in Gilbert, *Never Despair*, p. 290.

25. Churchill, *Step By Step*, p. 180.

26. Winston S. Churchill, *A History of the English Speaking Peoples*, vol. 3, The Age of Revolution (New York: Dodd, Mead & Company, 1967) p.77. For an in-depth treatment of the life and times of Churchill's most famous ancestor and a truly instructive reading on statesmanship, see Winston S. Churchill, *Marlborough: His Life and Times*.

27. Churchill, *Step By Step*, p. 53.

28. There are scholars who divide their understanding of international politics into three levels of analysis (the international system, individual states, and the individual). They argue that it is "reductionist" to try to understand the international system at the lower levels of the regime or the individual. So they disparage the practice of looking to ideologies, state traditions, regime principles, etc. (rather than remaining strictly on the level of balance of power) in order to explain state behavior. This author argues, to the contrary, that the examination of regime politics is essential to understanding how the third level, the international system, functions. See, for example, Kenneth N. Waltz, *Man, the State and War: A Theoretical Analysis* (New York: Columbia University Press, 1959) and his *Theory of International Politics* (Reading, MA: Addison-Wesley Publishing Company, 1979).

29. Aristotle, *Rhetoric and Poetics*, trans. W. Rhys Roberts and Ingram Bywater (New York: The Modern Library, 1954), *Rhetoric*, p. 56. See also*The Politics*, trans. Carnes Lord (Chicago: The University of Chicago Press, 1984), bk. 1, ch. 1.

30. Churchill, "To End War," *Churchill and War*, p. 348.

31. See for example Hans Morgenthau, *Politics Among Nations: The Struggle for Power and Peace* (New York: Alfred A. Knopf, 1978), pp. 179-183.

32. See, for example, Aristotle, *The Politics*, bk. 3, especially chs. 6 and 7, p. 95: "[T]hose regimes which look to the common advantage are correct regimes according to what is unqualifiedly just, while those which look only to the advantage of the rulers are errant, and are all deviations from the correct regimes; for they involve mastery, but the city is a partnership of free persons." As Churchill understood it in December 1950 (*Complete Speeches*, p. 8,138): "Totalitarian dictatorships are not concerned with public opinion, the mood of the times, or this or that wave of feeling. On the contrary, they do not allow any feeling except what is prescribed from on high by their machine."

33. Churchill, *Complete Speeches*, pp. 7,252-53 (emphasis mine). Churchill proposed nearly this same test to the people of Italy on August 28, 1944 and on May 8, 1946 to the States-General of The Netherlands. See also Churchill, *Triumph and Tragedy*, p. 127.

34. Winston S. Churchill, *A History of the English Speaking Peoples*, vol. 1, *The Birth of Britain* (New York: Dodd, Mead & Company, 1966), p. 120. See especially pp. 215-225, "The English Common Law." Ultimately, one would have to look as far back as Aristotle and Solon to discover the basis and earliest rationale for ruling by laws rather than the capricious dictates of rulers.

35. "The King should not be below man, but below God and the law." Churchill, *The Birth of Britain*, pp. xvi-xvii.

36. Winston S. Churchill, *The Second World War*, vol. 5, *Closing the Ring* (Boston: Houghton Mifflin Company, 1951), p. 124.

37. Churchill, *Complete Speeches*, pp. 7,565-7,566. See also Churchill's essay entitled "The Dream" in Gilbert, *Never Despair*, pp. 369-370. "The Dream" is a marvelous essay in which Churchill fantasizes a warm and exciting conversation with his father, who died when he was but nineteen. These paragraphs reveal Sir Winston's deep devotion to the idea that the will of the people must prevail in government.

38. Churchill, *The Story of My Early Life*, p. 133. See also Churchill, *Complete Speeches*, p. 7,912.

39. Churchill, *Complete Speeches*, p. 7,566.
   Some reverence for laws ourselves have made,
   Some patient force to change them when we will.

40. Winston S. Churchill, "Parliamentary Government and the Economic Problem," *Thoughts and Adventures* (Long Acre, London: Odhams Press Limited, 1949), p. 173.

41. Quoted in William Manchester, *The Last Lion: Winston Spencer Churchill; Alone: 1932-1940* (Boston: Little, Brown and Company, 1988), p. 131.

42. Winston S. Churchill, "Monarchy versus Autocracy," *The Collected Essays of Sir Winston Churcbill*, vol. 2,*Churchill and Politics* , Michael Wolff ed. (Bristol, England: Library of Imperial History, 1976).p. 65. Also, for an insightful analysis of Churchill's philosophy on tyranny and modern totalitarianism, see Charles Roger Smith, "Winston Churchill and the Rise of Totalitarianism: Statesmanship and the Challenge of Modern Tyranny" (Washington, D.C: Ph.D. dissertation, The Catholic University of America, 1982).

43. Churchill, *The Gathering Storm*, p. 70.

44. Gilbert, *The Wilderness Years*, p. 163.

45. See Aristotle, *The Politics*, (1312a38-1314al2 and 1315bl2-1315b39) pp. 174-179.

46. Churchill, *Complete Speeches*, p. 7,925.

47. Churchill, *Closing the Ring*, p. 384. See also p. 386.

48. This is not to say that Churchill denounced all of the kingships of the past, as long as they govern for the good of all and not only for private gain. (Churchill, *The Birth of Britain*, p. xv.)

49. See Churchill, *Step by Step*, p. 35, and *Thoughts and Adventures*, "Fifty Years Hence," p. 205. See also *Closing the Ring*, p. 386: "Stalin appeared to be, and at this moment certainly was, all-powerful in Russia. They could order; I had to convince and persuade. . . . The process was laborious, but I had no reason to complain of the way it worked."

50. Raymond Aron, *Peace and War*, pp 99-100 and 373-403 (emphasis mine).

51. "To End War," *Churchill and War*, p. 438. See also Henry Kissinger, *A World Restored: Metternich, Castlereagh and the Problems of Peace; 1812-1822* (Boston: Houghton Mifflin Company, Sentry Edition 1979), especially Chapter 1. Kissinger

discusses the disruptions to peace caused by the existence of revolutionary and status-quo powers in a single system. The peace-loving peoples, those favoring the salvation of the legitimacy of their order, seemingly invite war with their very efforts to avert it. "Whenever peace—conceived as the avoidance of war—has been the primary objective of a power or a group of powers, the international system has been at the mercy of the most ruthless member of the international community."

52. Churchill, *Complete Speeches*, p. 8,048. Indeed, despotisms seem to invite confrontation. "To make a permanent system of Dictatorship, hereditary or not, is to prepare a new cataclysm." (Churchill, *Great Contemporaries*, p. 41.)

53. Churchill, *Complete Speeches*, p. 7,308.

54. Martin Gilbert, *Winston S. Churchill*, vol. 4, *The Stricken World; 1916-1922* (Boston: Houghton Mifflin Company, 1975), p. 375.

55. Gilbert, *Never Despair*, p. 436.

56. Churchill, "Parliamentary Government and the Economic Problem," *Thoughts and Adventures*, p. 173.

57. See Churchill, *Complete Speeches*, pp. 7,284-7,285.

58. Quoted by Churchill, *Complete Speeches*, p. 7,587.

59. Cited by Mikhail Heller and Alexander Nekrich, *Utopia in Power: The History of the Soviet Union from 1917 to the Present*, trans. Phyllis B. Carlos (New York: Summit Books, 1986), p. 9.

60. Churchill, *Complete Speeches*, p. 7,303.

61. Churchill, *Complete Speeches*, p.7,806. While politics engages a multitude of opinions, it is nonetheless about a search for truth; see Churchill, *Complete Speeches*, p. 8,475. Both reason and revelation earn Churchill's deepest respect; see *Closing the Ring*, p. 533. See also Morton Frisch, "The Diplomacy and Statecraft of Roosevelt and Churchill" in Jeffrey Salmon, James P. O'Leary, Richard Shultz, ed., *Power, Principles & Interests: A Reader in World Politics* (Lexington, MA: Ginn Press, 1985), p. 233. Also concerning man's timeless nature, Churchill, The Birth of Britain, p. 6: "Biologists perceive important differences from the heads that hold our brains to-day, but there is no reason to suppose that this remote Palaeolithic ancestor was not capable of all the crimes, follies, and infirmities definitely associated with mankind."

62. Churchill, *Complete Speeches*, p. 7,285. See also Churchill, *The Gathering Storm*, p. 255.

63. "Of all the tyrannies in history the Bolshevik tyranny is the worst, most destructive and the most degrading." Churchill, *Complete Speeches*, p. 2,771.

64. Churchill, "Britain's Foreign Policy," *Churchill and War*, p. 214.

65. Churchill, "Boris Savinkov," *Great Contemporaries*, p. 127.

66. Winston S. Churchill, *The Aftermath: being a sequel to The World Crisis*, (London: MacMillan & Co. Ltd., 1941), p. 80. That such a state should be labeled as progressive was pure sophistry for Churchill. See Gilbert, *The Stricken World*, vol. 4, p. 365. Churchill: "And this is progress. This is Liberty. This is Utopia! What a monstrous absurdity and perversion of the truth it is to represent the communistic theory as a form of progress, when, at every step and at every stage, it is simply marching back into the dark ages."

67. See Alexander Solzhenitsyn, *The Mortal Danger: How Misconceptions About Russia Imperil America* (New York: Harper & Row, Publishers, 1981), pp. 3-17. See also Solzhenitsyn's replies to his critics, esp. p. 123, on how communism sacrifices the national interest: "The theory that communism is an essentially

Russian phenomenon . . . reduplicates the insane and self-defeating [racist] tactics of Hitler. . . . [N]o communist government cares about the interests of its citizens or relies upon public opinion; indeed they are even ready to sacrifice their populations in the interests of international victory" (parenthetical comment mine).

68. Churchill, "Army Estimates," *Complete Speeches*, p. 2,869. See also Smith, "Winston Churchill and the Rise of Totalitarianism," p. 170.

69. Churchill, *Complete Speeches*, p. 2,869.

70. Churchill, *The Aftermath*, p. 71.

71. Churchill, *The Aftermath*, p. 75.

72. "What Rome is to Catholics, Moscow is to the Communists of every country." (Churchill, *Step By Step*, p. 53).

73. Cited in Gilbert, *The Stricken World*, p. 365. See also *The Aftermath*, pp. 73-76; *Great Contemporaries*, p. 203; and *Step By Step*, pp. 36-37 and p. 203. The Soviet rulers used "Asiatic views of the value of human life and liberty" (Churchill, *Complete Speeches*, p. 7,588).

74. See Churchill, *Thoughts and Adventures*, pp. 210-211. Churchill's opinions about communism were to be entirely vindicated within his lifetime as news about the great terrors perpetrated in the Soviet Union surfaced gradually. In 1950 he wrote to his wife, Clemmie: "The book Randolph (his son) gave me, *The God that Failed*, is an impressive study of Communist mentality by those who have recovered from the disease" (Gilbert, *Never Despair*, p. 577). *The God that Failed* (1950) was edited by Richard Crossman and related the personal experiences of six disillusioned former Communists. The book began a vigorous reevaluation of communism.

75. See, for example, Churchill, "Mass Effects In Modern Life," *Thoughts and Adventures*, pp. 195-196.

76. Churchill, *Great Contemporaries*, p. 56.

77. Cited in Gilbert, *The Stricken World*, pp. 253-254. See also p. 260.

78. Churchill, "Army Estimates," *Complete Speeches*, p. 2,870.

79. Churchill, *Great Contemporaries*, p. 128.

80. Churchill, *Complete Speeches*, p. 7,805.

81. Churchill, *The Aftermath*, p. 263.

82. See Churchill, "Britain's Foreign Policy," *Churchill and War*, p. 217. See also Smith, "Winston Churchill and the Rise of Totalitarianism," p. 233. Martin Gilbert relates that Mary Bordon once observed: "Winston told LG one might as well legalize sodomy as recognize the Bolsheviks" (Gilbert, *The Stricken World*, p. 235).

83. Gilbert, *The Stricken World*, p. 418.

84. Churchill, *The Aftermath*, p. 173. To learn of Churchill's understanding of the principle of self-determination and the complexities involved when it comes to the application of that principle, especially as it relates to Wilson's Fourteen Points, see pp. 204-205. See also in Gilbert, *The Stricken World*, p. 321, Churchill's letter to Balfour (1919).

85. Gilbert, *The Stricken World*, p. 375.

86. Churchill, *Complete Speeches*, p. 7,769.

87. Gilbert, *The Stricken World*, p. 226.

88. Gilbert, *The Stricken World*, pp. 287-288. See also pp. 320 to 360 for the story of "Mr. Churchill's Private War" and "Denikin's Retreat."

89. Interesting parallels arise here between the foreign policies of Britain toward Russia in 1919 and the United States toward Nicaragua in the 1980s. In both cases the political enthusiasm to support democratic forces against the tyrannies of the

Bolsheviks, in the case of Britain, and of the Sandinistas, in the case of the United States, grew or dissipated according to the military ups and downs of the liberating armies. The reasons for withdrawing support in both cases (the desire to increase trade and proceed with normal relations, the pressures to stop the financial drain resulting from the expenditures on arms and logistical support, etc.) are strikingly similar.

90. Gilbert, *The Stricken World*, p. 412.
91. Heller and Nekrich, *Utopia in Power*, p. 97.
92. Heller and Nekrich, *Utopia in Power*, p. 97.
93. Gilbert, *The Stricken World*, p. 416.
94. Gilbert, *The Stricken World*, p. 399. See also p. 268; Churchill, being a man of action, did at one time believe that the vigorous use of British resources to aid the anti-Bolsheviks could have altered entirely the course of events in that country. Compare Churchill's efforts to shape an acceptable resolution to the civil war in Russia to the attitudes of President Wilson and Lloyd George, who appeared to have made up their minds early on in the campaign to let events play themselves out in Russia.
95. Gilbert, *Churchill's Political Philosophy*, p. 80 (mphasis and parenthetical insert mine).
96. Cited in Gilbert, *The Stricken World*, p. 234.
97. Gilbert, *The Stricken World*, p. 760.
98. See Gilbert, *The Stricken World*, pp. 776-785.
99. Gilbert, *The Stricken World*, pp. 268-269.

Chapter 3

The Grand Alliance: Grand Forces, Great Men, and a Grave New World

The purpose of this chapter is to examine the genesis of Winston Churchill's postwar Soviet policy. A more thorough understanding of the Grand Alliance will allow us to better comprehend the postwar period and the antagonisms inherent in the East-West relationship. In this stage of Churchill's career, he seriously entertained the idea of a thoroughgoing reconciliation with the Kremlin, and this despite what we have learned of Churchill's hostility towards communism in chapter two.

That chapter underscored the fact that the 1917 Russian Revolution brought to the world stage a radically different alternative to the existing international order. Churchill violently opposed formal recognition of the Soviet state several years after its inception. He thought this new regime represented the antithesis of the just political order. He threatened to resign from Lloyd George's Liberal cabinet in 1921 if the government recognized, formally or otherwise, the legitimacy of Bolshevik rule by negotiating with them at the Genoa Conference. Churchill wrote to the prime minister that the basis for nonrecognition rested upon the fact that there was no improvement in Bolshevik character or behavior. He stood firmly in his belief that the Soviet leaders could never reform themselves.[1] Only in 1924, on an initiative by the first-ever Labour government, did Great Britain grant *de jure* recognition to the Soviet government.

By the late 1930s and early 1940s, significant improvement in Anglo-Soviet relations had not been realized. In fact, one could say that diplomatic relations had worsened under Stalin's harsh rule over the people of Russia and the other Soviet republics. Soviet interference in British politics, the subsidizing of subversive activities, for example, culminated in a breach in diplomatic relations in 1927 that lasted about two years. However, with the rise of fascism in Germany, Churchill saw that instability in Europe had altered dramatically Great Britain's diplomatic priorities.

It will be demonstrated in this chapter that the war changed significantly the correlation of forces in the world. At war's end, the Soviet Union had vaulted itself into great power status, while Great Britain had been consigned to the realm of the lesser powers. The Nazi threat had forced Churchill to consider breaking with his past objections to a military association with a despised, outlaw regime and to entertain seriously the idea of a cooperative alliance with Moscow, even before the start of the war. Churchill's wartime experiences, as a principal leader in the wartime alliance, and his own elevation to power energized him to seek an accommodation with Moscow that could bring to the world a more stable peace. His ambitions led him on an adventurous quest to reach a settlement with Moscow that would carry over into the postwar period.

By war's end, Churchill desired to fashion an international order wherein nations would consult one another on issues of great political and strategic significance, wherein a few powerful states could throw their weight around in the interest of peace and perform a watchdog function around the globe to prevent war and potential catastrophe. A few positive developments in the East-West relationship gave him the hope that artful diplomacy could achieve a peace based on the continual cooperation of the emerging great powers.

This chapter also will demonstrate Churchill's consistent attachment to the principles of political sovereignty, liberty, safety, and honor. The wartime experience sharpened his own understanding of these ideas that were the driving force behind his foreign policy.

Men learn their greatest lessons, Churchill wrote in his tale of the birth of Britain, from "the grim needs of war."[2] The dangerous 1930s and the ensuing war against the Third Reich spoke to Churchill about the "grim need" to shift the focus from traditional political concerns concerning the "Red threat" to the pressing strategic threat in the heart of Europe. To keep some perspective, one must recognize that the struggle for survival in the face of the relentless German military machine dominated Churchill's wartime policy.[3] Survival and perseverance for the countries of Europe were of paramount concern. Lofty discussions about political principles are meaningless to citizens, after all, when the institutions of their country face extinction. Absent a body, the soul has no home; absent political and territorial integrity, national principles have no sanctuary.

The needs of survival forced Churchill to make bold decisions. Britain could not act alone to right the wrongs of the Nazis and restore lost sovereignty to the overrun nations of Europe. Britain led the fight in the early stages against Italy, which had invaded Abysinnia, modern-day Ethiopia, at a time when Hitler and Mussolini considered her a "frightened, flabby old woman." England did so, Churchill told Parliament, on borrowed time. Churchill acknowledged that although his country could not be the lawgiver and spokesman for the entire world, Britain must do its part to preserve order. "We must do our duty," he

The Grand Alliance

said, "but we must do it with other nations only in accordance with the obligations which others recognize as well."[4]

Churchill believed that Hitler's far-reaching military objectives and universal claims obliged the other European nations to fight side by side with Britain. Churchill's famed ancestor, the Duke of Marlborough, formed a military alliance against the French continental despotism by reminding other nations of the universal character of the terror wrought by Louis XIV. The tyranny of the "Sun King" gave strategic reason and political justification for the alliance of several states to oppose the aggressions on the grounds that France was a threat not simply to her neighbors but to all the nations of Europe.[5]

Churchill saw these same benefits accruing to the democracies in their struggle against Hitler; Europe, as a collective fighting force, would once again protest against the military domination of a single power. The question was, could the countries whose peace had been violated rally soon enough to thwart the aggressors?

Britain was once again engaged in battle with the continental despots, because, Churchill wrote to Roosevelt, "[d]emocracy has to prove that it can provide a granite foundation for war against tyranny."[6] The general reason for Britain's entry into the war was not "for profit and expansion, but only for honour and to do our duty in defending the right."[7] Specifically, Britain declared war to secure three honorable ends: to honor a pledge to rescue Poland; to preserve the balance of power on the continent; and to defend the rights of small nations.[8]

The compelling drama of the war ran its course, and Britain fought the honorable fight with Churchill leading the charge; but she would fail to realize her objectives. Nevertheless, at war's end, the balance of power in Europe would be distorted to the disadvantage of the democracies; and Poland along with other small nations in Central and Eastern Europe would fall under the subjugation of yet another alien political system.

Churchill's objectives and priorities were undeniable. He warned German Foreign Minister Ribbentrop that it was true that the British were on bad terms with the Soviet Union and that they hated communism as much as the Germans did. He also stressed that, even if France were protected, Great Britain would never disinterest herself in the political events in Europe so as to enable Germany to gain the domination of Central and Eastern Europe.[9] Churchill's warning to the Foreign Minister went unheeded.

Hitler's invasion of the Soviet Union in June 1941 disrupted the balance of forces in Europe in a grand way. The Nazi aggression against the Soviet Union resulted in a most unlikely and unforeseeable alignment of political forces. The realignment of power ultimately changed the political face of the continent and affected adversely the destinies of many nations for decades to come. The Nazi invasion resulted in a most awkward military alliance of liberal democratic and communist states. Democracy alone could not, in the end, provide "the granite foundation" to defeat tyranny. Democracy had to make its temporary peace with communism.

While "obligation" could hardly be said to have motivated Stalin's entry into the war against Hitler, Churchill welcomed the participation of his arch-foe in so grave a world crisis. The Alliance helped to form "a moral and intellectual impulse to unity" with the United States, whose leaders would join the Alliance soon after Hitler's aggression in the East, that would seal the victory.[10] Without unity, absent a "Grand Alliance," a satisfactory military victory may not have come, thus jeopardizing the liberties of many countries.

During the war as before it, when Churchill arduously fought against the plans of the Conservative members in the British Cabinet (Stanley Baldwin, Neville Chamberlain, Samuel Hoare, Lord Halifax) to strike a long-term agreement with Hitler, Churchill believed that a "permanent settlement" with the Nazi regime was impossible.[11] The end was simple, Churchill explained in 1941:

My one aim is to extirpate Hitlerism from Europe. The question is such a simple one. Are we to move steadily forward and have freedom, or are we to be put back into the Middle Ages by a totalitarian system that crushes all forms of individual life and has for its aim little less than the subjugation of Europe and little more than the gratification of gangster appetites?[12]

In the interest of liberty's preservation, Churchill sought an alliance with another gross abuser of liberty. This odd arrangement, together with the commitment to unconditional surrender and complete military victory, posed serious problems for Churchill and the American leaders once the Alliance achieved its victory. Churchill wrote in his memoirs about the possibility of German control of Europe in 1940 and concluded that it would be far better that the civilization of Western Europe "should come to a tragic but splendid end than that the two great democracies should linger on, stripped of all that made life worth living." [13]

The Alliance between the Soviet Union and the West did not come easily. As early as 1937 Churchill entertained some thoughts of an alliance with Soviet Russia in the interest of presenting a stronger posture to the more aggressive states such as Germany and Japan.[14] Before the beginning of open hostilities in early 1939, it seemed as though such an arrangement may materialize when, for fear of a German advance across Soviet borders, the Soviet government, through its ambassador M. Litvinov, tabled a secret proposal before Great Britain to form a "Triple Alliance," with France playing the third party. Such an alliance, believed Churchill, would have boldly confronted Hitler on two fronts and "struck deep alarm into the heart of Germany" and perhaps avoided the worst.[15]

For reasons that today remain obscure, the Triple Alliance never came to be. Some, like Churchill, thought it most probable that Stalin never intended the cooperative venture to materialize.[16] Others, like historian William Manchester, believed that the appeasement policy of the British Conservative Cabinet toward Germany was an effort to derail any attempt to ally the country with Moscow and to turn Hitler's ambitious designs away from England and France toward the Bolsheviks in the East.[17] Churchill too, to some extent, thought that the anti-communism of the conservatives foreclosed a valuable op-

The Grand Alliance

portunity to form a strategic alliance against the growing menace of Nazi militarism.

In 1936, Churchill did not share Stanley Baldwin's view that if there was to be fighting in Europe, it would be good "to see the Bolshies and Nazis doing it."[18] He considered it vital to Europe's safety to steer British sympathies away from Germany.[19] The clear and imminent threat came from Germany, not Russia. Unlike others in the British government, Churchill paid careful attention to Hitler's words and deeds; he deplored the consolidation of power by a party that operated on the principles of racial superiority; he warned his country, often standing alone, of the growing military might of the Nazi German nation. Consequently, there was an urgent need to form an immediate arrangement on equal terms with the Soviet Union of the most far-reaching character. Europe, he argued, needed the "solid backing of a friendly Russia" if it were to survive.[20]

As events played out, Soviet Foreign Minister Molotov, the successor to Litvinov, expressed a strong interest in a "Tripartite Pact," but only if Moscow's leaders were treated commensurately by the British as a full partner, and only if they had ample say in the new order in Europe and Asia.[21] Victory, Churchill knew, depended upon early recognition of Germany as the enemy and upon the successful formation of an eastern front. There could be no eastern front without the Soviet Union. He also knew that that the Alliance had a dark side, and that very little could forestall the growing Soviet influence over European affairs.

To justify an alliance with Moscow to his conservative co-Parliamentarians, Churchill reduced the basis of the association to that of naked "interest," not principle. Great Britain, like the Soviet Union, had "a great identity of interests" with the countries of northern Europe that would provide a solid foundation for a coalition to maintain stability in the region and protect British concerns. All along the whole of this eastern front, the major interests of Moscow were engaged, and therefore it fair to assume that they would "pool their interests" with other affected states.[22] An understanding with Russia, he argued, would provide the key to a Grand Alliance.

It is difficult to fault Churchill for fashioning an approach to Stalin based on self-interest. While Churchill despised both the Nazi and Soviet regimes on principle, only the Nazi regime was acting aggressively at that time. Interest, in any case, was not Churchill's only concern. The ultimate objective of his wartime diplomacy was to preserve the lives of the democracies and to place the purveyors of democratic ideals on a stronger footing. Thus, on some levels, interests and principles blend to the point where it becomes difficult to separate them. By way of analogy, President Lincoln, while he despised the institution of slavery, nonetheless sought first to preserve the Union and delay the expunction of that vile custom; for without the Union, there was an understanding that the ideas and principles of the Declaration of Independence might fade in significance on the North American continent. Lincoln saved the physical Union in order to preserve the metaphysical Union.[23] Quite unlike Britain, the Soviet Union had no principled objection to Hitler's activities. The rescue of political sovereignty, in Poland for example, and the vindication of liberty in other lands, were ends were not to be found within communist ideals or practices.

Churchill also realized that an effusive demonstration of kindness toward the Russians was the wrong approach to a rapprochement because that looked like weakness. He wrote to Anthony Eden in February 1941 that the "[b]est way of gaining [the] Russians was a good throw in the Balkans. . . . Events alone will convince them."[24] The appeal to interest was the last recourse to forming a Triple Alliance, and even this failed, in part because of British Conservative intransigence, which encouraged Moscow to seek a defensive alliance elsewhere. It also may have failed because of Stalin's own appetite for a greater piece of Europe or the understandable fright of Britain's allies in Central Europe and along the Baltic sea of relying upon a Soviet guarantee to protect their interests. Lithuania, Latvia, Estonia, Finland, Poland, and Rumania would have all been a part of the proposed alliance. These smaller states "did not know whether it was German aggression or Russian rescue that they dreaded more."[25] This torturous choice paralyzed British and French policy. So while the western nations were failing in their bid for a blockbuster coalition to secure the peace, the Axis powers were busy consolidating their own interests, which culminated in the infamous nonaggression pact between Nazi Germany and Soviet Russia.

The Axis powers offered Moscow "greater" assurances that the Soviet eastern borders would not be violated. Churchill believed that the vital link of the western powers with Russia at that moment had perished.[26] The agreement caused great alarm in the West and was a severe blow to Churchill's own defense plans.

The Molotov-Ribbentrop nonaggression treaty, signed on August 23, 1939, was enlightening on several levels. First, the pact represented a most serious failure of British and French foreign policy, a policy that extended back over a number of years.[27] The late 1930s were marred by a notable lack of strategic thinking by the Conservative government, the failure to recognize a mounting threat to British interests despite warnings from political leaders at home and affected individuals on the Continent.

Second, the pact emphasized to Churchill the vile nature of the government he attempted to befriend. Reminiscent of the 1922 Treaty of Rapallo between the Soviet Union and Germany, which attempted to cause a realignment in the balance of power in Europe by close economic and military cooperation between the two powers, Stalin chose to risk his own security for a roll of the dice with Adolph Hitler. To Churchill, this "violent and *unnatural*" turnabout "was a transmogrification of which only totalitarian states are capable."[28] Earlier, pro-Germanism had been decreed a heresy in the Soviet Union. Now support for the Nazis had become state policy, and those Soviet citizens who did not swing with the Kremlin were dealt with summarily. The Nazi-Soviet union, while unnatural on the level of competing interests (both countries had claims in Central Europe and the Balkans), was entirely understandable on the level of principle. Nazism and communism were, in fact, kindred movements. Churchill held that "Fascism was the shadow or ugly child of Communism,"[29] and Fascism, the

The Grand Alliance

Father of Nazism, was responsible for the catastrophe about to be visited upon Europe. "Germany and Russia," noted Churchill, "now worked together as closely as their deep divergences of interest permitted. Hitler and Stalin had much in common as totalitarians, and their systems of government were akin."[30]

Despite these revelations, Churchill pursued a patient policy to reestablish a cooperative relationship with Moscow, as he trusted that other antagonisms would one day destroy the pact. He firmly believed that Hitler would scrap the nonaggression treaty and recoil eastward (especially after Germany's defeat in the Battle of Britain during the summer of 1940).[31]

Finally, the pact served to demonstrate that territorial aggrandizement at the expense of weaker neighbors made up the hidden Soviet agenda. Stalin, in fact, harbored aggressive designs on Eastern Europe and the Baltic nations *before* Hitler's attack. He had hoped to avoid provoking Hitler and refrain from working closely with the British. Stalin thought he could avoid conflict with Germany despite his resistance to certain Nazi demands (for control over Middle Eastern oil, for example).[32]

Churchill characterized Soviet behavior in the Baltics as "a rush for the spoils." Severe military concessions and radical government changes were demanded of these tiny European republics following Soviet occupation.[33] After the break with Germany, Stalin attempted to wrestle from Great Britain and the United States assurances that what he gained from his pact with Hitler—the Baltic countries, parts of Poland, and Bessarabia—would remain in Soviet hands after the war.[34] Churchill, adhering to the provisions agreed to in the Atlantic Charter, repeatedly refused to affirm to Stalin's request to alter any frontiers until the great powers could meet at the peace conference following the victory over Germany.

Hitler turned on his Soviet ally in June 1941. If principle and interest could not bind together Great Britain and the Soviet Union before the hostilities, the panic for survival would succeed in forming an essential part of the victorious wartime coalition. As the League of Augsburg pulled different forces together for the sole purpose of supplanting Louis XIV's universal tyranny, so a Grand Alliance of dissimilar regimes would fight as one unit in this twentieth century struggle. Wrote Churchill in 1933 about the grand coalition led by his great ancestor: "Thus slowly, fitfully, but more than less surely, the sense of a common cause grew across the barriers of class, race, creed, and interest in the hearts of millions of men."[35] The Grand Alliance differed markedly from this seventeenth century coalition in at least one respect. There was nothing gradual about its formation. Hitler's assault on the East, in one fell swoop, generated a powerful centripetal force that gave birth to the Grand Alliance practically overnight.

This momentous realignment of forces was formalized on July 13, 1941, when Britain's Admiral Cripps and Soviet Foreign Minister Molotov signed a short treaty. Given the pressing need for urgent action, the treaty did not seek to deal with any political questions. Both powers pledged support to each other and agreed that under no conditions would they negotiate a separate peace with the enemy.[36] So desperate was the plight of the Soviet Union that the ever-suspicious Stalin even invited a sizable British force to fight on Soviet territory. When, after a number of months, events were to favor Moscow, the Allies would have trouble even trying to send observers to work with Soviet armies.[37] Much disagreement regarding the sharing of military plans, the control of armed forces, the best strategy to win the war, and the issue of future frontiers would heighten tensions among the Allies during the course of the war. However, the Alliance would succeed in accomplishing its primary objective: military victory.

To write that Churchill welcomed this turn of events, which he so accurately predicted even after the infamous pact, would be an understatement. It was the fateful moment he had awaited, counted upon, and swiftly used to his advantage when it arrived. His acceptance of the Soviet Union as an equal partner was immediate. He recognized that too much time had been squandered already. Every soldier was highly valued. Every weapon and piece of machinery available must be put to use. "One has to do the best one can, but he is an unwise man who thinks there is any certain method of winning this war, or indeed any other war between equals in strength."[38]

Even before Stalin's change of heart, Churchill attempted to share with him, and did share with FDR, vital intelligence findings that Germany was disposing her troops for a strike into the Russian heartland.[39] Now Churchill had Stalin's ear and heart. He would handle the partnership, in fact, in a most magnanimous fashion. Political differences, while real, did not obstruct Churchill's objective of welding together the most powerful wartime coalition in history. Wrote John Colville, Churchill's private secretary, about Churchill's attitude following a Tory disagreement by Eden and Cranborne concerning the extent of the alliance with Russia: "The PM's view was that Russia was now at war; innocent peasants were being slaughtered; and we should forget about Soviet systems or the Comintern and extend our hand to fellow human beings in distress."[40] If only to emphasize the utterly vile and evil nature of the Nazi order and the urgent need to smash that government, Churchill let it be known: "[i]f Hitler invaded Hell I would make at least a favourable reference to the Devil."[41]

In his broadcast to the British people following Barbarossa, the Nazi code name for the invasion of Russia, Churchill tailored a new British foreign policy. Despite the Nazi regime's obvious similarities to "the worst features of Communism," and despite Churchill's consistent opposition to the Communists, about which he would "unsay no word," Churchill called upon the British people to recognize the humanness of the Russians and the sacrifices made by the Russian people in the defense of their homeland. If the British people could not embrace the Soviets in principle, shared humanity must then provide the bond. The fall of Russia would spell doom for the British, as Hitler would surely direct his forces westward in his quest for the total domination of Europe. For this reason, "[t]he Russian danger is therefore our danger . . . just as the cause of any Russian fighting for his hearth and home is the cause of free men and free peoples in every quarter of the globe."[42]

Churchill expressed his wishes and goals to Stalin in a November 1941 letter.

Our intention is to fight the war in alliance with you and in constant consultation with you to the utmost of our strength, and however long it lasts, and when the war is won, as I am sure it will be, we expect that Soviet Russia, Great Britain, and the United States will meet at the council table of the victors as the three principal partners and agencies by which Nazism will have been destroyed. . . . *The fact that Russia is a Communist State and Britain and the United States are not, and do not intend to be, is not any obstacle to our making a good plan for our mutual safety and rightful interests.*[43]

Stalin, in fact, agreed that "the difference of the State organization . . . should not, and could not, hinder us in achieving a successful solution of all the fundamental questions concerning our mutual security and our legitimate interests."[44] The great question was, however, how did each side define "successful solution?"

Churchill's guiding principles for British wartime activities were clear. First, while the war continued unabated, the British would give assistance to "anyone who can kill a Hun"; and second, when the war was over, the British would look to "the solution of a free, unfettered democratic election" in the wartorn nations of Central and Eastern Europe.[45] While there was full agreement by Stalin and Churchill on the first of these principles, and while Churchill greatly admired the tenacity of the Russian people in their struggle (Churchill never hesitated to recognize and appreciate military virtue in the leader and people of a nation, be they friend or foe),[46] a great divergence on the second of the principles gradually manifested itself. The established foreign policy goals of both sides clashed even before the war's end, as we shall see in the remainder of this chapter. The inability of Churchill to realize the political goals of the contest, largely for fear of detracting from the more crucial military goals, left him to despair at times about his own plans for the future security of Europe.[47]

Churchill believed that if a working relationship with Stalin could be developed during the war, there would be a chance for postwar cooperation. Even in the youthful stages of this cooperative relationship with Moscow, Churchill knew that fundamental political antagonisms between the Soviet Union and the western democracies imposed certain hardships. Concerning an alliance with Russia, he wrote that he never had any illusions, knowing that they accepted no moral codes and acted on their interests alone. "But at least they owed us nothing. Besides, in mortal war anger must be subordinated to defeating the main immediate enemy."[48] Churchill at times questioned the metaphysical foundation of that alliance with communism, as he did while on route to his first meeting with Stalin in Moscow in August 1942:

I pondered on my mission to this sullen, sinister Bolshevik State I had once tried so hard to strangle at its birth, and which, until Hitler appeared, I had regarded as the mortal foe of civilised freedom. . . . We had always hated their wicked regime, and, till the German flail beat upon them, they would have watched us being swept out of existence with indifference and gleefully divided with Hitler our Empire in the East.[49]

Churchill worked openly with Stalin, as openly as the situation permitted, in order to convince the dictator that he and Roosevelt did not intend to isolate him.[50] With Stalin's cooperation and active participation, Churchill hoped to expand the working relationship forged within the Grand Alliance into a broader world instrument to keep international peace called the United Nations.[51] Other factors, however, would intervene to frustrate the realization of those noble goals.

POLAND

Endless military competition and intervening periods of oppression has marred the long history of Russian-Polish relations. Lenin viewed Poland as a launching platform for the injection of political turmoil, and ultimately communism, in to the heart of Europe, or Germany.[52] Poland was the potential "Red Bridge" to the West. John Colville, reflecting on the contentious Russo-Polish relationship, remarked in 1941 that "[t]o a Pole, a Russian has no advantages over a German—and history makes this very understandable."[53] By the middle of the twentieth century, Polish national integrity, raped by both harsh occupation and war, had been sullied like never before. The Polish tragedy commanded international attention both at the beginning and end of the hostilities of the second world war. Poland was the celebrated cause for the declaration of war by Great Britain against the Axis powers. She also would be the focus of international attention after victory, when the newly formed blocs of East and West struggled to include her in their respective coalitions.

The 1943 battle of Stalingrad, the valiant and successful attempt by the Soviet armies of this city, named after their leader, marked a turning point in the course of the war. According to Adam Ulam, the "war was to take on an increasingly political character, or, rather, the Soviets' solicitude about their political aims was to become, now that the military disaster had been averted, much more explicit."[54] In other words, the very *raison d'etre* of the Grand Alliance, which was based upon a common military interest, was beginning to deteriorate. The demands of survival no longer weighed so heavily upon Stalin, and he could look to pursue his political objectives in Europe. Much fighting remained, but a successful end to the struggle against Nazism was in sight.

This reversal in fortunes meant that the westward advance of the Red Army was only a matter of time. As Stalin's forces advanced, it became increasingly clear that Soviet Russia would be the new dominant power on the Continent. Stalin would have a new-found power to pursue old ambitions. The stretch to a warm water sea port, the movement of the communist front forward to points further west and south, and the control of the western passages into the Russian heartland by dominating the political systems of the Eastern and Central European nations were all traditional Russian goals that subsequently were advanced by the fortuitous events of 1943.

The ensuing dispute among the allies over Polish territorial and political sovereignty made Poland, in Churchill's opinion, a test case for the future relationship among the great powers. According to Churchill, far more than Poland was involved. The dispute over Poland would rage around the meaning of such terms as democracy, sovereignty, independence, and free and unfettered elections.[55] Stalin's insistence on propping up the puppet government in Lublin and his persistent interference in Polish politics, by drubbing the unfavorable elements (the opposition to Polish communist rule), was hardly indicative of Stalin's commitment to see sovereignty restored to Poland or to the other overrun countries of Eastern Europe.

The choice to defend Polish sovereignty before, perhaps even at the expense of, Poland's frontiers was one important aspect of the Polish debate. Britain went to war to defend Polish sovereignty, not her borders, although it would not tremendously strain the argument to point out that the two goals were closely linked. Churchill encountered much resistance from the London Poles, who insisted that Poland's territorial integrity not be violated in any manner and that the only satisfactory conclusion to the dispute was a reinstatement of Poland's pre-1939 borders in the east.

The Soviet Union insisted upon using the Curzon line as the future western frontier of the Soviet State along with certain modifications that compromised Polish territory still further by giving the resource-rich city of Lvov to the Soviets. The Curzon line was the eastern boundary proposed by the British in 1919. Stalin suggested that Poland could be compensated in the west with the annexation of comparable regions from Germany's eastern territory to the point of the Oder-Neisse line, or those regions known as Pomerania, East Prussia, and Silesia. Despite the fact that future Germans were bound to resent the transfer of their lands to Poland, Churchill strongly supported this Soviet claim. "If I champion this frontier for Russia, it is not because I bow to force. It is because I believe it is the fairest division of territory that can, in all the circumstances, be made between the two countries whose history has been so chequered and intermingled."[56]

At the Tehran Conference in 1943, Stalin expressed consternation over the future defense of the Soviet western frontier. He insisted that Poland be moved westward and that the next Polish government be friendly. Again Churchill did not resist these Soviet stances, to the disgruntlement of the London Poles, for he understood Stalin's interest in securing his borders from future aggressions.[57]

In exchange for his support of Stalin's position regarding a "friendly Poland," Churchill adamantly insisted that postwar Poland be free and strong. Churchill deemed the sacrifice of some territory to be an acceptable solution, if not a noble endeavor, if it spared Polish freedoms. He felt justified in making these decisions on Poland's future without prior affirmation from the Poles in

London, although he recognized that the negotiations over Poland's future would go nowhere without their involvement and acquiescence.[58]

While he took these liberties, Churchill fought throughout the duration of the war for Soviet recognition of the Polish exiles and the release of prisoners of war deported to the Soviet Union after the Soviet occupation of Poland in 1939. Churchill repeatedly warned the exiled leaders Wladyslaw Sikorski and later Stanislas Mikolajczyk that Soviet recognition and political power for the London Poles would not be forthcoming unless they accepted a truncated Poland.[59] While Churchill desired to reverse some of the gains won by Stalin in the Nazi-Soviet pact, he did so very delicately for fear of upsetting the Anglo-Soviet war alliance. Nevertheless, Churchill believed that the reestablishment of relations between the Polish leaders, who were forced to make a new home in England after the nonaggression pact was signed, and the Soviet Union was vital. Churchill had an unenviable balancing maneuver to perform. In the end, he was forced to assume the "invidious responsibility" of relying on Soviet good faith; he hoped that a fair settlement could be reached at the peace conference.[60]

Criticism of Churchill's handling of the Polish frontier dispute is understandable, but it generally tends to ignore the geopolitical realities of Eastern Europe at the time.[61] Aside from the cautious diplomacy displayed by Britain over Poland designed not to endanger the newly born war alliance, there was another factor that contributed to British weakness on this issue. The West was in no position to counter Soviet advances militarily and challenge Russian territorial claims in Poland. The British did not have the military clout in Poland to defend Polish interests.[62] Churchill tried to explain to his Polish ally Mikolajczyk on many occasions that Britain was "powerless in the face of Russia."

Although Churchill repeatedly reminded Stalin that all border disputes would be handled at the conference table after the war (in compliance with the principles of the Atlantic Charter and the Declaration of Liberated Europe), he knew that Soviet occupying forces were going to force the issue. Therefore, his advice to the London Poles was along this line: "concede while there was still something to preserve." For surely the advancing Red Army would, in a matter of time, make the decision for them.[63]

Another issue that fanned the flames of the Polish dispute revolved around the question of who legitimately represented the government of Poland. Stalin had set up a provisional government in Lublin, Poland in the summer of 1944 that would serve as Poland's new voice and decision-taking body. With Boleslaw Beirut, a Comintern official, at the head of the newly created regime, the Lublin government was composed of both Communists and political opportunists. Eventually, Stalin reorganized the Polish government along the lines of other Communist countries.

Britain and the United States thought the formation of a government in Lublin was imperialistic and counter to previous agreements regarding the treatment of the occupied nations. Upon learning from Mikolajczyk of Stalin's intentions to set up a puppet government and integrate Soviet Polish army divisions into a new Polish armed force, Churchill promised never to recognize the Lublin regime and reiterated his pledge to see to it that Poland did not become a satellite of Russia.[64] The London Poles had to have equal representation in the new government if the new Polish regime was to receive the full backing of Churchill and Roosevelt.

Stalin stubbornly stood against any significant involvement in politics by the "emigre" Poles. According to Adam Ulam:

[N]o amount of argument could swerve the Soviet determination that the Provisional [Lublin-Warsaw] Government be made the basis of the future, officially recognized regime. Yes, the Russians were willing that some "democratic" politicians be invited to join their puppets. But they would have to be in a minority and in inferior positions.[65]

While Churchill struggled with increasing frustration to get the London Poles, on the one hand, to accept the Curzon line, he wrestled with Stalin, on the other, before and during Yalta, over the nature of Polish sovereignty. He blamed the intransigent Polish leadership for allowing Stalin to so easily seal the fate of Poland and the rest of Europe.[66] After all, Churchill rightly believed that however Poland was situated at the end of the war, so the other occupied countries in Europe were likely to find themselves.

At Yalta, Stalin claimed the absolute right to determine who would participate in Polish politics. Churchill recognized that a failure to reach an agreement on the question of legitimacy would alert the world to the fact that fundamental differences existed among the Allies. The consequences of this for the future would be "most lamentable," as the world then would deem the Yalta Conference a failure, thereby dimming the prospects for future cooperation among the Allies. Postwar international cooperation was one of Churchill's grand strategic objectives, the other being the security of the rights of all sovereign states. The fissures in the Alliance and the problems that arose out of the fundamental antagonism could be resolved, at least temporarily, if East and West reached an agreement to allow free and unfettered elections in Poland. Churchill could not give his support to the Lublin Poles for the principal reason that they were not truly representative of Poland and were disliked by a majority of the Polish people.[67]

Stalin's intransigence concerning the dispute over recognition prompted a letter of supreme disappointment from Roosevelt as well, who believed that the Lublin Committee as constituted represented the people of Poland.[68] Justice demanded that the new government be national in character, made up of the different parties in Poland.[69] The future peace and prosperity of Central Europe depended upon the creation of a dignified Polish constitution and the empowerment of a just government. At Yalta, Stalin promised not to interfere in the proposed elections after the end of the war in exchange for recognition of this new government. Churchill wrote of this episode: "This was the best I could get."[70]

Commentary

To Churchill, the best deal for Poland would be one that preserved democracy and political freedom. Perhaps the acceptance of the Curzon line by the exiled government would not have yielded to them a Poland free of Soviet interference. This, however, would only have gone further to prove the point that diplomacy without the military advantage is often futile. Despite his weak negotiating position, there never was any doubt that Churchill would fight Stalin to the end on this issue of Polish sovereignty, as it was both a point of justice for the Poles and a security interest for Britain. Postwar Poland's eventual subjugation only lent further credence to Churchill's notion that power enforces and perpetuates political ideas. Whoever controls the political levers often has the greatest opportunity and leverage to propagate his principles, be they principles of freedom or slavery.

Churchill's preoccupation with Poland was not entirely altruistic. He believed the threat to Polish sovereignty was a threat to British interests in the entire region. Churchill worried that if Poland were weak and overrun by the Red Army, the result likely would hold great dangers in the future for the English-speaking peoples.[71] Poland also was a test case for British war objectives. Great Britain went to war against Germany so that Poland might be free of oppression. This being so, Churchill repeatedly stated, Britain could never accept any settlement that did not leave Poland free, independent, and sovereign.[72] This recognition of Polish sovereignty was a minimum requirement for his political and economic restoration plans. Beyond this, Churchill hoped that a solution regarding Poland would be the basis of a lasting settlement and friendship between Britain and the Soviet Union.[73] However, the "test case" was proving a different point. Churchill's early preoccupation with Soviet involvement in Poland graduated to consternation and even despair by his return from the Yalta Conference in February 1945. "Are their [Poland's] sovereignty and independence to be untrammelled, or are they to become a mere projection of the Soviet State, forced against their will by an armed minority to adopt a Communist or totalitarian system? It is a touchstone far more sensitive and vital than the drawing of frontier lines."[74]

Either out of deference to the force of circumstances, or from his heart (although greater plausibility should be given the former motive rather than the latter), Churchill publicly held out seemingly endless confidence in Soviet good faith and Stalin's pledges to carry out free elections in Poland. His concern that the Grand Alliance not unravel at this critical juncture helps to explain Churchill's curious statement regarding the Yalta agreements. Churchill told the House of Commons that he knew of "no Government which stands to its obligations . . . more solidly than the Russian Soviet Government."

Churchill evidently recognized that this statement did not stand very solidly on facts. His own experience would have informed him of that. He immediately declined "absolutely to embark here (in Parliament) on a discussion about Russian good faith." He emphasized that these matters touched the whole world,

The Grand Alliance 47

and that the fortunes of the world could be jeopardized if some "awful schism" between the western democracies and the Soviet Union arose. Churchill did not cave in on his convictions. His overly kind and exaggerated language should not hide the fact that he felt an almost unbearable burden to maintain the peace and harmony within the Alliance. Working for future peace, even before the end of the war, Churchill attempted to capture Russian trust by diplomacy and to guide East-West relations along more peaceful paths.[75]

Churchill chose to hope rather than to despair about the future. As firmly as he committed his hopes, however, with equal force and determination he promised that he would strive for rectification and justice should his hopes lie fallow.[76] In the end, Churchill did garner the support of the Commons for the Crimea agreements. It would have pleased him more to see evidence of Stalin's compliance with those agreements.

Stalin once made the argument that Britain and the United States should not be chastising him on the question of free elections in Poland. After all, DeGualle was not the freely elected leader of France, and so why were Churchill and Roosevelt demanding more of Poland than of France?[77] Stalin, in fact, twisted Churchill's often-preached notions of sovereignty and freedom. For Churchill, a just sovereignty or independence was derived from the freely voiced political opinions of the broad base of the people.

In France, while DeGualle did not go through a formal election process, he was nonetheless the freely recognized leader of France, empowered by the manifest consent of free Frenchmen. The General was the leader of the free French. DeGualle, therefore, contrary to Stalin's suggestion, could be recognized by nations like Britain as the legitimate source of authority in France. Stalin's interference in Poland made the difference between France and Poland one of kind rather than degree. The Lublin Poles, Churchill repeatedly pointed out, were lacking the broad-based consent of free Poles. Free elections were necessary in Poland, as they soon would be in France, in order to garner a sounder legitimacy.

The elections in Poland were, of course, a travesty. Any significant attempt by the West to monitor the voting was blocked by the Soviets, and real opposition to the Communists was non-existent. Taking the cue from Poland, again the "test case" for all of occupied Europe, the concepts of free elections and legitimacy were twisted and refracted out of proportion to their true meaning in subsequent elections held in postwar Eastern Europe. In February 1945, Churchill posed a more probing question about the darkening situation in Poland: "Are they to be free, as we in Britain and the United States or France are free?"[78] In other words, are the Poles to be masters in their own home and captains of their souls?

How important was the fate of Poland for the rest of postwar Central and Eastern Europe? In January 1945, Churchill made special note of the Russian advances along the eastern front from the Baltics to Budapest. These advances, he noted, "must produce consequences of a character and degree about which the wisest strategists and the most far-sighted prophets will reserve their opinion until the results are known."[79] The results were very soon in coming; Poland's fate was also to be the fate of Rumania, Hungary, Czechoslovakia, Bulgaria, and sections of Germany. If Poland, the object of intense moral concern to the democracies, were to become a Soviet satellite, what good would all of the Commissions and pledges for free elections do for the rest of occupied Europe?

The Soviet Army's blanketing of Eastern Europe had pinched off most influence from the West. Churchill's plan for a commercial federation made up of Poland, Hungary, and Czechoslovakia, seen as a sure way to make Central Europe prosperous again,[80] went only so far as Stalin's and Molotov's interest, which was not very far. Churchill's attempts to achieve justice and peace in Poland had failed. The injustice of Nazi rule gave way to further injustice when the Communists gained control. Some say that the Soviet occupation of Poland was even more terrible than that of the Germans.[81] Even peace eluded Poland, for it became a participant in a Cold War with the West for nearly forty-five years. The absence of military conflict did not mean that a true peace had been achieved. Adam Ulam summed up Poland's role in international politics when he stated that the "Polish problem was to cast an increasingly dark shadow over the Grand Alliance, becoming the source of those dissonances, recriminations, and, finally diplomatic crises that ripened into the cold war."[82] Poland was the prism through which the natural political differences splitting East and West reflected on the rest of the world.

THE BALKANS

Wartime developments in the Balkans, or the countries of southern Europe, shed additional light on Churchill's diplomacy. For here again the Grand Alliance was compromised by critical differences of opinion concerning military and grand strategy. It was in the Balkan nations of Greece and Turkey where the early principles of containment strategy were applied. The grand strategy of containment, followed by the United States since 1947, could be said to have evolved out of Churchillian wartime diplomacy. Churchill's strategy was to deny Stalin critical influence in the politics of Greece, Turkey, and Yugoslavia and to bar Soviet access to a permanent naval base in the Mediterranean. However, by the end of the war, Soviet entry into the Balkan region by force ensured Soviet leaders that they would have considerable influence in the daily affairs of Bulgaria, Hungary, and Rumania.

Immediately after the formation of the wartime alliance with Britain, Stalin requested a second front west of Germany to fight the Nazi forces while the Red Army hammered away at the front in the east. In fact, Stalin wanted some action on the second front strategy as early as July 1942.[83] A military operation on a militarily significant scale was clearly not feasible in these early stages of the war. The forces of Britain were not large enough nor in a position to launch a great cross-channel offensive against entrenched Nazi divisions, and America did not enter the war until the end of 1941. Churchill knew that a premature attack from the west would cost tens of thousands of British lives and, in fact, might not even succeed in securing a foothold on the Continent. His subsequent delays in executing the invasion maddened Stalin. Churchill and Roosevelt would be the recipients of many scoldings from "Uncle Joe," the term of endearment used by both when referring to Stalin.

Initially, Stalin did not display a great preference to the location of the second front, in the Balkans or in France. Stalin, in fact, seemed initially to prefer a British presence in the southern regions so as to complicate the efforts of the German southern armies.[84] Churchill recognized the urgency of a second front to relieve the Red Army, which in 1941 and 1942 was fighting for its life. The greatest concern was that the Soviet armies would collapse before the United States could commit itself to the war effort.[85] Immediately Churchill expressed an interest in attacking the Axis powers from the south by achieving successive victories in Northern Africa, the Middle East, and finally Italy.

Stalin's interest in this strategy of tearing away at the "soft underbelly" of Germany dissipated when there was mention of Anglo-American involvement in Turkey and the Caucasian mountains.[86] Indeed, Stalin began to wonder about the political advantages accruing to the Anglo-Saxons with the "Torch" strategy.[87] Stalin's reconsideration of the Balkan strategy indicated that he, like Churchill, had turned his thoughts to the shape of postwar Europe rather early in the war.

Stalin's passion for a second front in France rather than Italy may also be explained by a fear that the citizens in the overrun regions of the Soviet Union could have taken advantage of the instability in the region to rebel and secede from Moscow.[88] A quick victory on their western front would give the Soviet Union control over regions like the Ukraine, where the rise of anti-Soviet organizations was a very real prospect. If Britain and the United States could relieve the pressure from the German eastern front by attacking from France, the opportunities for a Soviet advance into the heart of Eastern Europe would also be enhanced. Stalin was understandably angered by the repeated delays in opening up a second front; he did not seem to understand the logistical impossibility of such an operation so early in the war.

Churchill also looked forward to opening a second front in France, and he did not believe his Torch plans would damage the chances of a successful Overlord operation, "Overlord" being the code name for the 1944 cross-channel invasion of France. In Tehran, Stalin threatened "bad feelings" within the Alliance if Overlord did not occur by May 1944.[89] Stalin's temperament on the question fluctuated from week to week. The possibility of an early fissure between the two sides of the Alliance weighed heavily upon Churchill, who desperately tried to reach an accommodation with Stalin on the issue of Polish sovereignty and who desired Stalin's favorable consideration on a number of other questions to be dealt with at the peace conference. Poland would remain a centerpiece on the negotiating table until the end of the war.

Privately, Stalin's scoldings and demands for sacrifices by the British and the Americans tried Churchill's patience. The Soviets, he maintained, "have never been actuated by anything but cold-blooded self-interest and total disdain of our lives and fortunes."[90] The second front was a case in point. Stalin allowed Hitler to fortify his front in the West after he signed the nonaggression pact in 1939. Stalin's complete indifference to the fate of Western Europe and Great Britain during 1939 and 1940 left him well short of reasonable ground to criticize Churchill's and Roosevelt's strategy throughout the remainder of the war. While publicly Churchill sought to convey the image of a unified Alliance, privately he seethed before Stalin's frequently vituperative messages to his partners in war.

Churchill strongly favored action against the Germans from the south that would allow them to join hands with the Russians in the East. He believed that an absolute commitment to Overlord that sacrificed attention to other strategies in the meantime, i.e., the plan favored by the Americans, most certainly would forgo valuable opportunities in the Mediterranean. He thought a campaign in Italy between October 1943 and the cross-channel invasion would force Germany to disperse her forces out of coastal France. If Overlord was to succeed, the Soviet forces would have to keep pressing in the East and the forces of the allies would have to be built up to adequate strength vis-á-vis the Germans in France.

Churchill argued vehemently against what he called a "lawyer's agreement" (referring here to the strategy agreed upon at the Quebec Conference between the United States and Britain) to send forces to Europe without regard to the changing circumstances in Europe.[91] Churchill was convinced that by building up naval and air superiority in the Aegean Sea, and by convincing Turkey to enter the war on the side of the Allies, the war against the Germans could be shortened. There was, after all, a growing resistance against the Germans in Greece and Yugoslavia that could be turned to Allied advantage. He wrote to Stalin that "the breaking down of Italy would lead to contact with the Western Balkans and with the highly hopeful (Serbian and Croatian) resistance."[92] Churchill suspected that for political reasons, Soviet acquiescence in a large-scale Balkan operation would not be forthcoming. He found himself isolated between America and the Soviet Union, both of whom wanted Overlord as soon as possible, for the Americans did not seem to hold a great interest in the final political structure of the Balkan region.[93] General Dwight Eisenhower, commander of the Overlord operation, made a similar observation.

Although I never heard him say so, I felt that the Prime Minister's real concern was possibly of a political rather than a military nature. He may have thought that a postwar situation which would see the Western Allies posted in great strength in the Balkans would be far more effective in producing a stable posthostilities world than if the Russian armies should be the ones on that region.[94]

Churchill's desire to balance the demands of justice and military exigency found expression in perhaps his most controversial diplomacy with Stalin. In October 1944, Churchill visited Stalin in Moscow to continue the discussions of the war effort and the future of postwar Europe. Churchill proposed that the business of the war and occupation be facilitated in the following manner. "Let us," he suggested to Stalin, "settle about our affairs in the Balkans. Your armies are in Rumania and Bulgaria. We have interests, missions, and agents there. Don't let us get at cross-purposes in small ways."[95] He then laid a piece of paper before Stalin detailing the following apportionment:

Rumania		
	Russia	90%
	The others	10%
Greece		
	Great Britain (in accord with U.S.A.)	90%
	Russia	10%
Yugoslavia		50-50%
Hungary		50-50%
Bulgaria		
	Russia	75%
	The others	25%

The inspiration for this somewhat cynical division of influence by percentages came out of Churchill's desire to reduce bloodshed and to restrain Stalin's ambition to extend his reach beyond those regions he already controlled. Churchill always maintained that this agreement was not an attempt to carve up the Balkans into spheres of influence as traditionally understood. The Balkans were not being set up for exploitation by the great powers. He explained to a skeptical and anxious Roosevelt that the planned arrangement applied only to war conditions.[96] Churchill believed, and evidence appears to support such, that the percentages were no more than a method to keep peace and order.[97] For clearly, Britain had no desire to maintain a presence in these Central European countries after the war, nor was it in a position to do so. His broad policy remained unquestionably that the people ought to choose their own form of government.[98] Churchill's actions and words before, during, and after the war support his firm belief that legitimate sovereignty only could come about through free and fair elections. He stood, as in the past, square against the establishment of any new tyrannies. In part, this sphere of influence agreement was meant to prevent the emergence of tyranny in the part of Europe supposedly controlled by Britain and the United States.

Roosevelt wrote to Churchill of his skepticism back in June 1944 and was convinced that the natural tendency for such decisions to extend outside the military fields would be strengthened by the agreement.[99] Roosevelt was, of course, correct. Once a nation has a military presence in another nation, the chances that influence would broaden to the political and economic spheres are favorable. But the fact was that in 1944 the Soviet Union already had advanced into the Balkans and was establishing its influence with or without western acquiescence. On this point the Americans opened themselves up to just criticism for their lack of foresight and diminished understanding of the unfolding geopolitical realities in Europe.[100] The Americans thought the agreement was Machiavellian in character and a violation of the Atlantic Charter—"a sinister scheme to further Britain's Imperial ambitions."[101] The American leadership failed to recognize what Churchill always had known, that Soviet Russia "naturally" had vital interests in the Balkans.[102] Churchill never altered his opinion that formal political arrangements would be addressed at the peace conference by the three great powers at the end of the war.[103] He recognized the overtly repulsive nature of the agreement, but nonetheless saw that it was necessary to take an interest in the shape of postwar Europe. Had western policy been based strictly on the American view, Greece might have been condemned to anarchy and then tyranny.

The purpose of Churchill's percentage agreement was twofold. First, there was an urgency to avoid strife within the Alliance that may have fed upon the developing civil wars (especially in Yugoslavia between the Croats and Slovenes) and the various Allied missions that worked at cross-purposes.[104] In 1944, though, there was little doubt that the forces of Hitler would be defeated, and Churchill's attention increasingly turned to geopolitics. Churchill believed the arrangements with Stalin were "the best possible." He wrote of the arrangements that coupled with successful military action, they should help save Greece and Yugoslavia from the arrival of Russian and Bulgarian forces under Russian command on the eastern flank.[105]

The second purpose of the percentage agreement, perhaps the most significant of the two, was to allow the western Allies some say in Balkan politics, especially in the strategically located nation of Greece.[106] The worry was that Britain would be "powerless in the face of Russia."

Churchill hoped that good relations with Stalin could be preserved and that he could pave the way by purposeful concessions, such as those implied in the percentage agreement and those that would allow the Soviets access to the Mediterranean via shipping lanes through the Dardenelles (an offer that violated the prewar Montreux Convention that gave sovereignty over these lanes to Turkey).[107] If these concessions had led to a broad-based peace in Europe, they would have been hard to argue against. Churchill did not, however, rely entirely upon Stalin's gestures of goodwill.[108] He was impotent to control the developments in Europe by force. Indeed, Stalin's military influence in the region was growing week by week. The percentage agreement, wrote Chester Wilmot, was an effort to circumvent this handicap. "Thwarted in his desire to forestall Russia militarily," Wilmot wrote, "Churchill endeavored to restrain her by striking a political bargain direct with the Kremlin."[109] Churchill argued from points of justice that the western forces ought to have a hand, as more hostile forces most surely would have one, in the political reconstruction of Greece and to assist in the resistance against the communist partisans. Churchill insisted that the British and Americans could not "leave Athens to anarchy and misery, followed by tyranny established on murder."[110]

Churchill's attempt to restrain communism on the Balkan peninsula by preventing the uncontested expansion of Soviet power created a special arrangement that would work in the interest of democracy and liberty. In 1942, during the youthful stages of new Anglo-Soviet cooperation, he noted that "it would be a measureless disaster if Russian barbarism were to overlay the culture and independence of the ancient states of Europe."[111]

By late 1944, Stalin had accomplished a *fait accompli*; certain European states were beyond rescue. Churchill's infamous slip of paper would let us know that he believed Rumania and Bulgaria to be beyond reach.[112] He could not justify military efforts to "run the same risk for them (Rumania and Bulgaria) as we have done for Greece and Poland." Whether this was one of Churchill's considerations is not clear, but both Rumania and Bulgaria were also at one time enemies of Great Britain. Cooperation with Stalin in the Balkans, so it was hoped, would encourage Stalin to favorably consider Britain's requests for the future composition of Poland. Churchill was willing, in fact, to sacrifice some interests in the Balkans to save Poland, his objective from the start of the war. In the end, though, Churchill was convinced that his backroom diplomacy saved Greece and forestalled the spread of communism in countries along the Adriatic and Mediterranean.[113]

Churchill's efforts to save Yugoslavia from communism failed. One could say that Churchill was hoodwinked here, first by Marshal Tito, the leader of the partisan movement against the Germans and the Yugoslav king, and then later by Stalin, who nullified the 50/50 percentage agreement with Churchill with his secret concessions to Tito. By June 1945, the tide had turned sharply against British interests in Yugoslavia.[114]

The ejection of the Germans by East and West had allowed Tito to solidify his hold on power. Churchill delivered much aid and support to the partisan's cause. His son Randolph even put on the uniform for their cause and fought with Tito's forces. Tito, for his part, used Churchill to gain valuable Allied recognition for his military and civilian authority and to denounce all of Tito's opponents, including the monarch.[115]

The Yugoslavian experience is another example where the ends of victory and justice clashed, justice here being freely decided local sovereignty. In fact, Nora Beloff accused Churchill of having inconsistent objectives. On the one hand, there was the push to aid the partisans both to fight the Germans and to shape postwar Yugoslavia. On the other hand, there was the declaration that *all* parties were to have a fair chance to participate in the new government.[116] Partisanship and free elections are at odds with each other. This is valid criticism but a little unfair to Churchill who, despite his aid to one faction over the others, did desire that the postwar environment in Yugoslavia be conducive to the eventual creation of a legitimate government, a government representative of all factions except the Fascists.

Tito promised Churchill, who discussed with Tito his notion of a democratic Yugoslavia based on peasant interests, that he would not bring communism to Yugoslavia.[117] Tito was to be the tool with which the ground would be cleared to accept the new political institutions. Tito's forces were also the best equipped and organized to combat the Germans and were naturally the recipients of great amounts of aid. But I see no reason to doubt Beloff's conclusion that, despite the fact that Churchill was seriously misled by his intelligence sources about the true character of Tito, "[t]he epic story of the gallant guerillas fired the Prime Minister's imagination and it took him more than a year before he realized that the gallantry was being expended in another cause."[118] Tito also had the support of the Communists in Moscow, and one can speculate whether Churchill's disassociation with Tito would have spared Yugoslavia her fate under communism. In either scenario, one would have difficulty impugning Churchill's motives.

The developments in Greece provided a platform for Churchill to expound further upon his notions of democracy. For Greece was embroiled in civil war, and there was evidence that Moscow desired to give the government of Greece a shape of its own liking. Since 1941, Britain had assumed the responsibility of ministering to the sick Greek nation where the Communists, supported by Moscow, were sowing the seeds of anarchy. Churchill hoped to reach at least a temporary accommodation with Stalin regarding a better working arrangement in Greece, an arrangement judged apart from the postwar settlement. Churchill appeared willing to give up certain British interests in Rumania in exchange for greater control over Grecian affairs.[119]

Churchill's efforts to bring democracy to the struggling nations of Europe were probably, outside of Poland, most keenly focused on Greece. The task of Great Britain was to see to it that relief was brought to the Greek people after a German surrender and then to ensure that a legitimate government took hold of the reins of power.[120] Churchill was angered not only with the intervention of the communist powers in Greece and the turmoil that was created by the German occupation. The Labour party supported the Greek communist guerillas (ELAS and EAM) as legitimate factions, and this deeply disturbed Churchill. His speech to his colleagues in December 1944 expressed ideas similar to those discussed in Chapter two, suggesting once again a remarkable continuity in Churchill's political thought:

The question however arises, and one may be permitted to dwell on it for a moment, who are the friends of democracy, and also how is the word "democracy" to be interpreted? My idea of it is that the plain, humble, common man, just the ordinary man who keeps a wife and family, who goes off to fight for his country when it is in trouble, goes to the poll at the appropriate time, and puts his cross on the ballot-paper showing the candidate he wishes to be elected to Parliament—that he is the foundation of democracy. And it is essential to this foundation that this man or woman should do this without fear, and without any form of intimidation or victimization. . . If that is democracy I salute it. . . . But I feel quite differently about a *swindle democracy*, a democracy which calls itself democracy because it is Left Wing. It takes all sorts to make democracy, not only Left Wing, or even Communist. . . . One must have some respect for democracy, and not use the word too lightly. The last thing which resembles democracy is mob law, with bands of gangsters, armed with deadly weapons, forcing their way into great cities, seizing the police stations and key points of government, endeavouring to introduce a totalitarian regime with an iron hand, and clamouring, as they can nowadays if they get the power [as they were attempting to do in Greece]. . . . Democracy is no harlot to be picked up in the street by a man with a tommy gun. . . . [W]e shall persist in this policy of clearing Athens and the Athens region of all who are rebels against the authority of the constitutional Government of Greece.[121]

Churchill's trip to Greece in December 1944 confirmed to him that Greece could be brought into the postwar world in much better form if the West were vigilant and guarded against a political imbalance that could result from the disruption and violence wrought by the anti-democratic forces (the Communists and Fascists). An institutionalized imbalance would result in what he called a "swindle democracy," if the ruling forces pretended to be one at all. Perhaps the greatest challenge to democracy in Greece recognized by Churchill was posed by his Alliance partner, Joseph Stalin.[122] The strength of the Soviet Union could not be counted on to promote democratic ideals. He knew that only the British action in 1944 could allow Greece to escape the fate of Czechoslovakia.[123]

Even before the end of the war, the political shape of Eastern Europe began to unfold. There were indications of a rupture in the Alliance as early as 1943, when the Soviets negotiated a treaty of friendship and alliance with Czechoslovakia. The treaty was a sign that small East European states had to seek an accommodation with Moscow and could not expect western support in any confrontation with the Soviet Union. It was an indication that Moscow expected those subject governments to be purged of all disagreeable parties in favor of the local Communists.[124] Events in Poland would continue to disturb the Alliance until its final dissolution. In January 1945, before Yalta, Churchill was convinced the western democracies were, politically and militarily, in a very disadvantaged position in Central and Eastern Europe. "Make no mistake, all the Balkans, except Greece, are going to be Bolshevised; and there is nothing I can do to prevent it. There is nothing I can do for poor Poland either."[125] There can be no doubt; had democracy not had such a devoted advocate as Churchill, more countries in Europe would have been subjected to Soviet influence, or at least fearful for their independence.

With little or no hesitation, Stalin solidified his gains in the Balkans. "By Christmas Eve [1944]—when the Germans in the Ardennes were but four miles from the Meuse—the Russians on the Danube had completed the encirclement of the Hungarian capital and, without waiting for its capture, had created for the liberated territory a government of their own persuasion."[126] The work in the previous months by Soviet forces to conquer territories in Rumania, Yugoslavia, and Bulgaria was instrumental to the solidification of their gains in Europe, for through these "liberated" nations vital supply routes were set up to feed the Red Army. Hungary, Germany, and Austria now lay before the Red Army. Difficulties in Italy also had begun, owing to "Russian intrigues."[127]

Despite the monumental military achievements of 1944, for Churchill, this year was marred by a growing anxiety concerning Soviet intentions and place in the postwar world. Rumania would provide the situation for the widening of the rift between East and West. The Soviets accused the British of meddling in Rumanian affairs while at the same time formed Communist cells within that same country. Churchill frequently expressed apprehension when he thought of the slim probabilities for the achievement of goodwill between Britain and the Soviet Union.[128] By March 1945, the mental strain wrought by the betrayals of Stalin in Rumania and the other nations of Eastern Europe took a toll, not only on Britain's honor, but also on the physical condition of the prime minister. For there were times when Churchill doubled over from exhaustion and anguish.[129]

Commentary

As the war progressed, Churchill increasingly worried about the spread of Soviet influence in the Balkan peninsula. By September 1944, Soviet advances into Bulgaria led Churchill to concern himself with the fate of Greece. The Balkan nations became yet another proving ground for the contest between the needs of military victory and the demands of justice in the occupied territories. As early as 1943, Churchill took note of Stalin's ambitions in this region and saw the need to impose restraints on them. The objective remained for Churchill not to leave the democratic cause politically weaker. Not only would a campaign in support of the Turks, Greeks, and Yugoslavs contribute to the winning of the war, it "would enhance the prospects of winning the peace."[130] Allied policy in the Balkans had three objectives: to nourish the resistance forces against the Germans; to bring Turkey into the war; and to promote chaos in the regions held by Germans.[131] Churchill's Balkan strategy also was designed to give the democratic Allies a more favorable position after the war vis-á-vis the Soviet Union.

Churchill did not push his Balkan campaign strategy out of deference to the United States. For, again, he shunned most behavior that threatened to drive a wedge between the United States and Great Britain. In a letter to Field-Marshal Smuts, Churchill reiterated that "British loyalty to 'Overlord' is [the] keystone of [the] arch of Anglo-American co-operation."[132]

Churchill tried many ways to excite American interest in the Balkans, including political arguments, to no avail. The United States failed to realize that "great prizes lie in the Balkan direction,"[133] and that the conquest of Italy would give the Allies leverage to bring Turkey into the war. Roosevelt neglected the growing Soviet hegemony in southeastern Europe. Chester Wilmot listed three reasons for Roosevelt's desire to keep out of the Balkans: first, FDR desired Soviet participation in the new world organization (he knew Anglo-American presence in the Balkans aggravated Stalin); second, FDR wanted to ensure Soviet participation in the war against Japan; and third, FDR did not want the American public to perceive him as following the British lead in the war, for 1944 was an election year.[134] To Churchill's utter disbelief, Roosevelt wanted southeastern European questions to be decided by Stalin, in effect, granting the Soviet Union control over most of the Balkan region.[135]

The Grand Alliance

Churchill's strategy was to fashion more tolerable political solutions in Europe than those advocated by Roosevelt. At one point he posed a series of questions to his Foreign Secretary Anthony Eden.

You should try to find out what the Russians really feel about the Balkans. Would they be attracted by the idea of our acting through the Aegean, involving Turkey in the war, and opening the Dardenelles and Bosphorus so that British naval forces and shipping could aid the Russian advance. . . . How great an interest would they feel in our opening the Black Sea to Allied warships, supplies, and Allied military forces, including Turkish? Have they any interest in this right-handed evolution, or are they still set only on our attacking France?[136]

Churchill was interested in accommodating Soviet interests for two purposes. First, Churchill desired to maintain optimum Soviet cooperation in the stretch for victory against Germany and avoid any fissure in the wartime strategy of the Grand Alliance. Second, Churchill hoped to have a cooperative relationship with the Soviets after the war and desired favorable consideration from Stalin on important political issues regarding control over the Balkan region. As in Poland, perhaps there was a way to compromise in the Balkans in order to save a portion of Central and Southern Europe from Soviet control.

Between the conferences at Tehran, where the beginning of the end game was discussed and the fate of Eastern Europe decided, and Yalta, where the decisions at Tehran essentially were ratified, the Soviets affirmed their new political and military presence in the world. President Roosevelt persuaded himself that the events in the Balkans were inconsequential; there would be no jeopardizing Soviet participation in the war against Japan. Churchill also acknowledged the significance of Soviet involvement as early as possible in the eastern conflict, but thought that Soviet participation should not be bought with concessions prejudicing freedom and justice in Central Europe or the Balkans.[137]

To Churchill, membership in the community of civilized nations depended upon the fulfillment of certain duties—the duty to respect the integrity of the individual and the sovereignty of legitimate states took first priority. In June 1945, Churchill was reminded of his old opposition to the formal recognition of the Bolsheviks as the legitimate government of the Russian and the other republics. Soviet atrocities in Bulgaria reminded him of how far the Soviets still had to come to join the international community. "Whenever these Bolsheviks think you are afraid of them they will do whatever suits their lust and cruelty. . . . Let them then behave, and obey the ordinary decencies of civilization."[138]

Churchill's sense for basic political and geographic realities during the war generated policies that may, arguably, label him the original architect of the "containment" policy, a strategy to meet the Soviets, where possible, in Europe with a combination of hard-nosed diplomacy and military muscle to block them from territories vulnerable to exploitation. His departure from office before the war's end deprived Churchill of the opportunity to be an official part of the initiation of the policy of containment, a policy so central to Western postwar defense strategy. That Greece and Turkey, the recipients of Truman's 1947 aid package that inaugurated the age of containment, would become hot spots in the world was no surprise to Churchill. He knew that the Grand Alliance was terribly imperfect, that it suffered from an acute divergence in purpose. He also knew that the Alliance had liberated Europe in a most dissimilar fashion, laying the seeds of conflict for generations to come.

GERMANY AND THE END GAME

Military and political events in Germany before the end of the war, like those in Poland and the Balkans, gave shape to a new Europe. The fate of Germany was a concern to all owing to her geographic situation on the Continent, territorial composition, and the character of her people. The centrality of the German state on the Continent meant a strategic advantage for any state fighting a land war in Europe. Germany's hearty industrial base and natural resources gave her obvious economic and military advantages. These advantages, combined with militaristic tradition, in Prussia in particular, lent compelling plausibility to the arguments that Germany would play a significant role in Europe's future.

There was little question that Germany would be divided after the war. Nor was there much doubt that she would be punished in some manner for her aggressive and atrocious behavior. Before the war's end, few had any concrete ideas as to how the Alliance relationships would evolve, or devolve, and what the consequent impact on the political order of Europe would be. The Allied policy of "unconditional surrender" for Germany, Italy, and Japan to end the war was, in part, responsible for this pervasive uncertainty. This policy, articulated by Roosevelt in 1943 at Casablanca, was accepted by Churchill as a general goal, but without Roosevelt's emotional attachment to it. While the desire to ask for the complete submission of the German people and state to the victorious powers was understandable given the Nazi's merciless military policies and barbarous political ends, the "unconditional surrender" policy was also dangerous and illogical. This slogan, or rallying cry, was looked upon at the time as an assurance to Stalin that the failure to open a second front in 1943 did not indicate any weakening in the resolution of the western Allies. But what effect would this have upon postwar Europe?[139]

In Britain too, there was no desire to accept a separate peace with Hitler, or to negotiate a settlement. Those who waged total war must be prepared to lose absolutely their standing in the world. The Americans easily adopted this idea of no compromises with the Devil. But in doing so, the continuation of the bloodshed to the bitter end was assured, as the Germans, with or without Hitler, lacked a diplomatic alternative for ending the conflict. Regarding the end game for Italy, Churchill expressed his consternation that "[m]erely harping on 'unconditional surrender' with no prospect of mercy held out even as an act of grace may well lead to no surrender at all."[140] Clearly, the most likely alternative to honorable capitulation for the Germans was a battle to the death.

Churchill provided his readers with a definition of "unconditional surrender" relative to Germany in his *The Hinge of Fate*:

By this we mean that their will power to resist must be completely broken, and that they must yield themselves absolutely to our justice and mercy. It also means that we must take all those far-sighted measures which are necessary to prevent the world from being again convulsed, wrecked, and blackened by their calculated plots and ferocious aggression. It does not mean . . . that we are to stain our victorious arms by inhumanity or by mere lust of vengeance.[141]

The emotional tide in the world against the Germans would have ensured unmitigated popular outrage toward any policy that called for less extreme measures. Churchill believed that the treatment of conquered Germany at the end of the war called for her disarmament, the suspension of her aviation activities, a trial of justice for those who committed atrocities and for those who led the war effort (without mass executions), and the division of Germany into separate states to break up the powerful confluence of resources and nationalistic spirit. The German people would not immediately be given the sovereign right to self-determination. Churchill stressed that the Allies would not be bound to the Germans at the moment of surrender by any obligation. He insisted that there would be no question of the Atlantic Charter applying to Germany as a matter of right and preventing just territorial adjustments in the enemy countries.[142]

For all of his support for terms of peace, Churchill still recognized, as did Stalin, the imprudence of their ambiguity. The quickest avenue to surrender, not necessarily the most prudent avenue, required the German leadership to be aware of what it was that the would-be victors demanded of them.[143] In actuality, there is no such thing as "unconditional" surrender. There always will be terms and conditions. Why would a government surrender unless it knew it would be better off by doing so? Perhaps death would be better than abject slavery to the victorious powers. Churchill believed that it was unlikely Germany would capitulate, and, therefore, the terms of unconditional surrender were appropriate and would not prolong the war.[144] One cannot help but wonder, however, that if the Allies were more flexible with their peace terms, German officers might not have been inspired to do away with their leader and save Germany the horrors of total military defeat and a national bloodbath?[145]

The proposed peace terms also were partially responsible for the eventual division of Europe. For this reason, the case could be made that the terms of peace were politically imprudent. By the end of the Tehran Conference, Churchill recognized that the Soviets had a long-term grand strategy and that the West was noticeably lacking in one. There was a political reason the Soviets wanted Britain and the United States to concentrate their forces in the western half of Europe and remain out of the south and east. This strategy, coupled with the consequences of unconditional surrender (which removed any opportunity for early German surrender, sparing Europe from further devastation and occupation), assisted the Soviet Union in achieving their dominance over Eastern and Central Europe.[146] The significance of the terms was that the war against Germany would not end until the forces from the West and the East met, probably in the very heart of Germany. Soviet domination over a portion of German territory was virtually assured. The Germans thought that these conditions would provoke a crisis within the United Nations as the Soviet armies gradually gobbled up parts of Eastern Europe and that they might be spared the sort of occupation that eventually resulted.[147] As it was, the Soviets were assured of reaching Berlin and beyond before East met West.

The capture of Berlin was imperative if the West was to ensure significant democratic influence in the construction of postwar Central Europe. The industrial centers of Germany would not hold nearly the importance of Berlin, the political center. As early as 1942, Foreign Minister Eden believed that the West ought not to gamble on the hope that the Soviet Union would be so exhausted at the war's end that "she will be forced to collaborate with us without our having to make any concessions to her."[148] There was no question of victory for the Grand Alliance; victory was theirs. What mattered during 1943 and 1944 was the political picture, the balance of power and political influence. Both sides recognized this. According to Wilmot, Churchill "was not to be deluded by any assurance from Moscow that Stalin considered Berlin had 'lost its political importance.'"[149]

There were, in fact, two wars in Europe. Moscow did not desire to coordinate the war effort within the Allied council as the English and the Americans did. For this would have meant western control over Soviet forces and the sharing of vital information about each side's war plans and, consequently, political intentions.[150] "United" nations these were not in spirit. Consequently, the frictions and events of war, instead of being to the disadvantage or advantage of the Grand Alliance, weighed in often against one of the coalition members. Hitler's transferal of Nazi troops from the eastern front to the western toward the end the war, to the obvious political advantage of the Soviet Union, is perhaps the starkest example of particular events benefitting certain members of the Alliance to the detriment of others.

After each successive meeting at Tehran, Quebec, Yalta, and then Potsdam, the question of how Germany was to be divided gradually became clarified. The rationale for the division was clear to Churchill at Tehran. The "root of the evil lay in Prussia, in the Prussian Army and General Staff." He recognized that all deeply feared the might of a united Germany. It would be possible and in the interest of a united Europe, he thought, to make a "stern but honourable peace with her" and at the same time "to re-create in modern forms what had been in general outline the Austro-Hungarian Empire."[151] Churchill believed disinterest in the West concerning the new division could very well become the cause of yet another war.[152] To divide Germany without giving due consideration to the geostrategic consequences might imperil the new Europe. According to Churchill's private secretary, Churchill "hardly liked to consider dismembering Germany until his doubts about Russia's intentions had been cleared away."[153]

Before and after Tehran, little thought was given to the extent of the Soviet zone of occupation. Churchill pointed out that general opinion in elite circles at the time about the Soviet Union was that it would not continue the war once it had reached its frontiers, that, indeed, when the time came, the western Allies may well have to try to persuade the Soviet leader not to relax his efforts.[154] Clearly at this time no one could see how the war would end. Plans eventually unfolded that would give the Russians control in the east, while the British and French controlled the northern and the Americans the southern sections of western Germany. Extreme eastern Germany, of course, went to the Poles as part of the overall border settlement.

Clear boundaries of control within Germany never were established until the presence of military forces made the question moot. The American forces extended their front further into eastern Germany than was expected initially. Instead of establishing their positions there, Roosevelt, out of concern for the political relationship with the Soviet Union, ordered his troops to withdraw 100 miles westward and to concede this territory to the Soviets. This decision tormented Churchill, who saw advantages in not giving up portions of hard-won land. For one, Churchill recognized that the Soviet Union would be controlling that portion of Germany considered the breadbasket of the nation. He feared that the burden upon the western Allies to feed their zones would be increased considerably without access to the arable lands to the east.[155]

Perhaps more importantly, the retreat meant thousands more would be subjected to Soviet rule. The Soviet geographic advantage in Central Europe would be increased further still. Territories under Soviet control included the Baltic states, occupied Germany, Czechoslovakia, Yugoslavia, Hungary, Rumania, Bulgaria, and the frontiers of Austria. The Russian advance to the positions retreated from on the Elbe, according to Churchill, constituted "an event in the history of Europe to which there has been no parallel, and which has not been faced by the Allies in their long and hazardous struggle."[156] The Allies now faced the likelihood of an indefinite occupation of eastern Germany by their ally, who would take years to exact reparations by the almost complete removal of industrial machinery and other resources from its section.

How strong should postwar Germany be? If Germany were made strong, would the world again be confronted by Hun militarism as it was twice before in this century? If it were made weak, would the western countries, out of concern for the well-being of millions of innocent Germans and the military balance in Europe, have to bear the economic, maybe even military, burden of supporting an emaciated Germany as they had done after World War I? There were some people in both the United States and Great Britain that argued that the world had no recourse but to economically and militarily weaken this aggressor nation. In September 1944, Roosevelt's Secretary of the Treasury, Henry Morgenthau, insisted upon a plan that called for the complete "pastoralization" of Germany, by denuding that vanquished country of its industrial capacity in order to keep it weak and dependent upon the exports of other states, especially steel exports. Churchill believed such a plan to both unjust and imprudent, although Churchill later agreed, with Roosevelt, to follow the plan to some degree. Lord Moran, Churchill's personal physician, recorded Churchill's reaction to the proposal at a round table meeting with Americans: "I'm all for disarming Germany," he said, "but we ought not to prevent her living decently. There are bonds between the working classes of all countries, and the English people will not stand for the policy you are advocating. . . . I agree with Burke. You cannot indict a whole nation."[157]

Tactically, the plan was believed by some to be a monumental mistake, for it granted the Nazi propagandist Goebbels an opportunity to rally the German population in the face of an enemy that was going to strip them of their pride and their living.[158] In accepting the plan against the wishes of his Foreign Secretary Anthony Eden, for the sake of amity within the Alliance, Churchill accepted the arguments that Britain's export trade would be wonderfully enhanced, and that the logic of the plan would lead to German disarmament. However, the developing threat from the East would turn Churchill eventually into an ardent supporter of a revived and strong German nation in league with the West.

Churchill believed that Germany would contribute one day to the security of the continent. This of course could only happen once every last vestige of Nazi tyranny and Prussian militarism had been extinguished. This would leave Germany psychologically mature to participate within the comity of nations.[159] At Tehran, Stalin expressed his doubts that a militarily responsible Germany could ever emerge, citing the industrious nature of the people, the economics of the land, and the militaristic nationalism that prevailed since Bismarck.[160]

Germany's dismemberment weighed heavily in the considerations of future European security. Churchill forwarded a policy that called for the isolation of Prussia from the rest of Germany, which would form a "Danubian Confederation" of Bavaria, Wuerttemberg, the Palatinate, Saxony, and Baden. As the Prussian region was the most "ferocious," it should be treated more harshly than the southern regions of Germany, regions that Churchill believed were not inclined to war. These lower regions, he said, should be dealt with in a more tolerable fashion.[161] Churchill informed Stalin, who displayed no sympathy for Churchill's attitude toward the German people, that he was not against the "toilers in Germany, but only against the leaders and against dangerous combinations."[162]

Roosevelt, in agreement with Stalin, believed the distinctions between the regions were unnecessary and that all of Germany should be made to pay for the sins of the Nazis. All Germans were the same. He proposed splitting Germany into five self-governing regions and two regions governed by the United Nations. This partition proposal was the one that most effectively would weaken Germany. According to Churchill, Stalin believed that it was better to break up and disperse throughout the land "the German tribes." He believed they always would want to reunite, and that this danger would have to be neutralized by various economic measures, possibly by force.[163] Milovan Djilas' reports in *Conversations with Stalin* confirmed Churchill's assessment.

Someone expressed doubt that the Germans would be able to recuperate within fifty years. But Stalin was of a different opinion. "No, they will recover, and very quickly. That is a highly developed industrial country with an extremely qualified and numerous working class and technical intelligentsia. Give them twelve to fifteen years and they'll be on their feet again."[164]

In addition to carving up the German nation, the Soviet Union demanded heavy reparations that effectively would force the German people to toil in the service of the victors for years to come. Churchill understood that these proposals would render Germany politically impotent and economically impoverished. Churchill did not believe that draconian reparations properly achieved the desired justice or stable political conditions. The profit gained from such processes, he wrote after reflecting on the Versailles treaty, bore no relation to the cost of the war.[165]

In his view, a punitive policy levied against all of Germany would have made that nation, or any part of that nation, insignificant in the balance of power in Europe, which would have been clearly detrimental to the security of other states on the continent. The Soviet occupation of Germany for an unspecified period of time had to worry Churchill still more given the American pledge to carry out a withdrawal from the continent shortly after the victory. Whose forces would move into the vacuum created by the withdrawal of the American troops? Even as late as October 1943, Churchill was aware that the political realities of Europe probably would be altered forever, and, evoking anger from Eden and his Cabinet, judged that "[w]e mustn't weaken Germany too much—we may need her against Russia."[166]

The negotiations at Yalta should be thought of for what they signified rather than what they accomplished. Lord Beaverbrook was right when he announced that the Yalta Conference in February 1945 was "[p]erhaps the most engrossing chapter since the early days of the war."[167] However, many major issues already had been decided, either by previous Alliance conferences and agreements or by force of arms. One legitimately can question the degree of influence each of the agreements exercised over the Allies. There was no question of who would determine political events in Poland; much of this already had been decided by private agreements among the great powers and sealed by the presence of Soviet military forces. Elections in Eastern Europe were, of course, "guaranteed" by the Declaration of Liberated Europe; Yalta would parade this illusion for a little while longer. In actuality, Soviet armies had the final say in many of the countries in Eastern and Central Europe.

Perhaps the most significant accomplishments of the conferences were to assure Soviet participation in the new United Nations Organization and Soviet involvement in the war against Japan after the defeat of the Nazi forces. While these objectives received Churchill's strong support, Roosevelt pushed for their acceptance more strongly.[168]

Churchill's concern revolved around two issues that did not receive full support from the American delegation. First, there must be solid agreement by the great powers on the recreation of a strong, free, and sovereign Poland.[169] By waiting for the three-power conference at Yalta to deal with the Polish questions,

Churchill believed that he might have been able to acquire some bargaining advantage that he lost to the Red Army.

Second, Churchill believed that great importance should be given to Britain's continued presence among the ranks of the great powers.[170] He therefore sought to enable a weakened Britain to play a major role on the world stage. A new balance of power would require a significant German presence and a France engaged in the affairs of Europe. It also would require the United States to assist Britain in the maintenance of a 300-year-old tradition of making sure no one power dominated the Continent. The Yalta negotiations would be the genesis of a new geopolitical order.

Churchill's confidence in the Yalta accords faded within days after their conclusion. Mikolaczyk, leader of the London Poles, was snubbed by the new provisional government in Lublin, nullifying the promise made by Stalin to accept a shared form of government. Freedom of movement promised to British observers in Poland also never fully materialized.

Yalta in fact would signal the beginning of the chill in East-West diplomacy for Churchill. He reported to his private secretary that he had "not the slightest intention of being cheated over Poland, not even if we go to the verge of war with Russia."[171] Colville recorded in March 1945 the emerging sense of despair over the alliance with Russia and the future of Europe.

It seems that we may be heading for a showdown with the Russians who are showing every sign of going back on the Yalta agreement over Poland and of enforcing aggressive Communism on an unwilling Rumania. The P.M. and Eden both fear that our willingness to trust our Russian ally may have been vain and they look with despondency to the future.[172]

Commentary

A great paradox was created in 1941 when the western powers allied themselves with an eastern power of radically different principles. At the very moment when the British and the Americans were cheering the Soviet armies on as they moved closer and closer to Germany, they also were rooting against their own interests and against the hopes of the peoples of Central and Eastern Europe.

Soviet political objectives were diametrically opposed to those of the western democracies. Consolidation of her gains across her western frontiers, rather than the stability of Europe accomplished by the general introduction of democracy into the region, dominated Soviet postwar foreign policy plans.[173] By dominating the polities of Central and Eastern Europe and the western regions of the empire, such as the Ukraine, Moscow hoped to eliminate any threats to those regions. A buffer zone of occupied states in Europe, a sign of entrenchment and separateness from the rest of the world, was the culmination of Soviet wartime policy that began with the turn of fortune at the battle of Stalingrad. Stalin's chief concern was power, not justice.[174]

Since Stalingrad, Soviet diplomacy aimed to create opportunities to capitalize on in Eastern Europe. Stalin's quick assent to the Yalta Conference immediately after Hitler turned his forces westward, and the early recognition of the Lublin Poles, reflected a savvy for strategic diplomacy. Stalin was not interested in participating in another Allied conference until his armies had secured the strongest military position possible.[175] By the time of the Yalta Conference, Stalin had within his grasp all the capitals of eastern Europe.

Churchill was under no illusions regarding Britain's weakened position. The ignorance of his American allies and of others in Europe regarding the ominous developments troubled him deeply. "People ought to be stirred out of their complacency," he said, "and given some sense of the forces moving in the world."[176] Weakness gave rise to the meaningless agreement at Yalta concerning the balance of power. Poland was not going to be saved; and Europe would have to contend with the presence of a new domineering power. Eliot Cohen reflected on these unwelcome facts. "Faced with now dominant Soviet power in the East and having failed to get Roosevelt to take a firm position on Poland and other Central European questions, Churchill now became anxious to strike the best bargain possible with Stalin before the Western negotiating position deteriorated still further."[177] Churchill recognized a cursed irony in Poland's fate a year before the conference: the reconstitution of Polish sovereignty and freedom depended upon Soviet victories against the German armies.[178]

The Declaration of Liberated Europe symbolized the hollow character of the united understanding regarding the fate of Europe. The Declaration was a pledge by the three powers "to solve by democratic means their pressing political and economic problems." As such, it was a follow-up to the principles outlined in the Atlantic Charter, which acknowledged the right of all peoples to choose their form of government and called for the restoration of sovereignty to those peoples deprived of it by the aggressors. Finding solutions to the problems on the continent, one of those solutions being free elections, was supposed to be a joint effort by East and West.

Difficulties with the document itself should have been apparent before the ink dried. For the Declaration was inconsistent with promises made by the leaders of the western powers, including Churchill, that Stalin would be allowed to ensure that all of the states contiguous to the Soviet Union had to be friendly. Indeed, how can one assure "free and unfettered secret ballot elections" in a political environment that demands an outcome favorable to one side? Considering the repression that followed in Eastern Europe, one could conclude that either Stalin did not himself take the document seriously, or that he had a different definition of "free and unfettered elections."

Though publicly supportive of the document, one is hard pressed to find evidence that Churchill placed faith in the Declaration as a guarantor of Europe's freedoms. The Declaration was largely Roosevelt's achievement, a moralistic response to Churchill's sphere of influence agreements with Stalin made in the previous year. These secret agreements by the British have been labeled by some as a principal cause of Stalin's subsequent control over Eastern Europe.[179]

Churchill had hoped that all the powers would live up to the Declaration, but the course of events informed him that such a prospect was unlikely. The advancing Red Army was reality; the Declaration was a wish, something very much beyond the control of just one or two of the great powers. Stalin accepted Roosevelt's Declaration on Liberated Europe, but he yielded nothing in so doing so since his armies were in possession of Rumania, Bulgaria, and Hungary.[180] What Stalin won on the battlefield, Poland's new borders included, he would not negotiate away. Stalin spoke very little about Soviet interests and intentions with Churchill and Roosevelt between the Tehran and Yalta Conferences. He did put himself, though, in *de facto* control of parts of Europe, giving himself the strongest hand for the peace negotiations.

Neither the German question nor the fate of Poland summarized the true concern for Roosevelt during the conference. These two issue, issues that Churchill took to heart, were bargaining levers for Roosevelt to ensure Soviet participation in the war against Japan. Yalta had exacted a political price from the western democracies.

The end game of the conflict shaped up to be one of great significance. The location of the Allied armies at the cessation of the war was an important element of that end game. Churchill believed that it was vital that the Western armies reach Berlin before the Red Army, that they reach, in fact, as far east as possible. This was especially important given the probable Soviet occupation of much of Eastern and Central Europe, including Austria.[181] That Churchill would form his military plans to this task in such a fashion gives one an indication of the growing mistrust he held for Stalin.

Churchill's attitude once again can be juxtaposed to that of the Americans. While Churchill sought to execute the political and military measures necessary to gain leverage when bargaining with the Soviets, the American objectives focused more squarely on military victory, oblivious to postwar power realities. The necessity of winning Soviet goodwill and Soviet assistance in the war against Japan determined much of the American political and military strategy during the European conflict. While it may be argued that the American insistence on Soviet participation in the East was prudent, it is fair to conclude that this position was held to the detriment of true peace in Europe.

Chief among Churchill's many preoccupations near the end of the war was the American withdrawal from Europe, which created a power vacuum at the very moment the Soviet Union was positioning its forces to dominate the political systems of Europe. Churchill remarked to Roosevelt in early 1945 that he thought the end of this war could well prove to be more disappointing than was the last one.[182]

Churchill believed that the western powers ought to strengthen their diplomatic hand by first, refusing to retreat from captured territories in the East to points agreed upon in Tehran earlier; second, by using the Black and Baltic Sea exits as carrots or bargaining chips with the Soviet Union, undeniably a land power looking for serviceable ports; and third, by reaching agreements before the American armies were withdrawn from their furthest points east.[183] Diplomacy without military strength would be ineffective. There was some question as to whether Roosevelt concessionary diplomacy to Stalin mitigated the suspicion that Stalin always had of American and British collusion. The Soviet leader had little incentive to grant negotiating points; for Roosevelt's pledge to remove troops from Europe within two years after the conflict meant that Stalin would benefit from a waiting game. "Why grant concessions on Poland and Germany?" he may have said. "The core of the Western forces will be gone in two years."

An American withdrawal in the face of new power arrangements was a form of unilateral disarmament.[184] This was dangerous in light of the experience following the last war, when the democracies chose to disregard the significance of unilateral rearmament by the more arrogant and bellicose states out of deference to the 1921 Washington Conference on Naval Disarmament and the 1930 and 1936 London Naval Treaties.[185] They also proved unwilling to enforce fully the Versailles Treaty provisions. During the interwar period, Churchill wrote that these unfavorable conditions were created by the victorious Allies in the name of peace. The lesson then was that states did have influence over the balance between war and peace. Military strength was far more vital than reliance upon world organizations.[186] Churchill indicated that the democratic powers after the second war bore the burden of checking the ambition of the powers less inclined to maintain the status quo.[187] He viewed the establishment of the Soviet Union in the heart of Europe as "a fateful milestone for mankind."[188] Not only did the withdrawal ensure an unshakable Soviet foothold in central Europe, it signified diplomatic weakness at a time when the western Allies had few trumps. There was also the need to give reassurances to the nations of Europe that their sovereignty would not again be violated by yet another ambitious military giant. In light of the great uncertainties surrounding Europe's future, it was clear that military withdrawal was a step away from this responsibility, irrespective of any previously signed agreement.

A GRAVE NEW WORLD

As the Allies were edging Adolf Hitler closer and closer to his fiery bunker, Hitler reflected on the nature of the coalition that blunted his ambitions for world hegemony. He noted that the coalition that had been formed against him was unprecedented in that it was composed of "such heterogeneous elements with such divergent aims." Capitalist states and ultra-Marxist states were allied as partners. He also recognized that these enemy states had competing political ambitions, with America attempting to become England's heir, England seeking to strengthen herself in the Mediterranean, and Russia vying for greater influence in the Balkans, the narrow seas, Iran, and the Persian Gulf. "Even now," he noted near the end of 1944, "these states are at loggerheads." And like "a spider sitting in the middle of his web," one could watch these developments and observe how these antagonisms grew stronger from hour to hour.[189] The front against Hitler was, in many ways, artificially bolstered. Common hatred of the

Nazis and their aggressions permitted the subordination of more deeply rooted differences among the Allies. Stalin, despite the fact that he probably did feel a sense of euphoria with each victory and probably was warmed by the comradery with Britain and the United States, nonetheless remained the ruler of a totalitarian political order and the head of a world communist movement.

Churchill continued to press for a meaningful diplomacy with Soviet leaders despite the fact that it was not clear that he could count on the Soviet Union as a beneficial influence in Europe or willing partner in maintaining world peace.[190] The Soviet state was a formidable new power, and the democracies could not afford to ignore its new-found influence. After Yalta, relations deteriorated gradually. Even Soviet cooperation in the creation of a new world organization was a point of constant friction. While Anthony Eden pressed for a western bloc to oppose communism earlier than Churchill, Churchill felt compelled to try to avoid the division of Europe, even though he agreed fundamentally that a coalition of democratic states opposing Soviet power was likely to be necessary. Churchill deemed an agreement among the three great powers to use their influence and the influence of a world organization to "compel peace upon the tortured world" as the best remedy.[191]

As alluded to, a part of Churchill's solution for peace was the cooperation of the Allies in a new United Nations Organization. The key to its success would be to dominate the world organization with nations that would not be inclined to use it in an aggressive manner.[192] The UN ought to be a meeting ground, he believed, a place for the powerful nations to settle differences and prevent ideological war; to serve the world, not to rule it. To Churchill, the new organization was primarily a vehicle to improve cooperation, not a vehicle for the eventual surrender of national sovereignty to a world government.

Both Churchill and Stalin opposed Roosevelt's suggestion to disallow the parties of disputes to render a veto. Churchill declared that he would "never consent to the fumbling fingers of forty or fifty nations prying into the life's existence of the British Empire.[193] This stipulation on the part of Churchill and Stalin was a reflection of their common understanding of the political realities (nations would look out for their own interests) and of Churchill's realization that such stringency, seeing that the great powers were not likely to give up the prestige that their power gave them, probably would have killed the world organization in it infancy. For similar reasons, Churchill opposed the American idea that the peace settlement be thrown to the newly created UN, a process that would have removed substantial influence from the victors to shape the world.[194] The idea for Churchill was not that the Big Three should relinquish their power, but rather that they should use that power to ensure future peace.

As much as Churchill hoped for an effective world organization, he realized that then-present impasses may have been too great. Both the prime minister and the president were pleased by Stalin's willingness to join the UN and to concede two critical points: due recognition of the rights of small states, and agreement to act in friendly concert to maintain and further the peace.[195] In retrospect, such concessions were meaningless; for what did rhetoric cost Stalin. He had no critical constituencies at home to hold him to his promises. In all probability, Stalin used Roosevelt's excitement about the UN as leverage to gain approval for his own plans in Eastern Europe, in Poland in particular. Churchill, on the other hand, placed Poland's sovereignty first on his agenda. Discussion about the world organization, even at Potsdam, Churchill thought was premature in light of the fact that Poland could not rule herself.[196] Poland, again, was the test case for future cooperation among the great powers.

By the meeting of the Big Three in Potsdam, much had changed since Tehran. The Alliance no longer was driven by the imperatives of war. Churchill was deeply distressed by Soviet ambitions and new position in Europe. Churchill did negotiate the integrity of Turkey's eastern frontier, a Soviet and British troop withdrawal from Persia, and the British and American occupation of part of Vienna, but the conference yielded nothing fruitful regarding Poland or the rest of occupied Europe.

New power relationships had given rise to a distressing situation in Europe. In a famous telegram (May 12, 1945) to the new United States President, Harry Truman, a man he highly respected, Churchill wrote of his forebodings. First, the withdrawal of western forces on the European continent was a threat to instability; second, the Soviet "misinterpretation" of the Yalta agreement and the utilization of "communist techniques" of maintaining huge armies in the occupied territories were highly distressing; third, the Soviets had drawn an "iron curtain" along their front; fourth, a ruined and prostrate Germany lay vulnerable to Soviet ambition; and fifth, it was of vital necessity to reach an "understanding" with the Soviet Union.[197]

Within the telegram, Churchill suggested a balanced approach to the European problem. On the one hand, there was the need to square off against "the Russian peril," and on the other, a vital need to seek an understanding with her (preferably through his own personal contact and effort).[198] Churchill remained with his balanced approach to the Soviet Union throughout the remainder of his career—giving more weight to one side or the other depending on the circumstances.

The charge that he was inconsistent in his Soviet policy is groundless, and the reasons why shall be developed in subsequent chapters. Suffice it to say at this juncture that Churchill always held that meaningful diplomacy could be advanced so long as it was convincingly supported by military might and determination on the part of the political leaders. Refusal to challenge flagrant violations or "misunderstandings" (a term Churchill no doubt used to give the benefit of the doubt to Stalin, as an expression of his hope that not all avenues to peace were foreclosed yet) would only lead to weakness. Churchill took the time to advise the new President that over the next two months, the gravest matters in the world would be decided.[199] The additional charge by A.J.P. Taylor, that Churchill "had no European policy" beyond the defeat of Germany and that Churchill's most important objective during the war was "a division of Europe into British and Soviet spheres of influence" is not only a torturous misreading of Churchill, it is also patently nonsensical.[200] Churchill's broader objective was a lasting peace in Europe. He did not desire "spheres of influence"; they were a matter of fact.

Among the new power realities was Britain's fall from the ranks of the most powerful. With Britain performing at perhaps the limit of her capacity during the war, and with FDR in no condition to respond forcefully in Eastern Europe, the defenders of Poland lost a critical edge in the competition with Stalin over geopolitical dominance in the region.[201] The passing of the scepter to the Americans did not go unnoticed in the United States. Secretary of State Stettinius saw reason behind Britain's motivation for increasing ties with America. He noted that the British longed for security, but that they were deeply conscious of their own decline to the position of a junior partner of the Big Three.[202]

Even before the end of the war, it became apparent that Churchill was not going to leave the fate of future peace to be determined by the Soviets. Churchill, the quintessential statesman, separating himself from the decline in his country's international status, set out to create opportunities that could lead to a favorable settlement with the Soviet Union. Exuding confidence in his own personal powers and statesmanship, Churchill, during and several years after the war, attempted to come to terms with Stalin. He believed that the sooner an agreement was reached between East and West the better; "this issue of a settlement with Russia before our strength has gone seems to me to dwarf all others."[203]

Already Churchill was building brick by brick the foundation of his postwar foreign policy, building from the ground up his vision of the grand strategy to be followed by the West. There was little doubt that if the three great powers were to be "the trustees for the peace of the world," a peace to last at least fifty years, a close-knit friendship had to be woven. The vital and most durable part of this trusteeship would be made out of the fraternal association of the United States and Great Britain, the alliance of the English-speaking peoples. Churchill believed the chances for a peaceful association with Soviet leaders had improved during the war years. Stalin's own expressions of unity and comradery, which some Soviet scholars believe ought not to be taken as entirely cynical, heightened Churchill's own expectations, that an elaborate system to resolve disputes among the great powers could be established.[204]

Churchill's major contribution to the understanding and the outcome of the conflict was his grand strategic vision. In September 1943, General Smuts, concerned about the strategic consequences of the Soviet victories, confided to Churchill his fears that Stalin would emerge as the diplomatic master by fighting and winning the bulk of the war against the Germans. Exiting the war on equal terms was vital to Britain's postwar status. Churchill responded by agreeing with his general, but emphasized that it was inevitable that Russia would become the greatest land power in the world after the war.[205] Seeing that Russian domination was more than probable, the task of facing this reality squarely naturally presented itself. The proposition was this: "I hope . . . that the 'fraternal association' of the British Commonwealth and the United States, together with sea- and air-power, may put us on good terms and in a friendly balance with Russia at least for the period of rebuilding."[206] The cultivation of the alliance with the United States, and the effort to ensure that it would work properly in war, remained a paramount concern throughout the war years. Clearly, the combination of force and diplomacy was the best chance to create a more stable world after the conflict.

Churchill's strategic vision remained steady throughout the conflict. Ever present were his concerns about the peace to come, having little doubt himself by 1943 that the Grand Alliance would prevail against the Germans. His most pressing concerns were the contours of postwar European borders and the sphere of influence Moscow was carving out of Europe with each victorious stroke. For this reason, Churchill had a keen sense of the geopolitical impact of the "liberating" armies, as these armies, by their very presence, would mold new political realities.

In the end, Stalin's territorial gains can be blamed partly on the inability of the democracies to maintain a united front. In particular, the strain in purpose that manifested itself between Roosevelt and Churchill, and between the American way of war and the British way of war, paralyzed the democracies to some extent from adequately meeting the new challenge posed from the East. As a result of the divergent views on how to "handle" Stalin and direct the war, the democracies sometimes found themselves at cross purposes. To Churchill was left the unpopular task of securing sections of Europe through deals with Stalin. His American counterpart chose to refrain from activities that may have kept Stalin out of the war against Japan and stridently protested against dealing with any political questions in Europe until after the armies closed the ring on Hitler. Wrote Adam Ulam of the hypocrisy:

America could be associated with the most draconian proposals on Germany. To Churchill could be left the "cynical" initiatives on spheres of influence (the mere term suggesting to the Americans something infinitely sinful and redolent of the wicked practices of Old World diplomacy). Naturally, the Soviets found themselves closer to the American position on most issues, and efforts to accommodate the Americans on some of the "stickiest" points were forthcoming during 1944.[207]

The problems encountered by the members of the Grand Alliance were understandable given the divergence on political principles and war ends. Anthony Eden suggested before Yalta that Stalin was the only one of the three who had a clear view of what he wanted and was a tough negotiator. Churchill, he said, was too emotional, while FDR was vague and jealous.[208] Although the judgments against Churchill and Roosevelt were probably too harsh, Eden was correct to give Stalin credit for knowing exactly what he wanted. It was for this reason that Churchill thought it most important that the United States and Great Britain stand together in the face of the harsh new realities.

One problem for the western democracies was created by Roosevelt's refusal, until just before his death, to acknowledge that Europe was imperiled by their Soviet ally. This fractured front, as early as 1943, allowed Stalin to shoot through the manifested cracks in the Anglo-American alliance to secure strategic advantages. British colonialism and Old World diplomacy, in Roosevelt's view, posed a greater threat than the Red Army or international communism.[209] Roosevelt believed that distancing himself from Churchill and attacking British foreign policy motives would remove the impression of a united front against Stalin, thereby winning for himself Stalin's confidence. There is little evidence to suggest that this strategy succeeded. There is evidence, on the other hand, that Stalin skillfully played Churchill and FDR off each other. Roosevelt's ambassador to Russia, Averell Harriman, gave this assessment in an interview with George Urban:

I did not disagree with Roosevelt's approach, but I was convinced that it would be far more difficult to establish a basis of confidence with Stalin than Roosevelt thought. Churchill was even more cautious. He too wanted a post-war understanding with the Kremlin, but he despised Communism and all its works and had his eye on specific political problems. He foresaw much greater political difficulties with the Soviet leaders after the war than Roosevelt did.[210]

Churchill's diplomacy was limited by many factors, chief among them was the American affinity for the Soviet Union. Churchill's power to act as he saw necessary was undercut by western public opinion, which was almost as strongly pro-Russian as it was anti-German. This development took away the necessary political support from the democratic governments to make joint policy designed to check Soviet ambitions. The development of pro-Soviet sentiment limited the room for action by political leaders and made Soviet domination of Eastern Europe all the more certain. FDR's own diplomacy was partially based on Anglophobia and a displaced faith in the promise of progress by Communism. Fundamental conflicts between East and West, in Eastern Europe, for example, where Roosevelt's statesmanship was notably deficient, lacked the attention it deserved thereby conceding an advantage to the more aggressive party. "Not for a moment," wrote Raymond Aron, "did the Russian authorities forget, but the Anglo-Saxons, and particularly the Americans, often acted as if they did not regard the hostility as fundamental."[211]

The very fabric of British democracy also limited Churchill. By the end of the war, Churchill felt the pressure for elections back home would damage the national coalition he formed when he became prime minister in 1940. Churchill remarked that he thought also of his own interest. He did not relish the thought of an early election (June or July rather than October 1945) when a loss would sink him from a national leader to a party leader. He believed himself to be the best man for the job of settling the emerging disputes in Europe, ending the Japanese war, and bringing the troops home. Though enfeebled by old age and the duties of the position, he nonetheless believed himself to be superior to others in overall capacity; for "I had the world position as a whole in my mind, and I deemed myself to possess knowledge, influence, and even authority, which might be of service."[212] The "Russian peril" demanded the united attention of the British government. "It is always difficult," he said, "for free democracies, governed in the main by public opinion from day to day, to cope with the designs of dictator States and totalitarians."[213]

Friction between the two Western allies in matters of diplomacy were complicated by differences in military strategy. Whereas Churchill and his generals fought the war to achieve political objectives, the Americans likened the conflict to that of a tournament, where winning the war dominated the military minds to the detriment of true strategy. According to Raymond Aron, "[i]t was the movement of armies that brought about the partition, not of the world, but of Europe. The West could have foreseen that the point at which their troops stopped would also become the outermost border of Western-type democracies."[214]

Coming out of the war, a major criticism of Churchill would have to be made concerning his confidence, at least as publicly demonstrated, in Stalin as a true partner. Churchill made the remark at Yalta that "the only bond of the victors is their common hate."[215] Was he justified in behaving as if it were otherwise? Many friendly gestures were exchanged among the Allies during the war and peace conferences. Churchill and Roosevelt affectionately referred to Stalin as Uncle Joe.[216] Understandably, Churchill displayed unbridled enthusiasm for Soviet military victories in the East.[217] Without much hesitation, he also was ready to welcome Russia as a great power on the high seas. He desired to amend the Montreux Convention with Turkey, which limited Soviet access to the Mediterranean, and he fought to assure Stalin a warm water port in the Pacific. If Churchill believed the Soviet Union posed such an enormous threat at the war's end, why bother to increase their strategic advantages?

Much of Churchill's public rhetoric gave little hint that the Soviet Union was a new power to be reckoned with. Rather, after Yalta, he declared that "the permanent friendship and association of the Three Great Powers has been proclaimed in a manner more precise and more authoritative than ever before."[218] With statements such as these, Churchill helped to lend legal and moral support to the decisions made at Tehran and confirmed at Yalta, effectively granting legitimacy to the new Soviet sphere of influence. Rather than speak in utopian terms, perhaps a more hard-nosed approach was called for once Churchill realized that the Soviet Union would attempt to dominate Europe in violation of international accords. Should the democracies have deceived themselves by believing a working relationship with Stalin was at hand? Churchill writes later that he had based himself on the belief that the Yalta Declaration would be carried out in both letter and spirit.[219]

Politics is often very messy. It does not leave many opportunities for decision-taking untouched by the ambiguities of human affairs. Churchill, it seems, had to make a decision to choose between publicly challenging Stalin over instances of Soviet noncooperation in Poland and Soviet intentions in the rest of Eastern Europe and keeping the Grand Alliance together. Despite the criticism he received from the Conservatives in Britain on his handling of Poland, by Lord Dunglass and Arthur Greenwood to name two, Churchill believed his only feasible option was to try to prevent the developing rift between East and West from growing larger. Toward the end of the war, he believed that alerting his nation to Soviet practices in Poland would have agitated British public opinion to the point where the Alliance could have been shattered.[220] Confronting Stalin during or immediately after Yalta would have probably achieved very little. Churchill preferred to see to it that the agreements were carried out, and he labored hard to make it so.[221] Churchill never lost hope that Stalin desired a good relationship with the West.

There is plenty of evidence today that Stalin never was prepared to exchange trust with the Western leaders. Near the war's end, Milovan Djilas recorded these sentiments of Stalin:

Perhaps you think that just because we are the allies of the English that we have forgotten who they are and who Churchill is. They find nothing sweeter than to trick their allies. During the First World War they constantly tricked the Russians and the French. And Churchill? Churchill is the kind who, if you don't watch him, will slip a kopeck out of your pocket. . . . And Roosevelt? Roosevelt is not like that. He dips in his hand only for bigger coins. But Churchill? Churchill—even for a kopeck.[222]

To be sure Churchill did question his approach and probably agonized over many of his decisions. The new complexity in world politics and the dangerous new political alignments rightly gave him great cause for concern.

By appealing to Soviet honor and glory in his correspondence and speeches, Churchill probably hoped to win Stalin's trust and to keep the shaky friendship alive. While his speeches appear quixotic today, back then it reflected his belief that opportunities did exist to firm up the relationship. Churchill consistently refused to link the person of Stalin to the ugly nature of communism. Perhaps this was intentionally done because direct criticism of Stalin might have shut the door on any negotiated settlement. Even after the 1944 Warsaw tragedy, Churchill believed he could deal with "the man of steel."[223] Perhaps Churchill's own words best answer his critics:

It is not permitted to those charged with dealing with events in times of war or crisis to confine themselves purely to the statement of broad general principles on which good people agree. They have to take definite decisions from day to day. They have to adopt postures which must be solidly maintained, otherwise how can any combinations for action be maintained? . . . What would have happened if we had quarrelled with Russia while the Germans still had three or four hundred divisions on the fighting front? Our hopeful assumptions were soon to be falsified. Still, they were the only ones possible at the time.[224]

Churchill explained, probably by way of apology, that he felt bound to proclaim his confidence in Soviet good faith in the hope of eventually procuring it.[225] Indeed, he seemed hardly to be in a position to do otherwise.

NOTES

1. Gilbert, *The Stricken World*, p. 785.
2. Churchill, *The Birth of Britain*, p. 67.
3. Winston S. Churchill, *The Second World War*, vol. 3, *The Grand Alliance* (Boston: Houghton Mifflin Company, 1950), p. 509.
4. Churchill, *The Gathering Storm*, p. 168.
5. Churchill, *Marlborough*, vol. 1, p. 229.
6. Gilbert, *Winston S. Churchill*, vol. 7, *Road to Victory: 1941-1945* (Boston: Houghton Mifflin Company, 1986), p. 65. A message sent to FDR in February 1942 when western interests were under assault in the Far East as well.
7. Churchill, cited in Gilbert, *Road to Victory*, p. 254.
8. See Winston S. Churchill, *The Second World War*, vol. 2, *Their Finest Hour* (Boston: Houghton Mifflin, 1949), p. 225: "We abate nothing of our just demands; not one jot or tittle do we recede. . . . Czechs, Poles, Norwegians, Dutch, Belgians, have joined their causes to our own. All these shall be restored." See also Chester Wilmot, *The Struggle for Europe* (St. James Place, London: Collins, 1952), p. 707.
9. Churchill, *The Gathering Storm*, p. 223.
10. Churchill, *Complete Speeches*, p. 7,098.
11. Gilbert, *The Wilderness Years*, p. 151.
12. Quoted in Kenneth W. Thompson, *Winston Churchill's World View: Statesmanship and Power* (Baton Rouge, LA: Louisiana State University Press, 1983), pp. 91-92.
13. Churchill, *Their Finest Hour*, p. 112.
14. Churchill, "The Wounded Dragon," *Step By Step*, p. 137.
15. Churchill, *Their Finest Hour*, p. 363. As we shall see, the "worst," the occupation of parts of Europe by yet another despotic power, eventually did come to pass anyway.
16. Churchill, *The Gathering Storm*, p. 363.
17. William Manchester, *Alone*, pp. 53, 61, 139, 174, 176, 206-207, 372, 475.
18. Churchill, *The Gathering Storm*, pp. 370-376.
19. Gilbert, *The Wilderness Years*, p. 161.
20. Churchill, *The Gathering Storm*, pp. 371, 375.
21. Wilmot, *The Struggle For Europe*, p. 68.
22. Churchill, *The Gathering Storm*, pp. 374, 349.
23. See Abraham Lincoln, "First Inaugural Address—Final Text," March 4, 1861, *The Collected Works of Abraham Lincoln*, vol. 4, Roy P. Basler, ed. (New Brunswick, NJ: Rutgers University Press, 1953), pp. 262-271; "Annual Message to Congress," December 3, 1861, *Collected Works*, vol. 5, pp. 35-53; "Letter to Horace Greeley," August 22, 1862, *Collected Works*, vol. 5, pp. 388-389; and "Annual Message to Congress," December 1, 1862, *Collected Works*, vol. 5, pp. 518-537.
24. Martin Gilbert, *Winston S. Churchill*, vol. 6, *Finest Hour; 1939-1941*, (Boston: Houghton Mifflin Company, 1983), pp. 1,015, 1,067.
25. Churchill, *The Gathering Storm*, p. 362.
26. Churchill, *The Gathering Storm*, p. 379.
27. Churchill, *The Gathering Storm*, p. 393.
28. Churchill, *The Gathering Storm*, p. 367-368.
29. Churchill, *The Gathering Storm*, p. 15.
30. Churchill, *Their Finest Hour*, p. 133.

31. Churchill, *Their Finest Hour*, p. 134. See also Wilmot, *The Struggle For Europe*, p. 709.
32. Wilmot, *The Struggle For Europe*, p. 709.
33. Churchill, *Their Finest Hour*, p. 136.
34. Gilbert, *Road to Victory*, p. 15.
35. Churchill, *Marlborough*, vol. 1, p. 232.
36. Adam B. Ulam, *Expansion and Coexistence: Soviet Foreign Policy; 1917-73*, 2nd ed. (New York: Holt, Rinehart and Winston, Inc., 1974), p. 318.
37. Ulam, *Expansion and Coexistence*, p. 319.
38. Churchill, quoted in Gilbert, *Finest Hour*, p. 1,206.
39. Gilbert, *Finest Hour*, pp. 1,050-1,051. Stalin apparently also ignored the warnings of his own intelligence organization, which warned of Hitler's invasion plans as early as November 1940 (*The Washington Times*, May 9, 1989, p. A2.)
40. John Colville, *The Fringes of Power: 10 Downing Street Diaries; 1939-1955* (New York: W.W. Norton & Company, 1985), p. 406.
41. Cited by Colville, *The Fringes of Power*, p. 404.
42. Churchill, *The Grand Alliance*, pp. 370-373.
43. Churchill, *The Grand Alliance*, p. 532 (emphasis added). This is not to say Churchill had compromised his notion of justice. Upon learning of Stalin's sacrifice of millions in his collectivization schemes, Churchill quoted Edmund Burke: "If I cannot have reform without injustice, I will not have reform" (Gilbert, *Road To Victory*, p. 204.)
44. Churchill, *The Grand Alliance*, p. 533.
45. Churchill, *Complete Speeches*, p. 7,116.
46. Churchill, *The Second World War*, vol. 4, *The Hinge of Fate* (Boston: Houghton Mifflin Company, 1950), p. 67.
47. Despite the fact that the tension between the political and military goals only intensified with time, Churchill continued to express his desire to realize both sets of objectives. Churchill, *Closing the Ring*, pp. 405-406. In a speech before the House in February 1945, Churchill proclaimed "(t)he Crimea Conference leaves the Allies more closely united than ever before, both in the military and in the political sphere." (Although this was not to say that they were always very close.) Churchill, *Complete Speeches*, p. 7111.
48. Churchill, *The Gathering Storm*, p. 448.
49. Churchill, *The Hinge of Fate*, p. 475. See also p. 581 in same; Colville, *The Fringes of Power*, pp. 476, 484, 487, 504; and Gilbert, *Road to Victory*, p. 778.
50. See Colville, *The Fringes of Power*, 523, and Gilbert, *Road to Victory*, pp. 328-329.
51. The phrase "United Nations" apparently had its origins in one of Byron's poems, *Childe Harold Pilgrimage*. The Allied and Associated Powers first assumed the new name in June 1941 (Gilbert, *Road to Victory*, n. p. 35).
52. Heller and Nekrich, *Utopia in Power*, p. 93.
53. Colville, *The Fringes of Power*, p. 422.
54. Ulam, *Expansion and Coexistence*, p. 338.
55. Churchill, *Triumph and Tragedy*, p. 422.
56. Churchill, *Complete Speeches*, p. 7,112. See also *Triumph and Tragedy*, p. 367, Russia's claim "was founded not on force but on right." Churchill cautioned as well against the excessive transfer of territory to the Poles from eastern Germany as serious ethnic problems would result. He put a limit of six million people to be trans-

ferred out of the newly annexed territory (Gilbert, *Road To Victory*, p. 1,231). See also Wilmot, *The Struggle For Europe*, p. 647. Despite West Germany's remarkable political transformation over its forty-year history, Poland's more representative leadership in 1990 has expressed the inveterate fear that future generations of Germans will make claims upon these lands and further compromise Poland's territorial integrity.

57. Churchill, *Closing The Ring*, pp. 394-398. A case can be made that these Soviet demands for territory were made not just out of a concern for security, but rather they were made in the interest of opening up a "gateway to the West." See Wilmot, *The Struggle For Europe*, p. 712. Historian Richard Pipes has argued that the theory that Russian aggression is a defense reflex is utterly facile. "(B)etween 1700 and 1870, Russia had spent 106 years fighting 38 military campaigns, of which 36 had been 'offensive' and a mere 2 defensive" (Richard Pipes, *Survival Is Not Enough: Soviet Realities and America's Future* (New York: Simon and Schuster, 1984), p. 38). Others have argued that the recovery of parts of White Russia, territory lost to Poland after World War I, made the shift to the west a matter of national pride. William L. Neumann, *After Victory: Churchill, Roosevelt, Stalin and the Making of the Peace* (New York: Harper & Row, Publishers, 1967), p. 58.

58. Gilbert, *Road to Victory*, p. 576.

59. Ulam, *Expansion and Coexistence*, pp. 365, 365, 366. See also Gilbert, *Road to Victory*, p. 701.

60. Churchill, *The Grand Alliance*, pp. 390-393. See also Ulam, *Expansion and Coexistence*, p. 320-321. Ulam viewed this concession to Stalin at the expense of another ally as a new precedent that would constitute a lesson for the western allies in their future dealings with the Soviet Union. For a critical view of Churchill, see also Morton Frisch, "The Diplomacy and Statecraft of Roosevelt and Churchill" in Salmon, ed., *Power, Principles and Interests*, p. 237.

61. See, for example, Frisch, "The Diplomacy and Statecraft of Roosevelt and Churchill," pp. 229-239.

62. Gilbert, *Road to Victory*, p. 1,015.

63. Gilbert, *Road to Victory*, p. 658.

64. Gilbert, *Road to Victory*, p. 734.

65. Ulam, *Expansion and Coexistence*, p. 376. See also Gilbert, *Road to Victory*, pp. 699 and 1,024.

66. Gilbert, *Road to Victory*, pp. 1,010-1,015.

67. Gilbert, *Road to Victory*, pp. 1,191-1,192.

68. Cited by Churchill, *Triumph and Tragedy*, pp. 334-335.

69. Churchill, *Triumph and Tragedy*, p. 367.

70. Churchill, *Triumph and Tragedy*, p. 671.

71. Quoted in Gilbert, *Road to Victory*, p. 671.

72. Churchill, *Triumph and Tragedy*, p. 368.

73. Gilbert, *Road to Victory*, p. 686.

74. Churchill, *Triumph and Tragedy*, p. 400.

75. Churchill, *Triumph and Tragedy*, p. 401. Churchill believed that a rift in the Alliance would not only burden the war effort against Germany and Japan, but it would signal also the *de facto* possession of the disputed Polish territory by the Soviets (Gilbert, *Road To Victory*, pp. 702-703.)

76. Cited in Gilbert, *Road To Victory*, p. 1,231. See also p. 671; Churchill privately stressed the importance of providing material support to the resistance in

Poland in order to fight elements of tyranny. This said, Churchill would tolerate many indignities by the Soviets in the interest of victory, including the discovery by the Germans of about 10,000 murdered Polish officers in Katyn Forest in June 1941. The evidence for Soviet culpability was undeniable even back then. See Churchill, *The Hinge of Fate*, pp. 758-761. Nevertheless, there was "no use prowling morbidly round the three-year-old graves of Smolensk," the cite of the massacre (Churchill in Gilbert, *Road To Victory*, p. 389). This again gives one a flavor of the balancing act Churchill had to perform in order that he might try to achieve both justice and peace after the defeat of the Axis powers.

77. Gilbert, *Road to Victory*, p. 1,193.
78. Cited in Gilbert, *Road to Victory*, p. 1,233.
79. Churchill before the House of Commons, *Complete Speeches*, p. 7,098.
80. Gilbert, *Road to Victory*, p. 1,026.
81. Colville, *The Fringes of Power*, p. 426.
82. Ulam, *Expansion and Coexistence*, p. 322.
83. Herbert Feis, *Churchill, Roosevelt, Stalin* (Princeton, NJ: Princeton University Press, 1957), p. 8.
84. Wilmot, *The Struggle for Europe*, pp. 1,180, 1,190.
85. Feis, *Churchill, Roosevelt, Stalin*, p. 8.
86. Gilbert, *Road to Victory*, pp. 181 and 182.
87. "Torch" was the code name for the planned invasion of Italy.
88. See Wilmot, *The Struggle for Europe*, pp. 438-439 and Ulam, *Expansion and Coexistence*, p. 327.
89. Gilbert, *Road to Victory*, pp. 442, 584.
90. Cited in Gilbert, *Road to Victory*, p. 433.
91. Gilbert, *Road to Victory*, pp. 536 and 541.
92. Churchill, *The Hinge of Fate*, p. 708.
93. See Thompson, *Winston Churchill's World View*, pp. 158. See also Bernard Brodie, *War and Politics* (New York: MacMillan Publishing Co., Inc., 1973), p. 40; Gilbert, *Road to Victory*, p. 536; and Robert Nisbet, *Roosevelt and Stalin: The Failed Courtship*, (Washington, DC: Regnery Gateway, 1988), pp. 102-110.
94. Dwight D. Eisenhower, *Crusade in Europe* (Garden City, NY: Doubleday, 1949), p. 301f.
95. Churchill, *Triumph and Tragedy*, p. 227.
96. Churchill, *Triumph and Tragedy*, p. 74.
97. See Churchill, *Triumph and Tragedy*, pp. 227 and 231-233.
98. See for example Lewis Broad, *Winston Churchill: The Years of Achievement* (New York: Hawthorne Books, Inc., 1963), p. 391.
99. Churchill, *Triumph and Tragedy*, p. 75.
100. Wilmot, *The Struggle for Europe*, p. 131.
101. Wilmot, *The Struggle for Europe*, p. 637.
102. Churchill, *Triumph and Tragedy*, p. 233. See also interview with Lt. Gen. Sir Ian Jacob in Michael Charlton, *The Eagle and the Small Birds: Crisis in the Soviet Empire; from Yalta to Solidarity*, (Chicago: The University of Chicago Press, 1984), p. 42.
103. Wilmot, *The Struggle for Europe*, p. 786.
104. Churchill, *Complete Speeches*, p. 7,084.
105. Churchill, *Triumph and Tragedy*, p. 238.

106. See Paul Johnson, *Modern Times: The World from the Twenties to the Eighties* (New York: Harper & Row, 1983), pp. 434-435. See also Gilbert, *Road To Victory*, pp. 991-992.

107. Apparently Churchill believed the sincerity of Stalin's concessions, and that there were other forces at work that might derail the arrangements. "Behind the horseman sits dull care" (Gilbert, *Road to Victory*, p. 1,027).

108. See Broad, *Years of Achievement*, p. 392.

109. Wilmot, *The Struggle for Europe*, p. 636.

110. Wilmot, *The Struggle for Europe*, p. 637.

111. Cited by Wilmot, *The Struggle for Europe*, p. 636.

112. Churchill recognized that the Soviet Union had special interests in Rumania, Hungary, and Bulgaria and would act to ensure them (Churchill, *Triumph and Tragedy*, p. 230). His worry was that Soviet influence would be extended to other nations contrary to their interests, and the geopolitical circumstances favored the expansion of Soviet influence throughout the Balkan peninsula. See Gilbert, *Road To Victory*, p. 1,089, and Michael Charlton, *The Eagle and the Small Birds*, p. 42.

113. Gilbert, *Road to Victory*, p. 1,056.

114. Gilbert, *Never Despair*, p. 44.

115. Nora Beloff, *Tito's Flawed Legacy: Yugoslavia and the West; 1939 to 1984* (London: Victor Gollancz Ltd., 1985), p. 111.

116. Beloff, *Legacy*, p. 115.

117. Gilbert, *Road to Victory*, pp. 641 and 890.

118. Beloff, *Legacy*, p. 96.

119. Churchill, *Triumph and Tragedy*, pp. 73, 76-78. Roosevelt continued to criticize the British for their ambitious games of power politics. Churchill reminded him (p. 77) that the Soviets were the only power that could do anything in Rumania, and that though he and Roosevelt had agreed that on the basis of their armistice terms, Moscow should try to give coherent direction to what happened in that country. On the other hand, he pointed out, the Greek burden rested almost entirely upon the United States and Britain.

120. Gilbert, *Road to Victory*, p. 906.

121. Churchill, *Collected Speeches*, pp. 7,051 and 7,052 (emphasis and parenthetical comments added).

122. Churchill, *Triumph and Tragedy*, p. 305.

123. Churchill, *Triumph and Tragedy*, p. 306.

124. Ulam, *Expansion and Coexistence*, p. 355.

125. Cited by Colville, *The Fringes of Power*, p. 555. "Russia had let us go our way in Greece; she would insist on imposing her will in Roumania and Bulgaria" (cited on p. 565).

126. Wilmot, *The Struggle for Europe*, p. 615.

127. Churchill, *Triumph and Tragedy*, p. 72.

128. Churchill, *Triumph and Tragedy*, p. 73. See also Gilbert, *Road to Victory*, pp. 754-56.

129. Gilbert, *Road to Victory*, p. 1,243.

130. Wilmot, *The Struggle for Europe*, p. 130.

131. Gilbert, *Road to Victory*, pp. 564-565.

132. Churchill, *Closing the Ring*, p. 131.

133. Cited in Gilbert, *Road to Victory*, p. 448.

134. Wilmot, *The Struggle for Europe*, p. 447.

135. See Nisbet, *Roosevelt and Stalin*, p. 70; Johnson, *Modern Times*, pp. 434-435; and Gilbert, *Road to Victory*, p. 829.

136. Churchill, *Closing the Ring*, p. 286.

137. Gilbert, *Never Despair*, p. 14.

138. Churchill, *Triumph and Tragedy*, pp. 759-760.

139. Wilmot, *The Struggle for Europe*, p. 123.

140. Gilbert, *Road to Victory*, p. 467. See also Broad, *The Years of Achievement*, p. 287.

141. Churchill, *The Hinge of Fate*, p. 688.

142. Churchill, *The Hinge of Fate*, pp. 689-690.

143. Gilbert, *Road to Victory*, p. 581.

144. Gilbert, *Road to Victory*, p. 310.

145. While not discounting this scenario entirely, Churchill doubted that Hitler's absence would have meant much (Churchill, *Complete Speeches*, p. 7,827).

146. Wilmot, *The Struggle for Europe*, pp. 140-142.

147. See Feis, *Churchill, Roosevelt, Stalin*, pp. 357-358, and Wilmot, *The Struggle for Europe*, p. 446.

148. Tuvia Ben-Moshe, *Churchill: Strategy and History* (Boulder, CO: Lynne Rienner Publishers, 1992), p. 228. Ben-Moshe argued, wrongly I think, that throughout the war Eden had seen more clearly the political consequences of Soviet military involvement in Europe.

149. Wilmot, *The Struggle for Europe*, p. 692.

150. Ulam, *Expansion and Coexistence*, p. 334.

151. Churchill, *Closing the Ring*, pp. 401 and 406.

152. Gilbert, *Road to Victory*, p. 490.

153. Colville, *The Fringes of Power*, p. 578.

154. Churchill, *Triumph and Tragedy*, p. 508.

155. Wilmot, *The Struggle for Europe*, p. 696.

156. Gilbert, *Road to Victory*, pp. 1,329-1,330. See also Churchill, *Collected Speeches*, p. 8,479.

157. Lord Moran, *Churchill: Taken From The Diaries of Lord Moran; The Struggle For Survival 1940-1965* (Boston: Houghton Mifflin Company, 1966), p. 190.

158. Wilmot, *The Struggle for Europe*, p. 548.

159. Churchill, *Triumph and Tragedy*, p. 399. See also Churchill, *Complete Speeches*, p. 7,112 and *Closing The Ring*, p. 159.

160. Churchill, *Closing The Ring*, pp. 394 and 400-403. See also Gilbert, *Road To Victory*, p. 574. Luigi Barzini, *The Europeans* (New York: Simon and Shuster, 1983), p. 72, wrote, interestingly, that the Germans did not always have such a fearsome military character. He reported that before the age of Bismarck, in the estimation of author Madame de Stael, there was nothing "odder than the German soldiers." She went on to inform her readers that "(t)hey fear fatigue or bad weather, as if they were all shopkeepers or literati.... Resolutions are slow, and despondency is easy.... Imagination, which is the predominant quality of the Germans, inspires fear of danger.... Among them a general who loses a battle is more assured of obtaining forgiveness than one who wins of being applauded."

161. Churchill, *Closing the Ring*, p. 401.

162. Cited in Gilbert, *Road to Victory*, p. 576.

163. Churchill, *Closing the Ring*, p. 401-403. See also Milovan Djilas, *Conversations with Stalin* (New York: Harcourt Brace Javanovich, 1962), p. 111.
164. Djilas, *Conversations*, p. 114.
165. Churchill, *The Gathering Storm*, p. 7, and Wilmot, *The Struggle For Europe*, p. 644.
166. Cited by Gilbert, *Road to Victory*, p. 518.
167. Cited in Kenneth Young, *Churchill & Beaverbrook: A Study in Friendship and Politics* (London: Eyre & Spottiswoode, 1966), p. 266.
168. Nisbet, *Roosevelt and Stalin*, pp. 101-107.
169. Wilmot, *The Struggle for Europe*, p. 628. See also Colville, *The Fringes of Power*, p. 561 and Ulam, *Expansion and Coexistence*, pp. 379-380.
170. Ben-Moshe, *Churchill: Strategy and History*, p. 230.
171. Colville, *The Fringes of Power*, p. 566.
172. Colville, *The Fringes of Power*, p. 570. See also p. 574.
173. See Charlton, *Eagle and the Small Birds*, pp. 19, 50, 53-54, 58, and interview with Leopold Lapedz, p. 14. See also Donald W. Treadgold, *Twentieth Century Russia* (Chicago: Rand McNally & Company, 1964), pp. 398-399, and Ulam, *Expansion and Coexistence*, p. 368.
174. See, for example, Djilas, *Conversations*, p. 153.
175. Wilmot, *The Struggle For Europe*, p. 630. "[T]he history of wartime and post-war diplomacy has made it clear that the Russians regard international conferences as opportunities for the recognition of situations which have already been created by the exercise of power, not as occasions for the negotiation of reasonable settlements, mutually acceptable."
176. Gilbert, *Road to Victory*, p. 1,230.
177. Eliot A. Cohen, "Churchill At War," *Commentary* (May 1987), pp. 40-49.
178. Gilbert, *Road To Victory*, pp. 664, 665.
179. Frisch, "Statecraft of Roosevelt and Churchill," p. 236.
180. Wilmot, *The Struggle for Europe*, p. 711.
181. Gilbert, *Road to Victory*, p. 480, and Churchill, *Triumph and Tragedy*, p. 344.
182. Cited by Gilbert, *Road to Victory*, p. 1,143.
183. Gilbert, *Road To Victory*, p. 1,330. Part of Churchill's strategy was to get France more involved as a player in that high stakes game to win geopolitical advantages. France would have been particularly important if the Americans had completely withdrawn from the continent (Wilmot, *The Struggle for Europe*, p. 645).
184. Churchill reminded his readers in *The Gathering Storm*, p. 102, that "(i)t is the greatest mistake to mix up disarmament with peace. When you have peace you will have disarmament." His arguments against an early American withdrawal reflected a similar logic.
185. These treaties failed to halt naval competition among the distrustful parties and did not stop Japan and Germany from deploying even more powerful navies with which to pursue their expansionist aims.
186. Churchill, *The Gathering Storm*, p. 14. See also, p. 13.
187. Gilbert, *Never Despair*, p. 6.
188. Churchill, *Triumph and Tragedy*, pp. 213, 609. See also Gilbert, *Road To Victory*, p. 1,303.
189. Cited in Wilmot, *The Struggle for Europe*, p. 578.
190. Cited in Gilbert, *Road to Victory*, p. 1,278.

191. Gilbert, *Road to Victory*, pp. 1,069-1,071.

192. Gilbert, *Road to Victory*, p. 585.

193. Cited by Wilmot, *The Struggle For Europe*, p. 646. See also Colville, *The Fringes of Power*, p. 521. Churchill announced that he would not tolerate an international body that interfered strongly in British affairs, i.e., her relations with her colonies (Gilbert, *Road To Victory*, p. 1,199). He also was skeptical about the efforts to promote international economic cooperation at the expense of British sovereignty over her trade interests, especially in the colonies (Gilbert, *Road To Victory*, p. 699).

194. Gilbert, *Never Despair*, p. 71.

195. Wilmot, *The Struggle for Europe*, p. 650.

196. Gilbert, *Never Despair*, p. 63.

197. Churchill, *Triumph and Tragedy*, pp. 572-574. This was the first use of the "iron curtain" metaphor (Gilbert, *Never Despair*, p. 7).

198. Gilbert, *Never Despair*, p. 6.

199. Churchill, *Triumph and Tragedy*, pp. 571-572.

200. See A.J.P. Taylor, "The Statesman," in *Churchill Revised: A Critical Reassessment* (New York: The Dial Press, Inc., 1969), pp. 56-57.

201. Colville, *The Fringes of Power*, p. 564.

202. Cited in Gilbert, *Road to Victory*, p. 1,295.

203. Cited in Gilbert, *Never Despair*, p. 7.

204. Gilbert, *Road to Victory*, pp. 495-496; Churchill, *The Hinge of Fate*, p. 710; Ulam, *Expansion and Coexistence*, p. 377; and Churchill, *Triumph and Tragedy*, p. 355.

205. Churchill, *Closing The Ring*, pp. 126-130. Chester Wilmot concurs for the most part, but indicated that greater strength on the part of the United States may have lessened the Soviet advantage. "In the triumph of the Soviet Union there was an element of the inevitable." The West's focus and resolve upon a military victory and the surge in sympathy for the USSR as a defender of progress ensure that Stalin's overtures would be well received (*The Struggle For Europe*, p. 713).

206. Churchill, *Closing the Ring*, p. 129. One cannot help but make note of Alexis de Tocqueville's prophesy made over 100 years before the war about two nations, America and Russia, that were destined to be great powers (*Democracy in America*, vol. I, trans. George Lawrence, ed. J.P. Mayer and Max Lerner (New York: Harper & Row, Publishers, 1966), p. 378).

207. Ulam, *Expansion and Coexistence*, p. 357.

208. Gilbert, *Road to Victory*, p. 1,140.

209. For a discussion of FDR's Wilsonianism and crusade against British imperialism see Nisbet, *Roosevelt and Stalin*, pp. 91-95. See also Wilmot, *The Struggle For Europe*, p. 638. FDR was apparently fond of Emerson's line: "The only way to have a friend is to be one."

210. George R. Urban, ed., *Stalinism: Its Impact on Russia and the World* (Cambridge, MA: Harvard University Press, 1986), p. 63.

211. Raymond Aron, *The Century of Total War* (Garden City, NY: Doubleday & Company, Inc., 1954), p. 49.

212. Churchill, *Triumph and Tragedy*, p. 590.

213. See Churchill, *Collected Speeches*, p. 8,033.

214. Raymond Aron, *Raymond Aron: The Committed Observer: Interviews with Jean-Louis Missika and Dominique Wolton*, trans. James and Marie McIntosh (Chicago: Regnery Gateway, 1983), p. 109.

215. Gilbert, *Road to Victory*, p. 1,171.

216. Churchill did later question the appropriateness of this appellation for Stalin. See Churchill, *Triumph and Tragedy*, p. 430.

217. Gilbert, *Road to Victory*, p. 1,277.

218. Churchill, *Complete Speeches*, p. 7,105-7,106.

219. Churchill, *Triumph and Tragedy*, p. 421.

220. Churchill, *Triumph and Tragedy*, p. 421.

221. Gilbert, *Road to Victory*, p. 1,242.

222. See Djilas, *Conversations*, p. 73.

223. Churchill, *Triumph and Tragedy*, pp. 208-209. In the summer of 1944, Soviet armies stood at the eastern gates of Warsaw while the German forces destroyed the city. According to Churchill, "(o)f the 40,000 men and women of the Polish Underground Army about 15,000 were killed." "When the Russians entered the city three months later they found but shattered streets and the unburied dead. Such was their liberation of Poland, where they now rule." (p. 145).

224. Churchill, *Triumph and Tragedy*, p. 402. It has been a familiar theme of Churchill's to contend that good people, people of moral stature and toleration and respectful of their fellow man, should not refrain from defending themselves or promoting their principles out of reverence to broad principles that ignore the circumstances of their predicament. Tyrannical men beholden themselves to no principle, leaving them virtually unrestrained to do injury to others. Good men must sometimes act outside their defined bounds to protect themselves.

225. Churchill, *Triumph and Tragedy*, p. 400.

Chapter 4

Churchill at Fulton: The Precarious Peace

Winston Churchill delivered perhaps his most famous speech at Westminster College in Fulton, Missouri on March 5, 1946 at the invitation of President Harry Truman. The speech, entitled "The Sinews of Peace,"[1] shall be examined fully both because it is commonly misunderstood and because the speech presented the basic principles followed by Churchill during his postwar career.

It is commonly understood in the West that Churchill's speech at Fulton marked, some might say even encouraged, the onset of the Cold War.[2] To the countries in the East, Churchill's speech was just another sign of capitalist adventurism. The Soviet leaders historically have pointed to this "slanderous" speech as the point of no return in East-West relations. Loyal Communists thought of this speech as an "ideological manifesto" whose author was bent on menacing and exploiting the peoples of the world through British and American imperialism.

In that speech, which was punctuated with vitriolic slander against the Soviet Union and the People's Democracies, Churchill called for a crusade against socialism and charted a programme for US-British world supremacy "not only for our time but for a century to come." Churchill's Fulton speech was the summons for the creation of an Anglo-US military and political bloc directed against the Soviet Union and other socialist countries.[3]

In fact, a chill in the relationship between East and West was noticed by some even before Churchill delivered his "iron curtain" speech. Soviet leader Stalin delivered a speech one month before that stressed the hopelessness of any constructive relationship between East and West. No peaceful international order was possible.[4] Churchill's oration reflected these recent political developments.

Nevertheless, several western luminaries denounced Churchill in rather harsh terms for riding roughshod over the delicate structure of peace and for dangerously heightening international tensions. The conclusions of the speech were not widely shared by the intellectuals, journalists, and politicians in the West. The speech terrorized Pearl Buck sufficiently for this popular American writer to conclude, "we are nearer war tonight than we were last night." The *Chicago Sun* deplored what it perceived to be a rallying cry for the domination of the world by Great Britain and the United States.[5] Within the week, the Labour Party of Great Britain tabled a motion of censure against Churchill, stating that the proposals in his speech were "calculated to do injury to good relations between Great Britain, the USA and the USSR, and are inimical to the cause of world peace."[6] Mr. William Warby, who tabled the motion, followed his censure with even greater condemnation in June 1946:

[Churchill's action] was an action as irresponsible and mischievous as that of a schoolboy, who, wandering in search of adventure, might come across a hand grenade and toss it casually into somebody's back garden. That speech has done more harm to the cause of world peace than any speech or action of any politician since Hitler and Mussolini ceased to trouble this world.[7]

Of course, there were political science scholars too that could see nothing other that vainglory in Churchill's speech.[8] Could Churchill have been so devilish, vainglorious, and indifferent to the fate of the world? What were his plans for East-West relations?

"The Sinews of Peace" was the first noteworthy public speech to articulate a comprehensive foreign policy for the West. It was the first speech to make a break from a past that gave the major western powers overweening confidence that peace would rule over the world's relations. By appealing to both their self-interest and sense of honor, Churchill presented to his American audience a patchwork of new political realities and offered what he believed were prudent policy suggestions for the future. His speech was a plea for vigorous statesmanship in "anxious and baffling times." Sharing his "true and faithful counsel," Churchill laid bare the architecture of his postwar politics and presented the fundamental political and moral justifications for those policies.

"The Sinews of Peace" called for action on the part of those states that were blessed with power and the international stature to build what Churchill called the "Temple of Peace" to guard the security and the liberties of the democracies. The common sense and urgency of this speech were undeniable, the persuasive power of which relied on the undaunted recitation of many dismaying facts and an appeal to America's kindred spirit to Britain. Ten days after his speech, Churchill confided that he intended to speak in "arresting terms."[9]

Churchill opened his address by expressing his gratitude for the opportunity extended to him by President Truman to speak to "this kindred nation," his own countrymen, and "perhaps some other countries too." He promised his audience that he would speak his mind about the "problems which beset us on the morrow of our absolute victory in arms" with an eye to preserving what had been gained by so much suffering in the last war. He reminded the Americans of their newly won stature in the world and of the shame that might befall them should they refuse to use their stature to help secure the "safety and welfare, the freedom and progress" of families everywhere. Clearly, America's policy would affect more than just Americans.

The security and welfare of men, he emphasized, must be shielded from "the two giant marauders, war and tyranny." Already, he announced, measures had been taken internationally to help prevent the recurrence of war. The new United Nations Organization would help the major powers, through concerted action, to confront future aggressors; this world organization would be "a force for action, and not merely a frothing of words." Churchill proposed that countries contribute portions of their air squadrons and armed forces to the world organization to give it international respectability. He warned, however, that countries ought not to disarm themselves immediately, nor should the United States rush to relinquish its control of the atomic bomb to the UN. The world would not rest so comfortably should other powers learn how to utilize the raw power of the A-bomb for unjust ends.

The second danger to man's welfare was tyranny. Tyrants deprived whole nations of "the title deeds of freedom" and used "all-embracing police governments" to consolidate their despotic rule. Churchill declared that all peoples had a right to choose the character of their government and to protect the exercise of their basic human freedoms. He enjoined all those living under free constitutions to preach this message of democracy and freedom to mankind. Once the scourge of war and tyranny were removed from the earth, man would then be free to apply his science to expand his material well-being, to bring on "an age of plenty," and then to address the vital problems of famine and insecurity.

Churchill then brought his audience to "the crux" of his speech; namely, that no advances would be made against war or tyranny without "the fraternal association of the English-speaking peoples." Not only should the United States and the British Empire continue to grow in friendship and mutual understanding, but an intimate military relationship between the two countries must be pursued in order to leave the forces of freedom stronger than ever to work "for the high and simple causes that are dear to us and bode no ill to any." This "special relationship" would help the UN to achieve its full stature and strength and provide the example for future international cooperation.

More than half way into his address, Churchill struck a few dissonant notes regarding the wayward ally in the Grand Alliance that shook many in his audience, in America and abroad. After having expressed his admiration for the valiant wartime efforts of the Soviet Union, Churchill graphically depicted the new geopolitical reality in Europe. Stalin, he reminded his audience, had thrown an "iron curtain" across Europe and had subjected the populations of the occupied countries to increasing control from Moscow. "Police governments are prevailing in nearly every case, and so far, except in Czechoslovakia, there is no true democracy." The Red Armies also threatened the security of other nations, Persia, Italy, Greece, and Turkey in particular. And the likelihood that part of Germany would become communist did not augur well for peace in Europe.

These facts justified policies on the part of the liberal democracies to establish a unified Europe. Churchill reemphasized that the United States had an important role to play abroad within the structure of the United Nations. France too must play her part. All of Europe must work to knock down the "Communist fifth columns" being established in the weaker democracies, to prevent them from imperiling "Christian civilization."

Churchill assured his audience that war was not inevitable, but that certain facts must be faced squarely and certain actions taken soon to ensure the "permanent prevention of war." From their position of strength, the democracies ought to reach a settlement regarding the outstanding differences with the Soviet leaders. And they ought to do this as soon as possible lest the leverage and balance tilt more to the advantage of the East. If the West were to divide itself, or falter in its duty, greater dangers certainly would threaten the peace. Churchill's peroration revisited the need for unity among the English-speaking peoples in order to realize "an overwhelming assurance of security."

If we adhere faithfully to the Charter of the United Nations and walk forward in sedate and sober strength seeking no one's land or treasure, seeking to lay no arbitrary control upon the thoughts of men; if all British moral and material forces and convictions are joined with your own in fraternal association, the high-roads of the future will be clear, not only for us but for all, not only for our time, but for a century to come.

THE THREE ELEMENTS OF PEACE

In "The Sinews of Peace," Churchill proposed that postwar democratic diplomacy follow three related goals. The three foreign policy guides for these "anxious and baffling times" were safety, liberty, and fraternity. These political ends gave unity to his speech and were a calculated tug at the American soul. To clear "the high-roads of the future" and to achieve "an overwhelming assurance of security," Churchill asked that a union of the liberal democracies be formed, a powerful coalition of states unified by the high ideals of liberty and a shared sense of destiny and purpose. Without the achievement of safety, liberty, and fraternity, man's obligations to other men would remain unfulfilled—his purpose impeded by war and chaos and his duties abandoned by his moral incertitude and decay.

Democratic leaders had a duty to provide for the security of their own countrymen as well as to work for peace and security in other lands. The duties of government, especially of a powerful and just government, had to assume an international character. Wars had become global and total. Expansionist, aggressive regimes had assumed an ideological and internationalist character. Great and liberal powers must not isolate themselves from the world's misfortunes and tragedies. Churchill's speech conjured up Edmund Burke and his observation that the only thing necessary for evil to triumph is for good men to do nothing.[10]

Safety

Safety led the list of Churchill's concerns. Without security, the weak nations would be forced to fend for themselves. The supreme task and duty of all free countries after the war was "to guard the homes of the common people from the horrors and miseries of another war." This Churchill termed the free world's "over-all strategic concept." It would be the end to direct all other ends. For Churchill, public service to the common people is the definition of just and good government.

The objects of Churchill's concern here were tangible and real. They were "the humble folk"; they were your neighbors. Governments must strive to simplify the lives of its ordinary citizens by dealing with the common concerns of famine, poverty, and shelter and by not adding unnecessarily to the "accidents and difficulties of life." Churchill believed that life was toil and grief enough. And when a government must involve itself in war, as clearly it sometimes must, it necessarily hinders material progress in its own country. "When the designs of wicked men or the aggressive urge of mighty States dissolve over large areas the frame of civilised society, humble folk are confronted with difficulties with which they cannot cope. For them all is distorted, all is broken, even ground to a pulp."

Churchill played hard upon the great irony of the twentieth century. Despite all of the prosperity and technological advances, men still were faced with death and deprivation. Wars in this century twice had involved entire populations, not just soldiers. Battle had pierced the serenity of almost every family. "Countless homes" in all the lands had experienced the horrors and miseries of war. Science, in the form of new weapons engineered to maximize destruction, had turned upon man and government and complicated the supreme task of guarding the livelihood of the family.

Liberty

The indiscriminate horrors of war were not the only violators of peace and safety. Churchill lectured that the homes of ordinary people also must be shielded from the arbitrary violence and unjust intrusion of tyranny. The preservation of liberty also was part of the "overall strategic concept." War and tyranny were "the two giant marauders" of the common folk, the twin pillagers of peace and security. Tyranny differed from war, however, in its intense campaign against liberty itself.

The idea and practice of liberty in America and Britain provided the spirit of life for all Britains and Americans. The "title deeds of freedom" are well known to free people everywhere, and Churchill recognized them as the lifeblood of the United States and Great Britain. Churchill expounded upon the purpose and functions of government by resting his arguments on the thoughts on government of John Locke and Montesquieu, thoughts that also guided the authors of

The Federalist and that poured life into the heart and soul of every American and every modern liberal democrat.[11]

Churchill proclaimed that a free people had the protected power "to choose or change the character or form of government under which they dwell," the freedom to express themselves in speech and press, and the blessing of independent and unbiased courts of justice to administer the laws approved by the people through the popular assemblies. A government concerned for the common people would refrain from intruding upon the ways of the family and the private "ethical conceptions" that are the mainstay of the family's inspiration and happiness. Ultimately, the family is the life of the community and the nation. The faith in freedom expressed daily by the English-speaking families had roots rich in honorable traditions and noble ideas.

> [W]e must never cease to proclaim in fearless tones the great principles of freedom and the rights of man which are the joint inheritance of the English-speaking world and which through the Magna Carta, the Bill of Rights, the Habeas Corpus, Trial by Jury, and the English common law find their most famous expression in the American Declaration of Independence.

The idea of liberty, Churchill implored, also must guide the West in its quest for peace. Churchill warned, however, that the West ought not to compromise itself by intruding unduly in the activities of other countries. "It is not our duty at this time when difficulties are so numerous to interfere forcibly in the internal affairs of countries which we have not conquered in war." (Churchill awkwardly qualifies this statement with the insertion of "at this time.") The statement follows his recognition of the persistence of despotic regimes, strongly implying that he was talking of their former ally—the Soviet Union. He evidently recognized the remote possibility that circumstances may involve the West in an intensive campaign to change the persistent radical behavior of, if not the nature of, the Soviet Union.

The Western democracies, however, were bound by an obligation to proclaim "in fearless tones" the "great principles of freedom and the rights of man." Freedom must be proclaimed by free men in an age when so many other men live under tyrannous conditions. "Every cottage home" should participate in these rights and freedoms. Free men should be actively involved in spreading the word and seeing that respect for the rights of man take root in other less fortunate lands. "Here is the message of the British and American peoples to mankind. Let us preach what we practice—let us practice what we preach." Churchill implied that there was a strong link between word and deed; he warned against passivity in the promotion of liberty. Simply put: a free people must be prepared to act in freedom's defense.

The systematic violators of liberty, be they Nazis, Communists or others, were the natural enemies of the liberal democracies. With freedom under such a broad-based assault, as it was at the conclusion of the war, the protection of freedom where it existed and the promotion of it where it could not be found would provide the moral justification and guidelines for Western foreign policy in the postwar world. While he carefully omitted any reference to the Soviet regime in his remarks on tyrannical rule, there is no doubt that the harsh criticisms of "police government" operating through "privileged party" and "oligarchic compact" applied to Stalin's state. Direct confrontation in the form of strident rhetoric would have almost certainly imperiled any chance for a general agreement on the postwar peace between East and West.

General reproach, though, of regimes that violated "the title deeds of freedom" did not escape his attention. "We cannot be blind to the fact that the liberties enjoyed by individual citizens throughout the British Empire are not valid in a considerable number of countries, some of which are very powerful." The "very powerful" depriver of the universal right to liberty is unquestionably the USSR. The speech at Fulton was replete with praise for democracy's virtues and open condemnation of the vices of tyrannical orders.

Do Churchill's ideas expressed at Fulton about the urgency of security and the requirements for liberty contradict his earlier appraisals regarding the natural place of war in the international system? He suggested the possibility that war and tyranny could be "removed" so that man could be freed from the threats to his life in order to concentrate on developing his "material well-being." What then are we to make of his earlier observation attributing a precarious nature to peace, that "the history of the human race is a history of war, and the records of thousands of years show only a few uneasy intervals of peace?" At Fulton, Churchill indicated that "if the dangers of war and tyranny are removed, there is no doubt that science and co-operation can bring in the next few years to the world, certainly in the next few decades newly taught in the sharpening school of war, an expansion of material well-being beyond anything that has yet occurred in human experience." There is here no contradiction, only a heightened sense of urgency to provide more assiduously for the safety of men. Churchill conditioned his optimism by the word "if," implying that unprecedented periods of tranquillity are not inevitable and perhaps not even possible.

He called upon men to labor even harder than their progenitors to build that "temple of peace"; for the twentieth century had made both wars and tyranny total in their destructiveness and indiscrimination. A strong message in this speech is that war could all too easily creep up on those countries that do not take measures to prevent the insolent aggression of other states; his words reminded his audience that peace is a labor of life. The preservation of liberty demanded vigilance as well, as freedom in this century seemed beset from all sides. "[T]here is no reason except human folly [war] or sub-human crime [tyrannical polities] which should deny to all the nations the inauguration and enjoyment of an age of plenty."

Churchill displayed for his audience a cautious faith in progress. The chief vehicle of progress since the advent of the industrial age was science. However, scientific progress and new technologies put even more destructive weapons in the hands of aggressor states. Science and technology also enabled tyrannies to fulfill their traditional objectives more effectively, to become even more encompassing and systematic in their injustice.[12] Mankind has suffered as a result of political repression and wars in this age of scientific enlightenment as it never had suffered in the past. Science has been a two-headed beast, serving both life and death, slavery and freedom. Churchill called upon mankind to redirect the energies of science to cultivate the earth "in justice and peace." Science ought to be used for good ends, to help unlock the treasures of material well-being guarded by mother earth. Churchill quoted approvingly his friend Mr. Bourke Cockran: "There is enough for all," said Mr. Cockran. "The earth is a generous mother; she will provide in plentiful abundance food for all her children if they will but cultivate her soil in justice and peace." Injustice and war, with the aid of science and technology, thus far have left many scars on this century.

The immediate prospects for abundance and security were not evident. "Now," he reflected, "at this sad and breathless moment, we are plunged in the hunger and distress which are the aftermath of our stupendous struggle." While Churchill's speech is generally upbeat and forward looking, he did not fail to remind his audience that "the Stone Age may return on the gleaming wings of Science." The security of the men and women everywhere, and in the free world in particular, demanded new efforts that were international in character and scope in order to prevent the slide back into war. The realization of greater security and broader freedoms in the world demanded that the West focus more upon the problems of defense.

Fraternity

Following his discussion of the principal maladies of the age, Churchill presented his audience with what appeared to be the only possible cure for both war and tyranny. In order to secure safety, liberty and progress, the English-speaking peoples of America and Great Britain must strive to form a special relationship or a "fraternal association." This, he informed his audience, was the "crux" of what he had travelled to Fulton to tell them.

The first half of the twentieth century saw Great Britain topple from its leadership position among the major powers. Faced with a diminishing empire and declining influence in the world, Churchill pressed home his point that the duty of keeping the peace had been passed to his American brothers. As successors to the guardianship, Churchill emphasized to his audience that "with the primacy in power is also joined an awe-inspiring accountability to the future." The sublime nature of his counsel reflected the solemn responsibility that the United States had assumed as the leader of the liberty-loving states. Churchill's blunt account of the state of the world at that time was spirited by his own recognition that the fruits of the victory over the Nazis would rot through inattention in America and free Europe. By focusing only on the problems of the present moment, these nations would once again imperil their peace and freedom.

While Churchill's preoccupations with American disengagement from the world seem frivolous to us today, it would have been presumptuous of him to assume that Americans would have accepted forthrightly their new role and shouldered their new burdens given their past proclivities to isolationism.

Churchill's speech recognized one of the great weaknesses of liberal democratic polities—their refusal to recognize that war is a permanent feature and ever present possibility of international relations. Liberal men generally view wars as unnatural and irrational folly in light of their belief that governments are set up to fulfill principally the end of self-preservation. War, by definition, threatens this very principle that brought men together to live in one society or political order under a social compact. Why would nations war with one another when their survival is of paramount importance? As strategic analyst Carnes Lord argued, "[l]iberal democracies are deeply disinclined to prepare adequately for war, or to foster the institutions and types of men capable of waging it."[13] Liberal regimes are rather more inclined to address international conflict through legal norms, which misleads its citizenry to believe that there are rules of "fair play" that states follow in order to achieve justice and improperly prepares them for war. Even in the state of nature, and nations are in a state of nature in relation to one another, natural law places limits on the conduct of men and governments; legality must rule over the passionate pursuance of vengeance or disproportionate justice.[14]

Churchill recognized that the liberal way of life was not conducive to adequate defense preparations, and that timely exhortation and exposition were needed from someone like himself who stood sufficiently apart from or above that liberal tradition (i.e., he understood the liberal tradition). Churchill's familiarity with the history and experience of war and his knowledge of the various types of governments gave him a vision of democracy's weaknesses that otherwise would be unavailable to a leader entirely raised and educated in the school of liberalism.

Churchill, therefore, intended his speech to shock Americans into action and into their proper role as the leading state of the free world. Inaction and indifference on the part of the liberal democracies was the bane of peace. Unless America utilized its newly discovered powers on behalf of peace and freedom, the threat of war and the reality of tyranny would have a controlling influence. Power without direction is only slightly better than power in the hands of despotic men. That is so if only because it enhances the powers of the tyrants by detracting from the influence of good men and decent political orders. Free nations had to take their stand in the world.

Churchill declared that Britain's old balance of power doctrine, which would allow a state to play on either side of an international dispute, was no longer welcome as the preeminent western strategy for peace. "We cannot afford, if we can help it, to work on the narrow margins, offering temptations to a trial of strength." A thriving cooperation between the English-speaking peoples would help assure that there would be "no quivering, precarious balance of power to offer its temptation to ambition or adventure." Rather, there would be "an overwhelming sense of security." Nothing pertaining to the West's security should be left to fortune. Indeed, the policy of "balancing" may well end in the disintegration in western unity, and this would leave the liberal political orders vulnerable to aggression and intimidation from states that scoffed at liberalism and traditional diplomacy. At this stage in history, regimes that were based on liberal principles had to prepare themselves to confront their enemies or else risk the return to total war. The achievement of security was the great task that lied before all the peaceful states, and before the United States (in league with her brother Britain) in particular.

Churchill related his proposal in a most brotherly fashion that reflected the common heritage of both countries and the profound agreement by British and American citizens on the principles of good government. The efforts to avert war would fail unless these common principles paved the way for a special relationship between the two countries. This fraternal association would be the most important sinew of peace in the collective effort to repulse the transgressions of tyranny and reduce the inclinations to war. Churchill's use of the word "fraternal" appropriately was suited to his purpose. Born to an American mother and British father of royal blood, Churchill was the perfect ambassador from England to America. In his calls for a special relationship, one that would be quite unique in the history of state relations, Churchill employed brotherly sentiments and appealed to "natural affinities and friendship" in order to arouse a sense of family. In the case of the United States and Great Britain, there were very strong bonds of tradition, principle, and blood. Family members are naturally under obligation to protect their own, their common principles, happiness, and property. Fraternal ties are solid ties. Only misfortune and unnatural, tragic acts break families apart, and usually to the detriment of all the members. Churchill's message was that as the family is a strong unity, so too would be the special alliance between the United States and Great Britain.

Churchill clearly indicated to his audience that unity in the defensive relationship was most important. Growing friendship and mutual understanding were essential to the "continuance of the intimate relationship between our military advisors, leading to common study of potential dangers, the similarity of weapons and manuals of instruction, and to the interchange of officers and cadets at technical colleges." Churchill presented both economic, logistical, operational, and strategic reasons for sharing naval and air force bases and for maintaining frequent military communications between the two English-speaking nations.

"[I]f all British moral and material forces and convictions are joined with your own in fraternal association, the high-roads of the future will be clear, not only for us but for all, not only for our time, but for a century to come." Common language, common culture, common laws, common principles, and common aims provided for a very formidable force in the world which ought to be employed in the protection and promotion of liberal principles everywhere.

Churchill also stressed common religion shared by the two countries, for he recognized that the citizens of both countries were overwhelmingly Christian. Christianity in America was particularly strong. He spoke of the "growing challenge and peril to Christian civilization" in order to stress once again that the broad commonalties between the two countries greatly outweighed the differences.[15] They would share a similar fate. Similarly, in his discussion of the "fraternal association," and of its welcomed place within a world organization, Churchill quoted directly from the Gospel of John (14:2): "In my father's house are many mansions." Again, the suggestion here is of a common fate and a common divine "parentage."

> Thus, whatever happens, and thus only, shall we be secure ourselves and able to work together for the high and simple causes that are dear to us and bode no ill to any. Eventually there may come—I feel eventually there will come—the principle of common citizenship, but that we may be content to leave to destiny, whose outstretched arm many of us can already clearly see.

And now the opportunity existed for *both* countries to shape a more peaceful and prosperous future. The association with the United States would accomplish two important tasks: first and most important, fraternal association would maintain most effectively the peace in a dangerous age; and second, the intimate bonds with America would help keep Britain's influence alive in the world.

INTERNATIONAL COOPERATION AND NEGOTIATED SETTLEMENT

If peace and liberty were to prevail in the world, the new fraternal relationship would have to lend its power and prestige to the multinational campaign to increase international cooperation, especially between East and West. Churchill believed the moral force of the American and British relationship would work on different levels, but especially within the newly chartered United Nations Organization.

The new world organization would be stronger than its predecessor because of the vital addition of the United States. America's absence from the League of Nations, in addition to other deficiencies, helped to make that organization ineffective in its attempts to prevent the greatest war of this century. The UN, as envisioned by Churchill, would be a significant and leading force in the world, quite unlike the present-day UN organization. Churchill's UN was to have a focused and defined purpose, restraining aggressive state behavior, and was to be endowed with the resources and constitution to execute that purpose.

> We must make sure that its work is fruitful, that it is a reality and not a sham, that it is a *force for action*, and not merely a frothing of words, that it is a true temple of peace in which the shields of many nations can some day be hung up, and not merely a cockpit in a Tower of Babel.

A clue to Churchill's ideas for the composition of the UN was found in his reference to "many nations" rather than "all nations." International cooperation among the liberty-loving states would form the leadership council rather than a hodgepodge of countries of varying aims and ideologies. (Although Churchill's reference to the Gospel of John—"In my Father's house there are many mansions"—seems to indicate that no country would be forever excluded from the international organization. Any state that could contribute to the maintenance of the peace and the promotion of liberty would be welcomed.)

Would the fraternal association between Great Britain and the United States hinder the development and operations of the newly founded UN? Where would the interests of both those states lie and how would they direct their bountiful resources? For Churchill, bilateral and multinational arrangements among states were natural and always would be an important part of international activity. Bilateral and multilateral cooperation was necessary to enhance peace. Absent these bilateral and multilateral activities, which develop out of mutual interests and benefits, how could one expect a world organization to succeed? Rather than constituting a hindrance, the special relationship "is probably the only means by which that organization will achieve its full stature and strength." Absent the union of these two great liberal democracies, two regimes that "harbor no design incompatible with the Charter of the United Nations," the world organization would lack proper definition and direction and, hence, strength and resolve.

As courts and other judicial bodies could not act effectively without sheriffs and constables, Churchill suggested, as a "practical proposal" for action, that the UN be equipped "immediately" with an international armed force. He recognized that states would only naturally and reluctantly give up a portion of their defensive forces. "In such a matter we can only go step by step, but we must begin now." While soldiers in the international army would retain marks of their own country and would never be requested to act against the interests of their home country, they must otherwise respond to breaches of the peace and accept direction from the world organization. These armies would start out with modest tasks that would grow with the confidence of those granting their charge. Churchill believed that such an arrangement after the first great war would have put significant barriers before the aggressive powers.

Despite Churchill's solid endorsement of the UN, he nonetheless displayed a great deal of caution by placing some significant restrictions on the power and jurisdiction of the organization. As armed international conflict is serious business, and as it always has been a threat to a state's well-being, several precautions must be taken. A nation's first line of defense must not be handed over to an international body in these early stages of its construction, and not until some very challenging conditions were first met. "Before we cast away the solid assurances of national armaments for self-preservation we must be certain that our temple is built, not upon shifting sands or quagmires, but upon that rock." What are these conditions? "Ultimately, when the essential brotherhood of man is truly embodied and expressed in a world organization with *all* the necessary practical safeguards to make it effective, these powers naturally would be confided to that world organization."

Upon reading this qualification, one has to wonder whether Churchill ever seriously entertained the notion of entirely trusting an international organization to provide for the defense of his own Britain. The success of this quasi-world government relied upon the embodiment of "the essential brotherhood of man" within the UN, a kind of intimacy and international unity never before experienced in history. And what else could be meant by "essential brotherhood" other than the common belief in certain fundamental principles? A brotherhood of "heritage" or "economy" would make little sense; a brotherhood of "humanity" would be too general as men always have shared this attribute. This notion of essential brotherhood must rest on an acceptance of common principles, a common understanding of the nature of peace, the good life, or justice.

However, history teaches that men always have harbored different notions of good government and the good life, some notions being quite different from others.[16] These many conflicting ideas on what is good and right often have been the source of fierce and violent international conflict, so often did they occur that Churchill considered war a part of the human condition.[17] As he pointed out later in the speech, men are often "unteachable" in regard to this condition and perennially throw themselves back into the maw of war. Consequently, the idea of universal brotherhood, particularly in the political realm, by most any measure appears to be somewhat distant.[18]

So why would Churchill tease his audience with this far-fetched objective? Perhaps he meant the brotherhood of man as a condition that all men ought to work for, but which probably would never be fully realized. Insofar as unity and fraternity were strong themes in Churchill's speech, it is very likely that Churchill believed that the achievement of this unity and cozy intimacy ought to be accomplished first by the free nations of the West. Brotherhood was certainly a conceivable end for Great Britain and the United States, and such a fraternal association might have marked the beginning of broader international cooperation as well as the possibility of a more ordered world.

If two of the workmen [on the Temple of Peace] know each other particularly well and are old friends, if their families are inter-mingled, and if they have "faith in each others purpose, hope in each other's future and charity towards each other's shortcomings"...why cannot they work together at the common task as friends and partners?... Indeed they must do so or else the temple may not be built, or, being built, it may collapse, and we shall all be proved again unteachable and have to go and try to learn again for the third time in a school of war, incomparably more rigorous than that from which we have just been released.

Fraternal association between the United States and Great Britain also would give the West strength for the coming negotiations with the Soviet Union. A settlement was needed among the former members of the Grand Alliance who, by the time of the speech, clearly had gone down separate paths. There were many outstanding differences that needed reconciliation. Time was of the essence, for "[n]obody knows what Soviet Russia . . . intends to do in the immediate future, or what are the limits."

Churchill bore no malice at Fulton, but he did bring with him a skein of harsh facts. Regardless of the temper then in America or Europe, Churchill acted out of duty to lay bare the new realities of the world and to give his "true and faithful counsel in these anxious and baffling times." His remarks on the most recent danger were prefaced as follows:

I have a strong admiration and regard for the valiant Russian people and for my wartime comrade, Marshal Stalin. . . . We understand the Russian need to be secure on her western frontiers by the removal of all possibility of German aggression. We welcome Russia to her rightful place among the leading nations of the world. We welcome her flag upon the seas. Above all, we welcome constant, frequent and growing contacts between the Russian people and our own people on both sides of the Atlantic.

These noble expressions of goodwill strongly suggest that the argument that Churchill's speech marked the onset of the Cold War is both rather tenuous and contrived. His speech touched most strongly on our humanity and marvelously expressed Churchill's own humanity.

Tragically, the behavior and the attitude of the Soviet leaders after the war sharply undercut these hopes. The most dramatic expression of this divergence of postwar objectives was the appearance of the "iron curtain" that stretched across the European continent and cut off "all the capitals of the ancient states of Central and Eastern Europe" from any participation in the free way of life. Churchill observed that the influence Moscow exercised over these captive lands was increasing day by day. The Soviet Union had done what Churchill had feared all throughout the war; it had begun to establish an old-fashioned sphere of influence in Eastern and Central Europe. All of the most important political and economic decisions were being transferred from Prague, Berlin, Warsaw, Vienna, Budapest, Bucharest, and Sofia to the Soviet capital of Moscow.

Would the Soviet leaders dare to go beyond their conquests in Europe in order to extend their influence in the Middle or Near East? What would become of the Asian political landscape, especially Manchuria? Do we dare wonder how much of "a growing challenge and peril to Christian civilization" the communist fifth columns will become in places like Italy that have weak political infrastructures? "These are sombre facts for anyone to have to recite on the morrow of a victory gained by so much splendid comradeship in arms and in the cause of freedom and democracy."

Churchill's speech demonstrated that he harbored no illusions about the viability and unity of the Grand Alliance. He saw its disintegration as a harsh reminder of the often tragic pattern of history. He pointed out to his audience that many felt war would be forever outmoded after the first great war of the century and with the emergence of the League of Nations, whose purpose was to keep order in a fractured world. Churchill recalled the confidence expressed by many statesmen in the new international arrangement, although Churchill himself had several reservations about the durability of the Versailles peace. Even less faith did he have at the conclusion of the war against Nazism. "I do not see or feel that same confidence or even the same hopes in the haggard world at the present time."

What worried Churchill in 1946 was the steady increase in Stalin's power and influence that resulted from the virtually unchallenged annexation of overrun territories. He had come to Fulton to express his consternation about the future to the leaders and the citizens of a major world power that had the economic and military strength to help provide greater security in Europe and some other parts of the world. The "Sinews of Peace" was a political and moral justification for the Americans to involve themselves intimately with the fate of Europe and use their military and economic strength as a force for liberty. American involvement would give the West something beyond the "narrow margins" of the balance of power to work with, a power that would reduce the "temptations to a trial of strength." By uniting forces behind a common and just aim, the West would strengthen the armies of liberty in order to challenge any further deterioration of their security.

I do not believe that Soviet Russia desires war. What they desire is the fruits of war and the indefinite expansion of their power and doctrines. But what we have to consider here to-day while time remains, is the permanent prevention of war and the establishment of conditions of freedom and democracy as rapidly as possible in all countries.

The immediate solution to the West's insecurity was not to bristle back at the threatening bear. Neither did the answer to the problem of peace and radical global disunity lie in appeasement or indifference. Churchill, instead, called for a "settlement" with the Soviet Union, the achievement of which rested on a convincing display of strength by the western countries. Churchill believed that "there is nothing they [the Soviet leaders] admire so much as strength, and there is nothing for which they have less respect than for weakness." Action *now*, while the West did have superior strength, and a faithful devotion to "the principles outlined in the United Nations Charter,"[19] would help to win the peace by achieving an historic settlement.

In 1946, strength for the West lay in the economic might of the United States as well as American military capacity, newly exalted to world superpower status by impressive victories during World War II and the invention and successful employment of the atomic bomb. This status could be used to bring the necessary leverage into the negotiations for a lasting settlement with Stalin. If war was to be averted and the crescendo of aggression (which already had approach the levels of total war) halted, high-level diplomacy with Moscow must be attempted by the West. Churchill explained that such a peace only could be achieved by reaching agreement as soon as possible,

by reaching now, in 1946, a good understanding on all points with Russia under the general authority of the United Nations Organization and by the maintenance of the good understanding through many peaceful years, by the world instrument, supported by the whole strength of the English-speaking world and all its connections.

The exact nature of the "understanding on all points" remained open to speculation, although a reasonable picture of this peaceful world order is not beyond our grasp. Natural spheres of influence probably would be respected for a significant period of time. The export of revolutionary doctrine to the detriment of the liberal states would be prohibited; this would mean, of course, that the Soviets would have to abandon the dream of world domination and the dissemination of communist propaganda. The West, in turn, would respect the current Soviet boundaries. As Churchill often confessed his dreams of a free and reunited Europe, East and West, we must assume that this extension of boundary recognition would not have reached into the occupied territories of Central and Eastern Europe. These boundaries would have been labeled as "inviolable," but not "unchangeable." Churchill declared, "no nation should be permanently outcast" from the "new unity in Europe." The Soviet Union would work within the existing international community and legal system in order to preserve it and to promote peaceful international relations. The West in turn would "welcome her flag upon the seas." Above all, Churchill emphasized, "we welcome constant, frequent and growing contacts between the Russian people and our own people on both sides of the Atlantic." In other words, the West would face the Soviet Union with open arms, but would refrain from all embraces until a more genuine trust was established. In a trusting relationship, the Soviets would enjoy the enormous benefits of trade, friendship, and genuinely peaceful co-existence with the western nations.

Although war was a natural phenomenon for Churchill, it seldom was inevitable. Churchill did not believe war between East and West was imminent. He was confident in his statesmanship and his own abilities to shape the future, even out of office, as his speech at Fulton would appear to indicate.[20] Fortune did not hold all the cards. This was the good message Churchill came to deliver. "It is because I am sure that our fortunes are still in our own hands and that we hold the power to save the future," he assured his audience, "that I feel the duty to speak out now that I have the occasion and the opportunity to do so."

ACTION AND HONOR

Churchill occasionally expressed his gratitude to Providence and to good fortune for the relative security that the West experienced since the conclusion of the war. Two of the references he made to these forces, forces beyond man's control (i.e., they could only be wished for or prayed for), were made in the context of his discussion of the atomic bomb. Indeed, the world had been spared a nightmare because the bomb found its way into the hands of a country that other men had no reason to fear.

No one in any country has slept less well in their beds because this knowledge and the method and the raw materials to apply it, are at present largely retained in American hands. I do not believe we should all have slept so soundly had the positions been reversed and if some Communist or neo-Fascist State monopolised for the time being these dread agencies.

He then continued his point: "God has willed that this shall not be and we have at least a breathing space to set our house in order before this peril [the peril of another state acquiring the bomb] has to be encountered." Fortune, in the above instances, had been kind to the West. Churchill indirectly had explained some of the old lessons of politics to his audience, that politics and war are influenced by fortune, and the victory of any battle and the success of any country will hinge, to some degree, on the frictions of life and on the unforeseen.[21]

In his discussion of the construction of the "Temple of Peace," however, fortune took on a darker meaning. Fortune had become the potential enemy of the liberal states. Churchill warned against allowing events to "drift," in essence either ignoring a significant turn of events or praying for favorable circumstance rather than acting to create or salvage the conditions of freedom.[22] Providence had seen to it that the destructive powers of the atomic bomb had found their way into the hands of the United States and Great Britain; but could the West continue to count on Providence to provide for their safety? What should happen if the totalitarian states developed atomic capabilities?[23]

Churchill came to Fulton to explain why the democracies ought to rely more on their actions than on distant and sometimes malicious fortune. Clearly he believed that the western leaders could, through statesmanship, shape the destinies of their countries. Otherwise, why bother informing the Americans about the sinews of peace? He said he came to speak because he was sure "that our fortunes are still in our hands and that we hold the power to save the future." At almost every juncture Churchill's words placed an emphasis on action. Action by the Americans to lead the West and guard the future; action within the UN to counter aggression; action to unite Europe; action to establish a fraternal association between Britain and the United States; and action by the democratic leaders to begin negotiations with the Soviet leaders.

Even action, though, without an understanding of purpose, without a clear grasp of the national security objectives, ultimately would be insufficient. Statesmen ought to embrace reason and a moral guide before they defined their purpose. Action must be reasonable and guided. Churchill reminded his audience that reason rightfully belonged within the political arena. "It is necessary that constancy of mind, persistency of purpose, and the grand simplicity of decision shall guide and rule the conduct of the English-speaking peoples in peace as they did in war." By referring back to their comradery in war, Churchill reminded his audience of the singularity of purpose that energized the free world to do noble deeds. There can be little doubt that Churchill wanted to harness that strength and energy found in the free world in peacetime by uniting the English-speaking peoples behind a simple yet noble goal. For statesmen to succumb to the illusion of a permanent peace and the flighty sentiment that the commotion of a great victory often stirs up would serve only to confuse western foreign policy objectives. Churchill's mention of "the grand simplicity of decision" reminded his audience that the choices were stark and obvious to any leader or citizen that understood the unfolding drama in Europe. The West once again must form a defensive alliance. The defense of the West had to be grounded in contemplation if the obvious choices were not to elude its leaders. Without proper understanding, the odds that an action would be appropriate or timely would be slim. Churchill took the time to remind his audience of the events leading up to the past war to encourage them to look more soberly upon the future.

There never was a war in all history easier to prevent by timely action than the one which has just desolated such great areas of the globe. It could have been prevented in my belief without firing a shot . . . ; but no one would listen and one by one we were sucked into the awful whirlpool. We surely must not let that happen again.

Churchill's rhetoric did not rely on persuading the Americans to lead the West by reminding them of their common fate with other liberal polities. He appealed also to their sense of honor and duty. "The United States stands at this time at the pinnacle of power. It is a solemn moment for the American Democracy. For with primacy of power is also joined an awe-inspiring accountability to the future." The stakes at hand were the liberties and security gained in the last war; the objective was to preserve them "for the future glory and safety of mankind."

There was glory and honor to be earned through the successful leadership of the free world. There also was ignominy to be apportioned to those whose foreign policies were inappropriate and embraced foolish objectives. "As you look around you," he said, "you must feel not only the sense of duty done but also you must feel anxiety lest you fall below the level of achievement." In order for the Americans to receive the glory that is rightfully theirs, they had to fulfill the duty that the course of world events had recently placed before them. To reject the "clear and shining" opportunities that had presented themselves would bring upon all of the leading liberal nations "all the long reproaches of the after-time."

Honor was closely linked with proper or good action on the part of the United States. Sufficient courage, which is needed to overcome adversity in the noblest of circumstances, was necessary to impel the Americans to accept their new responsibilities for preserving the common good. The future surely would provide hard tests of American courage. No longer could the United States hope to find sanctuary behind its two ocean fronts. Churchill reminded his audience that "[t]wice the United States has had to send several millions of its young men across the Atlantic to find war; but now war can find any nation, wherever it dwell between dusk and dawn." Clearly Churchill hoped to drive home his message that the United States had more than just a passing interest in the "pacification of Europe." The preservation of its very life may be jeopardized by events not entirely beyond its control. Churchill never thought of the Americans as cowardly, but he was not entirely certain that the Americans would have the will to assume their new responsibilities.[24] The duties of a great power were easy to shrink away from. The "sombre facts" could go unrecognized. It would not be easy to be the leading great power; there would be "an awe-inspiring accountability to the future." Churchill's emphasis on action, "timely action," reinforced the message of courage that he brought with him. Without courage, without "the persistency of purpose," no action was possible; without action, glory and honor (and perhaps even safety) were impossible.

Success in their duty would bring glory to America's leaders and safety to her citizens. The entire free world would benefit from America's success and leadership.

CONCLUSION

"The Sinews of Peace" is one of the earliest of the foundation documents of the western policy of containment. Indeed, "[t]he language of Fulton had become the policy of the Government of the United Kingdom and of the Administration of the United States."[25] Churchill's speech at Fulton was not a diatribe against the men in the Kremlin, nor was it a call for 1970s-style detente or appeasement. Rather, it marked the early stages of the West's new policy of containment, but with the additional hope that the West's superior strength would lead to fruitful negotiations and "a good understanding on all points" with the Soviet Union. It marked one of the earliest attempts to provide a political and moral justification for political and military action abroad. Churchill saw in his speech the kernel of a pre-NATO alliance structure for peace. Indeed, the Marshall Plan and NATO had followed Fulton and seemed to echo the ideas and sentiments found within Churchill's speech. Churchill desired the alliance to be based upon a special relationship between the United States and Great Britain, and that the objectives of the great powers be assisted by a flourishing world organization. Churchill's speech made clear, however, that international organizations were no substitute for a determined effort by the great liberal powers to counter Soviet expansionism. There was a growing strategic threat to security and liberty. American involvement in the practice of containment was entirely justified by her new position in the world and by the stake that all Americans had in the preservation of liberty all around the world, particularly in Europe.

The most dramatic event that immediately followed Churchill's "Sinews" oration was Stalin's withdrawal of his troops from Persia. This "retreat" was attributed by some to Churchill's assertive words and plans for action. *The New York Times* also noted that Washington had become noticeably firmer and that the prestige of the UN had swelled in the wake of his speech.[26] Perhaps Churchill believed of communism as Lincoln believed of the institution of slavery—that this vile system of rule that destroyed men's souls and ate away at their liberties would die out naturally if only it were not allowed to spread. At minimum, the policy of containing Soviet expansionism would not permit the communist regimes to pose as great a threat to the community of nations.

Hardly responsible for the beginning of the Cold War, this speech was a clear response to threatening Soviet postwar behavior, a response to the violation of the Yalta accords and the display of aggressive intent, and an attempt to prevent a new world struggle. The image of the "iron curtain" threw the world drama before the eyes of his American audience. Churchill laid down stark moral distinctions at Fulton that did not sit well with many. He painted a dark picture of totalitarian rule and expansionism.[27] He also extended a hand to Moscow as a gesture of peace, but insisted at the same time that peace would have to be compatible with western ideals and security. Churchill hoped that his audience would not distance themselves from the brutal facts he presented, and that they would nobly assume the leadership from Great Britain that he symbolically had handed over to them.

NOTES

1. This chapter is an interpretation of "The Sinews of Peace." All quoted material is derived from this speech unless otherwise indicated. The text of the speech can be found in *Complete Speeches*, pp. 7,285-7,293. All parenthetical comments and underlinings are the author's comments and emphases.

2. See, for example, James A. Nathan and James K. Oliver, *United States Foreign Policy and World Order*, 2nd ed. (Boston: Little, Brown and Company, 1981), pp. 56-58.

3. B. Ponomaryov, A. Gromyko and V. Khvostov, ed., *History of Soviet Foreign Policy: 1945-1970*, trans. David Shirvsky (Moscow: Progress Publishers, 1974), pp. 152-153.

4. Dean Acheson, *Present At The Creation* (New York: W.W. Norton & Company, 1969), pp. 150 and 194.

5. Cited in Gilbert, *Never Despair*, pp. 204 and 206.

6. Mr. Warby, Speech of 14 March 1946, *Hansard*, vol. 420 (London: Her Majesty's Stationery Office, 1946), c. 1293. According to historian Alan Bullock, *Ernest Bevin: Foreign Secretary* (New York: W.W. Norton & Company, 1983), p. 226, Warby's motion "made no impression" on either Churchill or Ernest Bevin, the Foreign Secretary at the time.

7. Speech of 5 June 1946, *Hansard*, vol. 423, c. 2064-5. Churchill received much abuse for his speech from the opposition parties over the next several years. He was accused of being a "warmonger," tying British interests too tightly to those of the United States, and political opportunism (see *Hansard*, vol. 423, cc. 2062, 2080, 2083; vol. 446, cc. 561, 590; vol. 459, c. 750). There were members who defended the Prime Minister, such as Major LeggeBourke, who suggested "that if everyone in this country and in the world took the trouble to read that speech again, they would see how very far from the truth is that suggestion [that Churchill was warmongering]" speech of December 10, 1948, *Hansard*, vol. 459, c. 757.

8. Perhaps the most cynical interpretation of Churchill's statesmanship was provided by A.J.P. Taylor who, in "The Statesman," *Churchill Revised: A Critical Assessment* (New York: The Dial Press, Inc., 1969), p. 57 (in which he was one of five contributing authors), wrote that "[s]ounding the alarm had become a habit with him and, having risen by championing liberty against Hitler, he could not resist repeating the performance against Stalin."

9. Gilbert, *Never Despair*, p. 215.

10. "When bad men combine, the good must associate; else they will fall one by one, an unpitied sacrifice in a contemptible struggle." From Edmund Burke, "Thoughts on the Cause of the Present Discontents" [April 23, 1770], *Selected Writings and Speeches*, Peter J. Stanlis, ed. (Chicago: Regnery Gateway, 1963), p. 141.

11. See for example, John Locke's *Second Treatise of Government*, chapters 2, 7, 12, and 13 (*Two Treatises of Government and Robert Filmer Patriarcha*, Thomas I. Cook, ed. (New York: Hafner Publishing Company, 1966) and Montesquieu's *The Spirit of the Laws*, book 11 (trans. Thomas Nugent (New York: Hafner Publishing Company, 1949)) on laws that contribute to the establishment of political liberty.

12. Tyrants always have had certain objectives that set them apart from other rulers, as Aristotle noted, but at the same time they also have had difficulty preserving their unjust rule. See Aristotle, *The Politics* , (1312a38-1314al2 and 1315bl2-1315b39) pp. 174-179. To preserve their rule, tyrants have resorted to "lopping off the preeminent and eliminating those with high thoughts—and also not permitting common messes, clubs, education. . . . Leisured discussions are not allowed. . . . Residents are made to always be in evidence. . . ; in this way their activities would escape notice least of all. . . . [There are] spies . . . and eavesdroppers." Aristotle noted that friends would be set against friends, and the poor made to hate the wealthy. Most of the ruled would be poor, so they would not have the leisure time to conspire. "It is also a feature of tyranny not to delight in anyone who is dignified or free." All of these measures, which we recognize to this day as features of totalitarian tyrannies, lacked the powers of preservation. Aristotle noted that tyrannies were the shortest-lived of the regimes.

The twentieth century has changed this. Ideology and modern science made it possible for tyrants to stay in power. Science provided the means to create systematic tyranny and "all embracing police government." Ideology gave moral justification to all the killings and radical restructuring of entire societies. Aristotle recognized all of the elements of totalitarianism, a form of government he could not yet have known, but he did not see how a total tyrant could maintain himself in power. Alexander Solzhenitsyn recognized this special power which justified injustice and political horror inherent in ideology. "To do evil a human being must first of all believe that what he's doing is good, or else that it's a well-considered act in conformity with natural law. . . . The imagination and the spiritual strength of Shakespeare's evildoers stopped short at a dozen corpses. Because they had no ideology. Ideology—that is what gives evildoing its long-sought justification and gives the evildoer the necessary steadfastness and determination." *The Gulag Archipelago*, trans. Thomas P. Whitney (New York: Harper & Row, Publishers, 1973), pp. 173-174.

13. Carnes Lord, "American Strategic Culture," *Comparative Strategy* (vol. 5, no. 3), pp. 269-93.

14. See John Locke, *The Second Treatise on Government* , ch. 2, sec. 7 and 8, p. 124. "And that all men may be restrained from invading others' rights and from doing hurt to one another, the execution of the law of nature is, in that state, put into every man's hands, whereby everyone has a right to punish transgressors of that law to such a degree as may hinder its violation; . . . And thus in the state of nature one man comes by a power over another; but yet no absolute or arbitrary power to use a criminal, when he has got him in his hands, according to the passionate heats or boundless extravagancy of his own will; but only to retribute to him, so far as calm reason and conscience dictate, what is proportionate to his transgression, which is so much as may serve for reparation and restraint."

15. In view of the devastating effects that Churchill believed communism had on the soul of man (Gilbert, *Never Despair*, p. 219), his reference here to "Christian civilization" is particularly apt, as the Christian man talks always of the possibility of

the soul's rejuvenation. With this point of opposition between Christianity and communism, Churchill demonstrated that there was an important unity of purpose among the people of God, especially in the Western world, where they also shared much else in common. In their common faith they shared a common fate, and in 1946 that fate was all too unclear to offer anyone any comfort about their future. See also *Complete Speeches*, pp. 7,645, 7,745, 8,096.

16. Some of Churchill's ideas on this phenomenon were discussed in the second chapter. Perhaps the most lucid and persuasive account of this understanding of the nature of political things can be found in Aristotle's *Politics* and *Nicomachean Ethics*. While Aristotle presented his understanding throughout these classical works of political philosophy, these points were clearly argued in *The Politics*, p. 35 (1252a1-1252a6), pp. 94-95 (1278b15-1278b25 and 1279a16-1279a22), pp. 199-201 (1324a5-1325a15).

17. Winston S. Churchill, "Will There Be War In Europe—and When?" *Churchill and War*, p. 436. See also Kenneth W. Thompson, *Winston Churchill's World View*, pp. 218-219.

18. Although a well-argued case for emerging universal liberalism, by way of resurrection of Hegel's philosophy of history, was presented by Francis Fukuyama in the pages of *The National Interest* ("The End of History?" Summer 1989, pp. 3-18).

19. The purposes and principles of the United Nations Organization are to be found in the Preamble and second article of the Charter and are as follows: a) to save succeeding generations from the scourge of war, which twice in our life-time has brought untold sorrow to mankind; and b) to reaffirm faith in fundamental human rights, in the dignity and worth of the human person, in the equal rights of men and women and of nations large and small; and c) to establish conditions under which justice and respect for the obligations arising from treaties and other sources of international law can be maintained; and d) to promote social progress and better standards of life in larger freedom. The Organization is based on the principle of sovereign equality; members must fulfill in good faith their obligations; peaceful means would be used to resolve international disputes and members would refrain from the use of force inconsistent with the purposes of the UN; good faith efforts should be made to assist the UN in any action; members must attempt to persuade non-member states to act according to the principles of the UN; and nothing would authorize the UN to impose itself within the "essentially" domestic jurisdiction of any state.

20. Churchill demonstrated his belief that he was not powerless to influence future developments even though he did not have a cabinet position. He announced that he had come to Fulton "to try to make sure with what strength I have that what has been gained with so much sacrifice and suffering shall be preserved for the future glory and safety of mankind."

21. Carl von Clausewitz's remarks on the nature of war emphasized the vital role which chance and other unforeseen events and circumstances could affect the outcome of a battle and a war. "This tremendous friction, which cannot, as in mechanics, be reduced to a few points, is everywhere in contact with chance, and brings about effects that cannot be measured, just because they are largely due to chance." Carl von Clausewitz, *On War*, ed. and trans. Michael Howard and Peter Paret (Princeton, NJ: Princeton University Press, 1984), pp. 119-121. See also pp. 87-89. See also Aristotle, *The Politics*, (1332a30-32), p. 218. "[W]e pray for the city to be constituted on the basis of what one would pray for in those matters over which fortune has authority"

22. Here Churchill once again echoed ideas discussed by Aristotle in *The Politics*. After Aristotle wrote that the city ought to pray in those instances where fortune is said to have authority, he reminded his readers that praying is an activity insufficient for the needs of the city. "[B]ut the city's being excellent is no longer the work of fortune, but of knowledge and intentional choice" ((1332a32-33), p. 218).

23. In this speech we find some of the earliest thoughts on the concept of nuclear or atomic deterrence. Churchill believed that the police governments would acquire one day the atomic bomb, and when that happened, the West must be sure of its strength in order to successfully counter the aggressive states attempts to intimidate other countries.

24. Churchill's speech did encounter much resistance in the United States. Although not necessarily a measure of cowardice, many high-level Americans did not accept Churchill's conclusions and were appalled at his audacity (Eleanor Roosevelt, Henry Wallace, and Senators Pepper, Kilgore, and Glen Taylor among them). See, for example, Broad, *Winston Churchill:*, p. 516.

25. Broad, *The Years of Achievement*, p. 516.

26. For a very good and in-depth treatment of the 1946 Iranian crisis and assessment of the impact of Churchill's Fulton speech on the Soviet withdrawal, see Fraser J. Harbutt, *The Iron Curtain: Churchill, America, and the Origins of the Cold War* (New York: Oxford University Press, 1986), pp. 209-266. See also Gilbert, *Never Despair*, p. 219, and Ulam, *Expansion and Coexistence*, p. 425.

27. Churchill remarked later that March: "I made it clear in my broadcast of June 22, 1941, that my support of Russia in no way weakened my opposition to Communism which means in fact the death of the soul of man" (Gilbert, *Never Despair*, p. 219).

Chapter 5

Churchill's Postwar Statesmanship Part I: Force and International Politics

In 1945 and 1946, Winston Churchill, no longer prime minister of Great Britain, continued nonetheless to focus on grand foreign policy questions. Despite his fall from power, or perhaps because of it, Churchill felt considerable apprehension for the future. He surveyed the devastation and the new political realities across the entire continent of Europe and understood that a much more difficult task awaited the statesmen of the western world. The great victory over the Axis powers was, in fact, only the beginning of a new collective effort to restore peace and security.

Four issues were of particular concern to Churchill during the immediate postwar period. First, no doubt first in priority too, as the Fulton speech emphasized, was the formation of a fraternal association with the United States. These special ties, strengthened by blood, heritage, and shared principles, and solidified by military and economic interests, were supposed to be the core of the collective western security alliance, an alliance intended to exercise vigilance before the growing threat from the East.

Second, a lasting peace demanded the nonaggressive association of all the leading powers which, in this new international order, would stand on equal terms with one another and behave toward one another in good faith and goodwill. A settlement with the Soviet Union on the outstanding contentious issues was critical if there were to be true peace.

Third, Churchill understood that Britain's own prestige in the world hinged upon its ability to maintain the special relationship with the United States and Canada in the realm of defense and to work jointly with the only existing nuclear power on the manufacture of the atomic bomb. By withholding the secrets of the bomb from Moscow, the security interests of the West could be protected. A monopoly on this super weapon would give the West important leverage in any future negotiations over the fate of Europe.

Finally, Churchill believed that many of the best opportunities for international cooperation rested upon the success of the United Nations Organization. The significance for Churchill of these four issues, alluded to in the previous chapter, will be elaborated upon in the pages to follow.

Even in 1945, the achievement of all of these objectives had been jeopardized by an unwelcome turn of events. Abroad, he noted, "our relations with the United States have become more distant, and those with Russia more obscure. We are told the Big Three are never to meet again, which I heard with great grief. ... The condition of Europe is a nightmare."[1] The absence of a commitment from Stalin, supported by deed, to realize peaceful relations between East and West was most troubling. The world appeared to be heading inexorably toward another tragic conflict. No sooner had the Big Three accomplished their military objectives than were these friends in war to become mortal enemies in peace.

Churchill's speech at Fulton laid down the facts about the newly divided world, including the possibility that events of that period would have the major states careening towards one another, locked once again in mortal combat unless bold initiatives were seized upon by the leading statesmen. Churchill contended throughout the final course of his career that the world had reached this precipice, referred to by some as the Cold War, because the Soviets had succumbed to the spirit of aggrandizement in the hour of allied victory.[2] Stalin, in disagreement with Churchill's assessment of the true source of international instability, was asked by reporters to state what he considered to be the greatest threat to peace. "Instigators of a new war," he answered, "in the first place Churchill, and those, his partisans, who think like him in Great Britain and the United States."[3]

The magnanimous spirit of Churchill's public response to Stalin's remarks indicated that, even in these very stressful times, Churchill did not lose sight of his dream of placing East-West relations on a firmer and safer footing.

I have a regard and respect for Premier Stalin, and always remember all we went through together. I also wish to see the Russian people, who fought so bravely for their native land, safe and glorious and happy. It was always my desire that when the war was won the Soviet Government should play one of the leading parts in the rebuilding of our shattered world. By the Anglo-Russian treaty made when I was Prime Minister in 1941, we are bound not to interfere in each other's internal affairs or system of society. Therefore I do not see why we cannot all be friends and help each other, and thus advance the whole basic standard of livelihood of the broad masses of people in every land.[4]

Given the Soviet reaction, Churchill believed his paradoxical speech (which called for both peace and confrontation) at Fulton was entirely justified. He thought it proper to ask the United States to exercise greater vigilance and prepare for a period of prolonged confrontation. "Fulton still holds its own," he said upon learning from a top secret report of Soviet military strength and organization.[5]

Churchill never flinched before his obligation to western security—and this despite his earnest desire to reach a meaningful agreement with Moscow. He remarked in March 1950: "I try to pursue, as it seems to me, a steady theme and my thought, as far as I can grasp it, is all of one piece. It is the building up of effective forces of resistance to tyranny and aggression in any form, or from any quarter."[6] For this reason, Churchill wholeheartedly approved the new policy of President Truman to rally U.S. forces to contain what was believed to be an expansionist Soviet Empire.[7] Indeed, the objectives of the so-called Truman Doctrine paralleled many of the objectives spelled out by Churchill at Fulton more than one year before "containment" became official strategy.

The balance one finds in Churchill's postwar Soviet policy, between strength and vigilance before the communist menace on the one hand and Churchillian "appeasement" on the other, is truly remarkable for its underlying, if not quite obvious, consistency. Churchill's objectives, in fact, were rather straightforward: to keep the peace at almost any cost (as he surmised that World War III likely would surpass the previous war in destruction and barbarism); and to approximate justice as best he could by preserving the sovereignty of decent regimes and working to spread it to the less fortunate countries. Together with the establishment of political systems that functioned according to the rule of law and majority consent, another important element of justice for Churchill was comfortable economic prosperity for the great mass of ordinary people.

When Churchill's methods for achieving these ends are examined, however, one finds inconsistency. For how could he have expected to reach a settlement with communist Russia, a regime notoriously duplicitous, and at the same time call for a collective military arrangement, one eventually involving West Germany, to contain this aggressive state? Did Churchill truly understand the nature of the Soviet threat? Had he gone "soft" on communism? With infirmity advancing more quickly upon him in his final years in politics, had senility finally claimed the mind of this great statesman who once was known for his incisive understanding of world politics?

On the contrary, Churchill's carrot and stick approach (for lack of a better phrase) was characteristically holistic in conception. His diplomatic and defense initiatives were fashioned side by side to achieve a common aim—peaceful relations among the leading powers and a better approximation of justice in Europe. There is at least one obvious correlation in the linkage of these two initiatives, and it was made evident as early as 1946 at Fulton; namely, a settlement on favorable terms could not be accomplished unless the democracies possessed the leverage that superior military strength and geostrategic position could offer.

There is, however, another element in Churchill's approach that easily could be overlooked. A negotiated settlement with the Soviet leaders would not necessarily lessen the long-term danger that its revolutionary policies still would pose to the West. Churchill consistently took pains to point out to the world that the Soviet state still hungered for greater power and influence and that it would not stop short of total domination of the Eurasian landmass.[8] Recognizing this dilemma, Churchill's quest for peace was oriented both toward the short- and long-term. Clearly, an effective peace, a peace with more lasting benefits, must take into account Soviet ambition for a greater position in the world. Communism, he warned at Fulton, posed the greatest threat to liberty and decent political orders. If the threat of communism could be neutralized, or at minimum contained, the threats to peace and liberty would be diminished substantially.

Churchill believed that a more thoroughgoing cooperation with Moscow was possible only if Soviet political objectives could be modified. This is not to suggest Churchill supposed the modification of communist state goals would be easy or even likely. There is evidence, however, to suggest that one of Churchill's principal aims in his quest for an East-West settlement was to incorporate this rogue state into the community of nations. This agenda, as it developed in the late 1940s and early 1950s, formed what was to be one prong on Churchill's foreign policy pincer, the other prong being the policy of containment.

The resulting policy involved a concerted effort by Churchill to moderate Soviet foreign policy by an artful combination of force and persuasion, by robust containment measures and by farseeing diplomacy. If he had succeeded in reintroducing the Russian state back into the mainstream international community, the "Cold War" would have taken on a much different character, or it might have died in its infancy; for success would have meant the death of communism in Soviet Russia.

The failure of his initiatives, the most famous of which is treated in some detail in the chapter to follow, did not rid the world of the Cold War. Most importantly, it must be emphasized, his foreign policy did not subject the free states to any new dangers or deprive them of the shields needed to defend themselves, despite the bold nature of his initiatives. Churchill's insistence on a united and militarily superior West helped prepare it to both prosper in peace and prevail in adversity. While his bold statesmanship was not reflected fully in Prime Minister Attlee's administration and did not structure official British policy in Churchill's peacetime premiership, his "hidden agenda," the transformation of the Soviet polity, had been in place at least implicitly, and at least since his famous speech at Westminster College in Fulton.

Churchill's principal ideas about foreign policy and defense matters were formed in 1911, and were inspired by the Agadir crisis facing Great Britain.[9] On July 11, Germany sent the gunboat *Panther* to the Moroccan port of Agadir (then controlled by the French) as a demonstration of their dissatisfaction with Spanish, British, and French disregard for German claims and interests on the African continent. This "gunboat diplomacy," which amounted to a challenge to French sovereignty in Morocco, had its intended effect. Germany already was a formidable land power and had given notice at Agadir that it also had aspirations to dominate the high seas. This action taken against Britain's natural ally, France, opened the eyes of many in the British Cabinet, including Churchill, to Berlin's growing, and potentially limitless, ambitions.

The lessons he formed were as follows. First, Churchill recognized the connection between a country's unity and its ability to defend itself; domestic unity, of course, gives a country strength as well as resolve. Second, he was keenly aware of the crucial link between a nation's foreign policy and its defensive preparations. Third, he believed that aggression could be deterred if the threatened states acted in unison. And fourth, the states of Europe will always find danger, he believed, when a single power dominates the continent.

Every one of these elements found there way into Churchill's policies after the war. After the second world war, for example, Churchill admired the efficiency with which his national government operated. Unity of purpose for his country, and for the western alliance, consistently could be found to be among his primary objectives as a leader, despite the fact that internal harmony was at times very difficult (a problem that commonly afflicts democratic polities).

Clearly, a state's foreign policy or diplomacy, without military power to weigh in on its behalf during times of crisis or even in the normal course of its international relations, can be undermined by a hostile power. In a democracy, defense and social programs are frequently at odds with each other. Democracies often are unwilling to devote a large percentage of their budgets for defense in times of relative peace. Churchill himself did not hesitate to pare down defense expenditures if danger was not present. He nonetheless recognized the importance of having an economy that was prepared to provide for its people in both manners. For example, he once said that "[e]ver since we took office [1951], the Government have been pursuing the twin but divergent objectives of financial solvency and military security. Solvency is valueless without security, and security is impossible to achieve without solvency."[10] He also believed that "[i]n these times of rapid scientific progress when new and improved weapons are being constantly evolved, one of the most vital factors in the nation's preparedness for war is the progression of an adequate and flexible armaments industry capable above all of speeding expansion."[11] Following the war, the defensive shield formed by the conventional forces of the western nations would be critical to their safety, given the ambiguous nature of Soviet intentions. Britain, as well as her allies, had to exert themselves over the long haul (through conscription, maintenance of a war industry, and alliance cohesion) to remain militarily capable of meeting the Soviet threat.[12]

When threats of aggression surface across several fronts, the weak or threatened states best preserve peace by standing in alliance with one another. After the second world war, the union of the British Commonwealth, the United States, and a United Europe was needed to meet the uncertain threat posed by the Red Army. Churchill deemed alliances were deemed as vital for the future prosperity and well-being of Europe; for no power should be allowed to build up a dominant position on that continent, especially a power that also dominated Asia.

STATESMANSHIP AND FORCE

It is true, Churchill noted in his account of the life and times of his great ancestor the Duke of Marlborough, that the fate of all war conquests "depended upon the ultimate peace treaty."[13] Indeed, the fate of whole nations, not to mention the character of the peace, often has been twisted or changed by violent events of war as well as by the decisions made by the victors in the more relaxed and sober atmosphere around the armistice table. Peace is never a sufficient end in itself. Churchill recalled in *Marlborough* how the French despot, Louis XIV, sought peace in Europe. It was, he noted, still "only a French peace: and at any moment a turn of fortune would revive his full claims."[14] There is, in other words, good peace and bad peace. A peace that severely compromises justice, that creates the conditions for future confrontations, or that allows for the rise of tyrannical states can hardly be worthy of the name.

In 1945, the world gratefully welcomed the end of a worldwide international conflict. Many called it a time of peace. Others were not so sanguine about their new fortunes or the new relationship that had developed among the major powers after the victory. There still remained a powerful disturbance in the international system; for the world had been divided at the moment of triumph and never quite reached that point where it could enjoy fully or appreciate what had just been so heroically accomplished.

Churchill wrote in a letter to Stalin, dated April 29, 1945, that he had been extremely disappointed by the tragic turn of events. He took particular exception to Stalin's breach of the Yalta agreement, especially on the Polish question, and he insisted that the will of the people to choose their own government must be the "root principle" of any common understanding between East and West. He concluded with a sober reflection on the "peace" that appeared to be taking root in the world. A quarrel between East and West, he noted, would "tear the world to pieces" and would be shameful before all history. He concluded with this caution: "[D]o not, I beg you, my friend Stalin, underrate the divergences which are opening about matters which you may think are small to us but which are symbolic of the way the English-speaking democracies look at life."[15]

Churchill later recalled in a 1953 speech before the Scottish Unionist Association that he could not understand why the Soviet Union did not join with the western Allies in seeking a just and lasting treaty of peace. Peaceful and quiet times are most attractive conditions for the majority of countries. However, his appeals to Stalin went for naught, and the gross violations of the Yalta accords gave shape to a new Europe and a new world. Stalin had further despoiled his reputation in the eyes of many by committing egregious lies. The Red Army had overrun much of Europe, free elections in occupied states were disallowed, and the Soviet Union showed no intention of demobilizing its vast and powerful military machine. The West had to face up to the reality that a major power of measureless ambition had settled in its midst. If war were once again to revisit the continent, there was no doubt who the enemy would be. Acknowledging both Britain's diminished standing in the world and the grand forces then at play, Churchill believed that if war came, it would be because of world forces beyond British control. "Whatever happens," he spoke, "we shall stand up with all our strength in defense of the free world against Communist tyranny and aggression."[16]

Standing at the dawning edge of this new age in Europe and the world, Churchill pondered over the appropriate foreign policy for the West. He remarked to Henry Luce in November 1947 that the drift of events that took place prior to the second world war cast striking parallels when compared to the events of the early postwar years. He explained to Mr. Luce that the reason the world was journeying down a path frighteningly similar was because "there happened exactly what is happening today, namely no coherent or persistent policy, even in fundamental matters, among the good peoples, but deadly planning among the bad."[17] The postwar years to Churchill were dire times that demanded bold and insightful leadership.

The policy that Churchill recommended for the liberal democracies was strikingly similar to that conjured up by George F. Kennan, the former U.S. Ambassador to Moscow. In the July 1947 issue of *Foreign Affairs*, and earlier in his famous "long telegram" to President Truman, delivered February 22, 1946, Kennan argued that the United States must prepare itself to meet a new series of geopolitical threats and challenges posed by the Soviet Union with the "adroit and vigilant application of counterforce at a series of constantly shifting geographical and political points." In "The Sources of Soviet Conduct," Kennan argued that the United States should aim to contain Soviet expansionism in the hope that eventually it would collapse through its own internal contradictions. In later years, many people disagreed with Mr. X's message (Mr. X being the pseudonym under which Kennan published his article). Kennan himself disputes the suggestion that his "containment" policy called for actions that were more military than political in character. It cannot be denied, however, that his geopolitical and social analysis contributed to the formulation of the Truman Doctrine, or the policy of supporting "free peoples who are resisting attempted subjugation by armed minorities or outside pressures."[18]

This policy of the strategic defensive, while very similar to Churchill's proposals, appeared to exhibit more confidence in the ability of the United States to be competitive with the USSR over time. Time was on the side of the West, Kennan believed. While Churchill also saw the virtues of this waiting game, his message to the United States and the other democracies was that time was also of the essence in the struggle to establish a new peace. A militarily strong West could contain Soviet territorial ambitions, but what might happen should the Soviet Union reach parity or even superiority? What would happen when they developed the nuclear bomb? Could the United States and her allies summon the will and the resources to endure a protracted Cold War and remain willing to engage the enemy when the war became "hot"? Churchill pondered endlessly over these types of questions; for he recognized the inherent inclination of democratic political orders to back away from military preparedness.

As events played themselves out, Kennan had been vindicated. By 1990, significant internal contradictions within the world's communist political orders had manifested themselves and were leading them toward collapse forty-four years after Kennan first diagnosed the infirmities. The United States, with the help of the NATO allies, had been able to carry the containment strategy through successfully. The West marshaled both sufficient will and material resources to endure the Cold War contest, although at times the military execution of the strategy left something to be desired (the tragedy of Vietnam being perhaps the most obvious example).

Churchill's policies did not conjure up vivid images of communism in collapse (if only because such proclamations would have been fatal for postwar defensive preparations). Churchill too understood Soviet society to be radically deficient in that it lacked the mechanisms to govern the citizenry properly. As we shall see in Chapter six, Churchill set about attempting to take advantage of some of these systemic weaknesses.

Before any actions could be taken to stem the tide of growing hostility between East and West and to cultivate a prosperous peace, the West had to make sure that it did not abandon the use of force and the power of deterrence. For Churchill believed communism to be an immediate menace, and that to act from a position of weakness or to behave cowardly might leave the free democracies in a militarily weakened position. Kenneth Thompson also took note of some very striking parallels in Churchill's thought. "In strictly chronological terms, the opinions that Churchill offered on the prospects of World War III are roughly equivalent to those he set forth between 1919 and 1926 on the chances of a second major struggle."[19]

NEW THREATS TO THE WEST

In one sense, the reality of several divisions of hostile armies facing off against one another in Europe made the task for statesmen of persuading their countrymen to accept the sacrifices necessary for a strong defense less difficult. The stakes in this contest were enormous—freedom versus slavery, self-rule versus despotism, the rights of man and the Declaration of Independence versus the march of history and the Communist Manifesto. "[W]hen you look at the picture as a whole," Churchill reiterated in a 1950 election address, "you see two worlds ranged against one another more profoundly and on a larger scale than history has ever seen before."[20] Indeed, he often reminded his audiences of the moral stakes of the contest. "They [the Communists] have condemned Christian ethics and civilization, as we have known them, to a formidable struggle."[21]

What of the future? The Soviet Union's postwar strategy was obvious to Churchill. He believed it was Moscow's design to drive a wedge between the British and the Americans, and between the Americans and Europe. Thus, he stated in early 1952 that "[a]nything that secures that unity must be considered a service not only to freedom but to peace."[22] In the eyes of many western leaders, the "very able men" in the Kremlin had an advantage over them: an aspiration for world domination, little to no opposition among the ruling elite, an obedient populace, and a war-supporting industry. The Soviets appeared to be ready to march.[23]

Clearly, there were many ominous events that justly concerned the West in the late 1940s. Moscow had achieved, after all, what Germany had only attempted to do—the domination of Central and East Europe. Soviet foreign policy and its military presence in Europe was less than reassuring. With the rise of communism in Asia, Churchill was concerned that the world, especially the United States, would divert its attention from Europe. In October 1946 he noted that the Soviets have over two hundred twenty-five divisions on a war footing beyond the Russian frontiers in the occupied territories of Europe, compared with about twenty-five British and American divisions.[24] The risk of a diversion of resources from Europe increased with the onset of the Soviet-inspired aggression in Korea. Churchill believed that it would be strategic folly to become entangled in a war with China while the situation in Europe seemed so perilous.[25] "There may soon be Communist attacks upon Tibet and Persia. But the supreme peril is in Europe. We must try to close the hideous gap on the European front."[26]

Soviet caution in its relations with China in 1948 contrasted sharply with the Moscow's bold actions in Europe, most notably the Berlin blockade, which threatened to result in a clash with the United States.[27] Nineteen forty-eight also marked the end of a period of restraint in military spending and production for Stalin. "From 1949 they [the Soviet armed forces] grew to the point where in 1955 they would be twice as large as they had been in 1948."[28] In these times, the West believed itself to be under assault from many directions.

WESTERN UNITY: "PEACE THROUGH STRENGTH"

The foundation of Churchill's postwar policy toward the East was Western unity, beginning with the powerful and special association of Great Britain and the United States.[29] Churchill laid out the moral and geopolitical justification for the union of the English-speaking peoples in Fulton and elaborated on it in subsequent years. "The inheritance of the English-speaking world," he stated on July 4, 1950, "derives its glory as a moral unity from thought and vision widely spread in the minds of our people." Churchill also spoke of the "common creed" on both sides of the Atlantic so "amazingly laid down" in the Declaration of Independence.[30] The strength of this union was the heart of the strategy to contain Soviet Russia and put pressure on her to live up to the agreements made at Yalta. Without this foundation, the postwar peace structures built by negotiation and settlement would collapse.

Churchill did not assume that this natural association between the United Kingdom and United States was inevitable.[31] The very possibility that fissures could develop in the relationship kept Churchill alert to any actions or words that might cause a breach. Harsh words concerning the American retreat from eastern Germany in 1945 were lifted from Churchill's account of the war in *Triumph and Tragedy* so that the new American leader, President Eisenhower, would not be offended. For similar reasons, Churchill confined his unkind thoughts of John Foster Dulles to himself.[32] Truman's Agriculture Secretary, Henry Wallace, an avowed pacifist and pro-Soviet in his views, caused Churchill to be concerned about the future course of the Anglo-American security relationship. Truman later replaced Wallace.[33]

American forces found a home in Britain for several years after the war. Although the U.S. presence aroused much discontent and criticism among the English, Churchill nonetheless defended the stationing of troops on British soil as "an essential feature in the cold war."[34] Relations never soured to the point of rupture. The growing threats to American ideals and interests attracted U.S. leaders to the alliance strategy conceptualized by Churchill. According to historian Paul Johnson, by 1946, British and American air forces began exchanging war plans and intelligence agencies resumed their mutual networking. "By midsummer the Anglo-American alliance was in unofficial existence again."[35] In many ways, Churchill maintained, Stalin was responsible for the coming together of the two great English-speaking peoples. Without Stalin, the alliance might not have happened for generations. "The architect of the Kremlin builded better than he knew."[36]

Strategic insight inspired Churchill's dreams for a trans-Atlantic partnership. He thought the special and privileged friendship ought to become "for strategic purposes one organism." Not only would this enable a more friendly and trustful relationship with the Soviet Union, it would pave the way for the more successful construction of the UN. Without the fraternal association of Great Britain and the Commonwealth with the United States, there could be no peace. He believed that strategically, the two countries were bound together, perhaps enabling them to win the respect of the Soviet Union and possibly its friendship.[37] As he indicated at Fulton, Churchill's aspirations went beyond diplomacy. He envisioned the eventual creation of a unified military structure where the two countries would share air and naval bases around the world and have the benefit of organization around a single purpose. Herein would lie the key to a West that would increase in strength by at least fifty percent. Churchill gave his full support to Attlee's cabinet in "developing the closest possible unity with the United States on moral issues and in military measures." [38]

Although such an intimate arrangement was never to be, the leaders of both countries were nonetheless on friendly enough terms to influence each other's policies. Churchill's conceptions and ideas for European recovery, detailed in his famous speech at Zurich in September 1946, played a decisive role in the U.S. relief effort. His ideas had a profound influence on General George Marshall, who in turn was the source of inspiration for the June 1947 Marshall Plan, an economic rescue effort that Churchill believed was a turning point in world history.[39]

"The Great Powers must seek to serve and not to rule," were the words echoed by Churchill in the House of Commons following the Yalta

Conference.[40] Nobility in their rule would be evidenced by the prosperous conditions of their people and the measures taken to ensure their safety. Harmony with the United States would go far in fulfilling many of these ends. "I feel that [the special friendship] is more than survival. It may even be safety, and with safety, a vast expansion of prosperity."[41] Americans and Britons should stand together "in malice toward none, in greed for nothing but in defense of those causes which we hold dear not only for our own benefit, but because we believe they mean the honour and the happiness of long generations of men."[42]

Unity was beneficial for the United States as well as for Europe, for the fates of New World and the Old World were linked. In September 1946, Churchill reminded his audience at Zurich University that "but for the fact that the great Republic across the Atlantic Ocean has at length realized that the ruin or enslavement of Europe would involve their own fate as well, . . . the Dark Ages would have returned in all their cruelty and squalor."[43] Churchill believed that if the English-speaking world, the British Empire, and a United Europe were linked together, there was "no force or combination which could overthrow them or even challenge them."[44] This was the essential message of his speech in Zurich.[45] The "tragedy of Europe" was a tragedy for the West; but it could be overcome through unity. It is for this reason that Churchill urged the West so strongly to "recreate the European Family, or as much of it as we can," an idea that President Truman also endorsed.

It was at Zurich that Churchill let fly another one of his bombshells. After those in Germany guilty of war crimes had been punished, he declared, it was critical that the retribution not widen in scope. Rather, the West must turn and once again face the future. "There must be what Mr. Gladstone many years ago called 'a blessed act of oblivion.'. . . . Is it the only lesson of history that mankind is unteachable." This act of faith toward the German people was necessary if Europe were to be brought out of her misery.

Not only must Europe as a whole accept Germany back into the fold. France, continually Germany's mortal enemy for centuries, must be at the front of the line to welcome her.[46] A partnership between France and Germany would be the first step in the re-creation of the European family. "In this way only can France recover the moral leadership of Europe. There can be no revival of Europe without a spiritually great France and a spiritually great Germany."

The union of France and Germany made sense on two levels. First, if the animosities between these two countries could be overcome, Europe's acceptance of Germany would be virtually assured. Second, France and Germany, geopolitically, were the two major players on the western half of the continent. (Germany is automatically a major European power due to her size and geographical location at Europe's center.) If Germany were to become a pariah state, a critical void would appear in the heart of Europe. In partnership, these two states would become the backbone of a rejuvenated Europe.

Churchill's concluding remarks at Zurich hit once again upon his long-term goal, revealed earlier in the year at Fulton. "In all this urgent work, France and Germany must take the lead together, Great Britain, the British Commonwealth of Nations, mighty America, and I trust Soviet Russia—for then indeed all would be well—must be friends and sponsors of the new Europe and must champion its rights to live and shine." After Zurich, as leader of the new movement for unity in Europe, Churchill prepared a Statement of Aims to demonstrate the urgent need to all who expressed doubts about the enterprise.

> In the mechanized world of today the small nation States of the past can scarcely hope for political or economic survival as isolated units. The peoples of Europe, or as many of them as are willing to make a start, should come together in order to create an effective European union, not aimed against any other nation but designed to maintain their common peace, to restore their common prosperity an above all to preserve their common heritage of freedom.[47]

A unified western Europe was necessary, and not only to rekindle the engines of prosperity and well-being for European citizens. Unless Europe once again came together by putting aside traditional hostilities and suppressing long-held prejudices, she would jeopardize her freedom. Moscow's intentions were anything but certain. There was little evidence to suggest that Stalin meant well. Force, in the form of a robust defensive alliance of European states and the United States, would help ensure European security. The modern age had made an alliance indispensable. Churchill wrote on this subject in the pages of *The Gathering Storm*: "In modern wars of great nations or alliances particular areas are not defended only by local exertions. The whole vast balance of the war front is involved. This is still more true of policy before war begins and while it may still be averted."[48]

While reflecting on the expected shape of the postwar world, he wrote in a later volume of his memoirs that "[f]orce would clearly be required."[49] The countries that were most directly affected by the tragic turn of events after the war had to exert themselves above the exertions of others if an acceptable result was to be obtained. Duty called from across the ocean to America to assume her role in securing the peace; but it called much more loudly to the Europeans to assume a role in the leadership. Tyranny and war, after all, were at their doorstep.

First things were first; a collective defense had to be established. To Churchill's mind, the alliance need not pose a threat to the Soviet Union. None of the efforts to unify Europe or to provide a collective defense, NATO included, ever posed a serious threat to the Soviet Empire. NATO was essentially a defensive arrangement designed to prevent further expansion by the Soviet Union, and it was not intended to modify the political character of the countries in East and Central Europe.[50] Churchill believed that the creation of a healthy, unified Europe would be, on one level, in the best interest of the Soviet Union, for it would provide stability in their (recently acquired) backyard.[51] After all, wars that originate in Europe could easily spread into Eurasia. Indeed, European wars commonly included parts of far eastern Europe and Asia.

Although the Soviet leader looked upon this line of argument as mere propaganda, Churchill thought it was important to stress continuously the non-aggressive function of the alliance. Indeed, even considering the Soviet point of view, it would have been difficult for a coalition of western forces to act in concert on any aggressive initiatives. Indeed, for all of its oversimplifications, the Soviet thesis that the imperialist camp was beset by internal contradiction was, in part, true. Different western opinions and interpretations of interest did frustrate plans for an alliance.[52]

Thinking of the long-term peace, Churchill believed that these new arrangements should not stand in the way of progress toward a peaceful settlement of the most important outstanding differences between East and West. For this reason, he was particularly careful in his rhetoric. Misguided rhetoric also might keep the liberal states from associating with one another in a constructive fashion.

We should brush aside these terms of prejudice, which are used only to darken counsel and which replace, in certain minds, the ordinary processes of thought and human feeling. If the liberal nations of the world—the Western Democracies, as they are called—are to be turned from their natural association and true affinities by bugbear and scarecrow expressions like "bloc" and "ganging up," they will only have themselves to thank when once again they fall into misfortune.[53]

It was not to array themselves against a particular race or a nation that Churchill called upon the free states to combine. The free states had to take a firm stand against tyranny wherever it held sway.[54]

The new order was to be nurtured by a compelling purpose. Sharply delineated formulas and constitutional abstractions would not take proper regard for the true purpose of union and would likely ignore the many different points of view that had to find their focus in the future order. The new European order ought to be directed and instituted according to the "tide of facts, events, and impulses rather than by elaborate constitution making."[55] Churchill stressed the organic nature of the whole endeavor. The common threads for the proposed alliance were simply the love of freedom, hostility to totalitarianism, the search for truth, and the respect for the individual.[56]

The Soviet repression in Czechoslovakia in the spring of 1948 heightened Churchill's sense of urgency for a United Europe. He gave a speech at the First Congress of Europe at The Hague in May 1948 calling for unity, courage, and clarity of purpose. Some sacrifice of national sovereignty would be necessary, he believed, but not to the extent that national traditions and diversity would be expunged. "His speech at The Hague," wrote Martin Gilbert, "was proof of an energy which he could still command; and of his broad and inspiring view of the future."[57]

Churchill let it be known that he was not content to unify only western Europe. All Europe would be invited in the hope that one day they could join. He noted in his Hague speech that "[d]istinguished exiles from Czechoslovakia, and almost all the Eastern European nations" were in his audience. The union would welcome "the eventual participation of all European peoples . . . , making all allowances for the different points of view." Europe was politically, culturally, and economically distinct from their Asian neighbors, he noted. There was one important precondition for membership: "We welcome an country where the people own the Government."[58]

Needless to say, Churchill's ideas for a United States of Europe did not escape the criticism of the Labour Party, the party then currently in power. Prime Minister Clement Attlee argued that the objects aimed at by Churchill's proposed organization would be better achieved through the United Nations rather than a separate union, which he believed could be misunderstood and misrepresented.[59] The Labour Party, in fact, had refused to participate in the Hague Conference, believing that the subject of European unity would be entrusted to unrepresentative interests.[60]

When the Shuman Plan for the European Coal and Steel Community, the forerunner to today's European Economic Community, was introduced in 1950, Churchill's concepts and priorities appeared to have been unaltered. "First, there is the Empire and Commonwealth, secondly, the fraternal association of the English-speaking world; and thirdly, not in rank or status but in order, the revival of united Europe as a vast factor in the preserving of what is left of what is left of the civilization and culture of the free world."[61] However, the party in power also refused to attend the conference on the Shuman Plan. Churchill deplored the absence of Attlee's government, saying that their refusal to participate deranged the balance of Europe. The participation of Britain and France, he believed, would be needed in Europe to prevent Germany from dominating the coal and steel pool.[62]

Churchill also deplored the institutionalization of the European Defense Community (EDC), a plan preferred by his own Foreign Secretary, Anthony Eden. Churchill initially fought against it on the grounds that such an army would be international in character and would not be an organization that properly reflected the various national interests. Such an army, he believed, would conflict with national traditions, language, and sovereignty and was unlikely to inspire sufficient spirit (due to its international rather than national character) in the troops, troops who would much rather fight for "home and country."[63] Clearly Churchill believed that some kind of defense force was needed (he welcomed the formation of NATO), to close "the hideous gap" in the protection of western Europe from the Soviet "onrush."[64] At Strasbourg in August 1950, echoing themes from his Zurich speech, he laid out his own proposal for a European Army that was sensitive to national elements. "I had in mind . . . the formation of a long-term grand alliance under which national armies would operate under a unified allied command. . . . My conception involved no supranational institutions and I saw no difficulty in Britain playing her full part in a scheme of that kind."[65]

Churchill searched for a way to include Germany and France in the collective defense, but both countries balked at his ideas. "Germany must make her military contribution to the safety of Europe," he stated in December 1953.[66] NATO already had been formed, but did not include Germany. He later looked upon the EDC as the stepping stone to his broader alternative. The EDC, of course, never materialized, and the problem of Germany's contribution to the defensive efforts in western Europe would not be solved until her inclusion in NATO in 1955.

The Korean conflict, begun in the summer of 1950, was one of a number of important tests for the western alliance (the contest over Berlin in 1948 and the growing Soviet military preponderance at the end of that decade being two others). Churchill gave his full support and the support of his party and government to the United Nations and the United States in their efforts to resist the unprovoked aggression against South Korea. Before and after his second premiership (October 1951), Churchill called for "prompt, resolute, and effective" action by the government to forestall a communist victory, including the bombing of China if it was in any way involved with the aggression.[67] It was for the purpose of meeting these very threats that Churchill aspired to bridge the gulf between the New and Old Worlds. "I still hope that the unities now being established among all the Western Democracies and Atlantic Powers will ward off from us the terrors and unspeakable miseries of a third world war," he said in July 1950.[68]

There were, to be sure, instances of disagreement during the cooperative relationship. Both parties in the Commons were unsettled by the United States' refusal to consult adequately with Britain about vital bombing missions. Explained Churchill, the UN "had entrusted the conduct of the Korean campaign to the United States; and we should be well-advised to avoid a position in which we shared the responsibility without the means of making our influence effective."[69] Churchill, nonetheless, cautioned members to avoid public statements that suggested a divergence of views between the United States and Great Britain on the Korean issue. Labour failed in some instances to heed his warnings. The United States, he emphasized, was a vital member of the new alliance. He promised in January 1953 to speak to the newly elected President Eisenhower about the continued need of a common Anglo-American front "from Korea to Kikuyu and from Kikuyu to Calais."[70]

The final element in Churchill's grand scheme for western unity was alluded to above and dealt with in the speech at Fulton. It was a viable United Nations Organization. It was clear after his Fulton speech that Churchill believed the new world organization should be reasonably energetic in the world and not just a rubber-stamp body or a nice place for well-paid diplomats to congregate. Upon the initial Soviet refusal to withdraw troops from Persia after the Fulton speech, Churchill warned that "the Security Council of the United Nations must show that it is a reality and not a pretense; that it deals with facts and truth. I trust that we shall not find that the World Organization allows itself to be confronted with a *fait accompli*."[71] Strong actions were needed to prevent conflict. Over the years, the activity at the UN became somewhat of a disappointment for Churchill. He continued to support it, however, as the "citadel" of the free world.[72]

The purpose of the world government was to complement the emergence of a United Europe, to become a part of the network established to secure the peace.

Generally, Churchill placed the greater portion of his faith in his national initiatives. However, on occasion, Churchill's rhetoric soared, and he dreamed of fantastic possibilities for the new international body.

> We do not of course pretend that United Europe provides the final and complete solution to all the problems of international relationships. The creation of an authoritative, all-powerful world order is the ultimate aim toward which we must strive. Unless some effective World Super-Government can be set up and brought quickly into action, the prospects for peace and human progress are dark and doubtful.[73]

Churchill's efforts were aimed at setting the stage for the day when a world government could be put in place to rest upon the main regional groupings. However, the UN was not ultimately designed to supersede the "ordinary channels of friendly diplomatic intercourse."[74]

Churchill's aspiration to build an effective world organization was restrained by his political experience and knowledge. There was, after all, the likelihood that not all states could join the UN. China, for example, in the early 1950s was at war against the UN. How could she become a member? While in the UN "there must be tolerance, the recognition of the charm of variety, and the respect of minority rights," the UN also must strive to be "indivisible and invincible." "A world organization, open to all and all-forgiving, might be both diffuse and powerless."[75] The major powers, including Soviet Russia (friendly or not by consequence of her position after the war), especially the western democracies, were to have more than just a hand in controlling the UN. Churchill never believed it was right that small nations should exercise influence beyond their true power or representation, and he deplored this trend in the UN.[76]

The fortunes of an effective UN depended heavily upon the nature of the East-West relationship. At the end of the war, the world was deeply divided. Disagreements with the Soviets over the purpose of the new world body existed from the very outset. The Cold War naturally jeopardized the hope for peace through organized interstate cooperation. "If no such unity [Great Power unity] exists in Poland, which is after all a major problem of the post-war settlement, what, it will legitimately be asked, are the prospects of success of the new World Organization."[77]

Churchill believed that these questions concerning the division of the world were unavoidable. There was much work for statesmen; certain answers to these questions were better than others, and these had to be sorted out. Regardless of the answers, however, the West could not afford sacrifices to the new world organization that would jeopardize its security and freedom. If the deep divisions were to manifest themselves, Churchill believed, it would be better to accept this "than tamely to accept a continued degeneration of the whole world position. It is better to have a world united than a world divided; but it is also better to have a world divided, than a world destroyed."[78] And elsewhere: "We must persevere, and if the gulf continues to widen, we must make sure that the cause of freedom is defended by all the resources of combined forethought and superior science."[79]

By exerting themselves to prepare their defenses, to clash if necessary with the great land power in Eurasia, Churchill believed that, by a law of opposite effects, the world had a chance to become more unified. It does not follow, he stated, that "in a world divided there should not be equilibrium from which a further advance to unity might be attempted as the years pass by."[80] The difficulty of securing peace was never lost upon Churchill. As he explained in his work on Marlborough, his ancestor utilized a seemingly contradictory or paradoxical approach to find an answer to this eternal problem, an approach that Churchill too would use for the benefit of peace in a divided and war-torn world as we shall see in Chapter six.

We must admire the dual process to which the Allies were now committed of earnestly seeking peace while at the same time preparing for war on an ever greater scale. Nearly always Governments which seek peace flag in their war efforts, and Governments which make the most vigorous war preparations take little interest in peace. The two opposite moods consort with difficulty in the human mind *yet it is only by the double and, as it might seem, contradictory exertion that a good result can usually be procured.*[81]

NOTES

1. Churchill, *Complete Speeches*, p. 7,262.
2. Churchill, *Complete Speeches*, p. 8,532.
3. Gilbert, *Never Despair*, p. 281. Many of the citations in this chapter and the one to follow are culled from this final volume in Gilbert's eight-volume biography. Gilbert's work to compile what has become the definitive account of Churchill's life is the single most valuable source for Churchill scholars, replete as it is with page after page of citations from Churchill's speeches, works, private letters, and official documents, many of which remain unavailable for routine public examination to this day. Analysis of Churchill's activities is not the strong point of this massive biography. Gilbert remained faithful, however, to the theme of the work (begun by Churchill's son Randolph, who met an untimely death) that "[h]e shall be his own biographer."
4. Gilbert, *Never Despair*, p. 281.
5. Gilbert, *Never Despair*, p. 289.
6. Churchill, *Complete Speeches*, p. 7,980.
7. Gilbert, *Never Despair*, p. 326.
8. See for example Gilbert, *Never Despair*, pp. 24, 26, 32, 45, 154, 194-195, 536, and 842.
9. Gilbert, *Churchill's Political Philosophy*, pp. 59-60.
10. Churchill, *Complete Speeches*, p. 8,459.
11. Churchill, *Complete Speeches*, p. 8,460. Churchill spoke here on the benefits of having an arms export industry, one of which would be the ability to keep the nation's industries prepared for total mobilization in the event of war.
12. See for example Gilbert, *Never Despair*, pp. 320, 477-478, 518, 530, 539-540. Churchill also believed Britain, especially during the administration of the Labour Party between 1945 and 1951, had to maintain her defenses if Britain was to

sustain its otherwise "fading influence in world affairs" (Gilbert, *Never Despair*, p. 320). See also Broad, *The Years of Achievement*, pp. 537-538.

13. Churchill, *Marlborough*, bk. 2, vol. 3, p. 49.
14. Churchill, *Marlborough*, bk. 2, vol. 3, p. 215.
15. Churchill, *Triumph and Tragedy*, pp. 494-497.
16. Cited in Gilbert, *Never Despair*, p. 670.
17. Gilbert, *Never Despair*, p. 358.
18. For a lively discussion of the meaning of the "X" article and the significance of the containment strategy, see Martin F. Herz, ed., *Decline of the West? George Kennan and His Critics* (Washington, DC: Ethics and Public Policy Center, 1980).
19. Thompson, *Churchill's World View*, p. 206.
20. Churchill, *Complete Speeches*, p. 7,943.
21. Churchill, *Complete Speeches*, p. 8,048.
22. Churchill, *Complete Speeches*, p. 8,352.
23. All of this is not to deny that western leaders might have exaggerated the degree and the proximity of the danger from communist advancements after the war. Not only was Stalin militarily and economically strapped with his newly won empire and burdened by economic and organizational problems during these years, he was probably unable to risk a confrontation with a formidable western alliance led by the fully mobilized Americans who had, additionally, the atomic bomb. Stalin must have felt threatened to a degree by the 1947 Marshall Plan. After all, he must have believed, the plan would assist the resurrection of European prosperity and strength and restore Great Britain and France to their great power status and present an irresistible attraction to the recently cowered satellites in Central Europe. See Ulam, *Expansion and Coexistence*, p. 436. For whatever reasons, Stalin chose to hide these weaknesses and unwillingly he contributed to the founding of a very successful western defensive alliance.
24. Gilbert, *Never Despair*, p. 277.
25. Churchill, *Complete Speeches*, p. 8,346.
26. Churchill, *Complete Speeches*, p. 8,072. See also p. 8,181. While Churchill vehemently opposed any escalation in the Korean conflict, he fully supported UN and U.S. efforts to squelch the communist invasion across the 38th Parallel. "[W]hat the Communists have begun in Korea should not end in their triumph." (p. 8,039). He did emphasize, though, that whatever happened in Korea would be only a "small part of the pressures under which our free civilization lies, and which it must face or perish" (p. 8,049).
27. Ulam, *Expansion and Coexistence*, p. 487.
28. Ulam, *Expansion and Coexistence*, p. 498.
29. Churchill, *Complete Speeches*, p. 8,417.
30. Churchill, *Complete Speeches*, p. 8,032.
31. This theme was struck several times over at Fulton and many more times throughout Churchill's career. "The unity of policy that exists throughout the English speaking world does not arise from any bargaining or treaties, but from the fact that there is a natural agreement between Great Britain and the United States on almost all the questions which arise. That is because we pursue the same ideals and have a common inheritance of literature and law." *Complete Speeches*, p. 7,525. See also, pp. 7,299-7,301, 7,383, 7,484, 7,540, 7,712, 7,972.

32. Gilbert, *Never Despair*, pp. 792 and 810. Churchill, once said of Dulles that he was "clever enough to be stupid on a rather large scale." Cited by Lord Moran, *Diaries*, p. 469.
33. Johnson, *Modern Times*, p. 438.
34. Gilbert, *Never Despair*, p. 777.
35. Johnson, *Modern Times*, p. 438.
36. Cited by Gilbert, *Never Despair*, p. 685.
37. Gilbert, *Never Despair*, p. 167.
38. Churchill, *Complete Speeches*, p. 7,712 and Gilbert, *Never Despair*, p. 69.
39. Gilbert, *Never Despair*, pp. 337 and 463.
40. Churchill, *Complete Speeches*, p. 7,124.
41. Churchill, *Complete Speeches*, p. 7,244.
42. Churchill, *Complete Speeches*, p. 7,296.
43. Churchill, *Complete Speeches*, p. 7,380.
44. Churchill, *Complete Speeches*, p. 7,712.
45. This speech can be found in the *Complete Speeches*, pp. 7,379-7,382.
46. See Broad, *The Years of Achievement*, pp. 536-537.
47. Cited by Gilbert, *Never Despair*, pp. 278-279. As the leader of the movement for European unity, Churchill felt obliged to form a "Steering Committee" to accomplish two critical tasks: to form a non-political group to prevent the catastrophe of a third world war and to stimulate the world's opinion leaders. His whole project for unity was the one way he believed war could be stopped. See pp. 290-291.
48. Churchill, *The Gathering Storm*, p. 274.
49. Churchill, *The Hinge of Fate*, p. 805.
50. Ulam, *Expansion and Coexistence*, p. 423. Ulam also pointed out (p. 498) that, from one point of view, NATO, as a response to potential Soviet aggression, was an overreaction of sorts during the late 1940s. The Soviet Union had real weaknesses in the early postwar period, including economic devastation and the formidable tasks of imposing communism on Eastern Europe. After 1950, regardless of how much NATO increased its strength, the West would never be in such a commanding position vis-á-vis Soviet Russia.
51. Churchill, *Complete Speeches*, p. 7,487.
52. Ulam, *Expansion and Coexistence*, p. 503.
53. Churchill, *Complete Speeches*, p. 7,348.
54. Churchill, *Complete Speeches*, p. 7,640.
55. Churchill, *Complete Speeches*, p. 8,066. See also p. 7,639. Churchill's vision for the new order (p. 7,486): "We hope to see a Europe where men of every country will think as much of being a European as of belonging to their native land, and wherever they go in this wide domain will truly feel 'Here I am at home.'"
56. Churchill believed that "[t]hese moral values, founded alike on Christian faith and charity and on the critical spirit of rationalism, are the messages of our 2,000 year-old European civilization and culture" (Churchill, *Complete Speeches*, p. 7,793).
57. Gilbert, *Never Despair*, p. 408.
58. Churchill, *Complete Speeches*, p. 7,637.
59. Gilbert, *Never Despair*, p. 287.
60. Gilbert, *Never Despair*, p. 397. In part, Churchill blamed Labour's foot dragging on the "closed shop" behavior of left-wing political parties (p. 398). He

accused the government of trying to form an exclusive union of the Socialists of Europe.

61. Churchill, *Complete Speeches*, p. 8,023.
62. Gilbert, *Never Despair*, p. 535.
63. Gilbert, *Never Despair*, pp. 779-780.
64. Churchill, *Complete Speeches*, p. 8,082.
65. Churchill, *Complete Speeches*, p. 8,588-8,589.
66. Churchill, *Complete Speeches*, p. 8,519.
67. Gilbert, *Never Despair*, p. 705. By February 1952, the Labour Party accused Churchill of wanting to make war with China in order to end the deadlock in Korea. He deflected the accusations by his co-Parliamentarians that he was a warmonger (an accusation with which he was thoroughly familiar) with a bombshell of his own when he brought to light before the entire Commons that Attlee's government was, secretly, fully prepared to participate in the bombing of China if necessary. When the pandemonium abated, Churchill had emerged the clear victor in his position to support any retaliatory measures against China that the United States thought necessary (Gilbert, *Never Despair*, pp. 704-706).
68. Cited by Gilbert, *Never Despair*, p. 537. He stated to the Commons in January 1952: "I thought it important to try to give the impression to the American people that we rejoice in their effort to defend the cause of world freedom against Communist aggression and penetration and that we will aid them in this purpose, which is ours also, with all our strength and good will." (Churchill, *Complete Speeches*, p. 8,330).
69. Gilbert, *Never Despair*, p. 737. See also p. 746, where this principle was applied in the making of political and military appointments.
70. Colville, *The Fringes of Power*, pp. 657-658.
71. Cited in Gilbert, *Never Despair*, p. 217-218. The UN was to be a "strongly-armed body," one that would "not shrink from establishing its will against the evil-doer, or evilplanner, in good time and by force of arms" (Churchill, *Complete Speeches*, pp. 7,110-7,111). See also, Churchill, *Triumph and Tragedy*, p. 209; *Complete Speeches*, p. 7,792.
72. Churchill, *Complete Speeches*, p. 7,401.
73. Churchill, *Complete Speeches*, May 1947, p. 7,488. Churchill's priorities generally did not begin with the UN, although he expected this body to perform an important function. Given his past experience, it is very doubtful Churchill desired to have a world government in which states would relinquish their most cherished sovereign rights—including the right to have an army. If I have misinterpreted him in this instance, I can only attribute this apparent weakness in his "political philosophy" to his heavy reliance on history as a guide to understanding politics. History is essential to understanding political things. However, it is not sufficient for this task as it cannot faithfully evaluate competing political ends. This task is one for political philosophy. The ancient philosophers would have looked upon the creation of a political order based on principles of excessive unity as the initial step to tyranny; a strong indication of this can be found in Aristotle's *Politics* (book 2, chs. 1-5) and Plato's *Republic* (which is a criticism of politics and its tendency to degenerate into either tyranny or anarchy). Churchill's hesitancy to rely upon "abstractions" (as Edmund Burke would call them) or political principles that may have dissuaded him in this instance may have led him astray. Statesmen need to guard against political unity that operates without regard for the parts in a political order (states and indi-

viduals). Even if a world government did not become despotic, it is not likely to stop international conflict. See, for example, Walter Berns, "The Case Against World Government" (American Foundation for Political Education, 1955) and Lee D. Neumann, "World Government," *Fateful Visions: Avoiding Nuclear War*, ed. Joseph S. Nye, Jr., Graham T. Allison, Albert Carnesale (Cambridge, MA: Ballinger Publishing Company, 1988), pp. 197-214.

74. Churchill, *Complete Speeches*, p. 7,111. See also *Triumph and Tragedy*, p. 356: "(T)he World Organization in no way destroyed normal diplomatic intercourse between States, great or small." See also *Triumph and Tragedy*, p. 610: "I have always held the view that the foundation of a world Instrument should be sought on a regional basis." Localities know their problems better than any super-organization.

75. See Churchill, *Complete Speeches*, p. 7,322 and also Churchill, *Triumph and Tragedy*, p. 649.

76. Churchill, *Complete Speeches*, p. 8,683. Still politically observant in July 1957, Churchill decried the swelling of the United Nations by numerous small countries. The UN, he said, was moving away from its original design. "But it is anomalous that the vote or prejudice of any small country should affect events involving populations many times its own numbers and affect them as momentary self-advantage may direct. This should be changed."

77. Churchill, *Triumph and Tragedy*, p. 433. Here Churchill also tells us that Foreign Secretary Molotov's behavior at the San Francisco Conferences left a deep and bad impression on him.

78. Churchill, *Complete Speeches*, p. 7,353.

79. Churchill, *Complete Speeches*, p. 7,806.

80. Churchill, *Complete Speeches*, pp. 7,353-7,354. See also pp. 7,317-7,318.

81. Churchill, *Marlborough*, bk. 2, pp. 521-522 (emphasis added). Marlborough was also one to quote the old Roman maxim that you have to be resolved to make war in order to keep the peace (bk. 2, p. 236).

Chapter 6

Churchill's Postwar Statesmanship Part II: Negotiation and Persuasion

Those who know how to win are much more numerous than those who know how to make proper use of their victories.

—Polybius

The plight of mankind is all the fault of the human mind being made in two lobes, only one of which does any thinking, so we are all right-handed or left-handed; whereas, if we were properly constructed, we should use our right and left hands with equal force and skill according to circumstances. As it is, those who can win a war well can rarely make a good peace, and those who could make a good peace never win.

—Winston Churchill

The conclusion that one must draw from the preceding chapter is that no foreign policy can have validity if there is not adequate force behind it and a national willingness to make the necessary sacrifices.[1] Churchill understood that nothing would be so foolish in the quest for normal relations with Soviet Russia than for the western democracies to abandon their unity or their arms. Above all, there was always the possibility that war once again would rain down its misfortunes over the entire world. Unity, stability, strength, and a common purpose, the guarantors of safety, also were the preconditions, the "essential basis," for an understanding with the East.[2]

Churchill's postwar diplomacy was inspired by the urgent need to avoid a third world struggle, which meant making sure the Allies did not repeat the same short-sighted mistakes that permitted Nazi imperialism and aggression, organizing forces and policies around this single purpose, and finding a profitable approach to better relations with the Soviet Union. Force was a necessary component. A measured military policy can provide "the means of gradually approaching the situation when relations between world Powers may express themselves in normal terms and not only be measured in the strange and novel methods of the atomic age."[3]

Churchill began and ended his postwar political career with a faithful dedication to building the noble structures on which he believed peace must rest. In this manner only could peaceful science advance and bring prosperity to mankind. Churchill was convinced of his path—having superior strength and "then acting with reason and fairness. This is the plan for the battle of peace and the only plan which has a chance of success." Churchill believed from the closing days of the war until his retirement from politics that the West "ought to close no door on the attempt to establish some understanding between these two opposed worlds."[4]

CHURCHILLIAN POSTWAR DIPLOMACY

If any man in this century understood the power of rhetoric and persuasion, it was Winston Churchill.[5] Rhetoric, when force does not hold sway, is the essence of politics. Speaking to his London audience in 1947 on the possibilities of unity within Europe and peace with Russia, Churchill noted that "[w]e are not acting in the field of force, but in the domain of opinion. We cannot give orders. We can only persuade."[6] There is little doubt that Churchill judged his own abilities as a statesman and high-level diplomat to be preeminent. A further incidence of world war, caused by the shortcomings of diplomats and the errors of statesmen, could not be tolerated and must be avoided at almost all costs.[7] In the first part of this century, Churchill, reflecting his remarkable consistency over the years (and the wisdom of Marlborough cited at the end of the last chapter), related these ideas as follows:

In place of arguments for coercion, there must be arguments for conciliation; and these must come from the same lips as the former. But all this may be capable of reasonable and honourable explanation. Statesmen may say bluntly, "We have failed to coerce; we have now to conciliate," or alternatively, "We have failed to conciliate; we have now to coerce."[8]

In other words, applying these thoughts to the most recent challenges, Churchill believed that the circumstances shaping the postwar world made conciliation between East and West the most favorable and sensible option, especially since the West carried the upper hand in terms of military strength.

The common bond of hatred for the Nazi regime had dissolved, and with it, Churchill believed, the hope for a just peace—that is, unless a fair settlement on the terms of peace from the last war and the rules of future international conduct could be reached among the major powers. The prospects for conciliation and agreement among the United States, Great Britain, France, and the Soviet Union were dim. Churchill acknowledged in 1946 that the Soviets appeared at times to delay purposefully all final settlements of peace.[9] If the negotiations were to begin, another source of commonality had to be sought.

After the war, Churchill recognized and accepted a *de facto* balance of power between East and West, and he crafted his postwar positions with these new facts in mind. From the war's conclusion, he championed a working association with the Soviet Union and resented any suggestion that Britain pursue an anti-Russian policy.

> Even if as, alas, is possible—or not impossible—we should develop strong differences on many aspects of policy, political, social, even, as we think, moral, with the Soviet Government, no state of mind must be allowed to occur in this country which ruptures or withers those great associations between our two peoples which were our glory and our safety, in the late frightful convulsion.[10]

So compelling were the imperatives to establish a new peace, that vital political and moral differences had to be, if not entirely ignored, pushed back into the shadows.

Churchill's position on Britain's relationship with Soviet Russia was subtle and complex, and demonstrated that Churchill was not simply a Realpolitik statesman. The Soviet Union had a vital role to play in providing future stability in the world, and all exertions to accomplish her entry into the new world order ought to be made, but not at the price of one's soul, so to speak. In the above quotation, Churchill spoke of "a state of mind" that must not be allowed to manifest itself within British foreign policy. This also could be read as "emotion" or "popular sentiment," either of which, when firmly in control of the hearts of the people and politicians in a democratic country, could lead to a foreign policy unguided by reason. Such a circumstance in these times, Churchill believed, would have been dangerous and deplorable. Therefore, his ideas expressed in the following quotation, while apparently inconsistent with the one cited above, really add a significant dimension to his understanding of morality and politics, and policy and the public mind. He wrote in a May 1945 note to Anthony Eden:

> It must be remembered that Britain and the United States are united at this time upon the same ideologies, namely, freedom, and the principles set out in the American Constitution and humbly reproduced with modern variations in the Atlantic Charter. The Soviet Government have a different philosophy, namely, Communism, and use to the full the methods of police government. . . . The Prime Minister cannot [i.e., "should not"] readily bring himself to accept the idea that the position of the United States is that Britain and Soviet Russia are just two foreign powers, six of one and half a dozen of the other, with whom the troubles of the late war have to be adjusted. Except in so far as force is concerned, there is not equality between right and wrong. The great causes and principles for which Britain and the United States have suffered and triumphed are not mere matters of the balance of power.[11]

Churchill did not approach the Soviets wearing moral blinkers. As it often does, politics in this situation pitted several moral positions against one another, the two most obvious being the imperative to avoid a third world war and the crying need to redress Soviet injustice in Europe.

"The gulf which yawns between the two worlds," Churchill recognized, made for extreme difficulties in securing a meaningful settlement.[12] Failure would mean—would demand—a further intensification of the Cold War.[13] He, therefore, knew the dangers of cultivating false hopes of a speedy friendly settlement with the Soviet Union. "It may be," he lectured in 1948 to his Conservative colleagues, "that some formula will be found or some artificial compromise effected which will be hailed as a solution and a deliverance. But the fundamental danger and antagonisms will still remain."[14]

Churchill's postwar policy toward the Soviet Union, from the closing days of the war to the final days of his political career, was characterized by remarkable consistency. This was particularly the case with regard to his drive for a negotiated settlement with Moscow. According to Kenneth Thompson, "[b]y the 1950s, Churchill had called on no less than forty occasions for an approach to the Russians based on a peaceful settlement."[15] Churchill reemphasized his position to the Commons in December 1948, a time when relations between East and West were at or near their nadir. "It has always been my earnest desire, which I do not yet abandon, that a peaceful settlement may yet be reached with Soviet Russia if it is within the bounds of possibility."[16] Indeed, in November 1954, Churchill admitted that the issue that most governed his thoughts when he wrote his famous "iron curtain" telegram to Truman was "an understanding with Russia."[17]

Over the years, several elements have marked Churchill's approach to an East-West settlement. One characteristic feature of his diplomacy was the recognition that negotiation, diplomacy, and conciliation were vital international activities. "Well was it written," he wrote in 1937, " 'Agree with thine adversary quickly whilst thou art in the way with him.' "[18] This adage indicates the complexity of diplomacy, that there are times to negotiate, times to stand back, and times to prepare for war. The postwar period, characterized by the disintegration of one of history's great wartime alliances, was one of those times, considered Churchill, when a settlement with the Soviets was one of the most important diplomatic ventures that statesmen of this period could pursue.[19] Even when catastrophe loomed, Churchill did not despair over the chances for peace, as Martin Gilbert indicated about Churchill's attitude while delivering a speech to the U.S. Congress in January 1952 (before Stalin's death and before Churchill famous May 11, 1953 speech to the House detailing his new diplomatic initiative): "Churchill's concluding words were not . . . words of warning, but words that looked forward to a healing of the wounds and a reconciling of the differences."[20]

Churchill's cautious understanding of summits was the second element of his diplomacy. Summits, or high-level meetings among the major powers, are not ends in themselves. Larger political objectives, in this case the safety of the

West, the avoidance of war, and the spread of democratic principles to less fortunate lands, must help guide all diplomatic objectives. Additionally, the results of a summit may not play favorably. Churchill noted in March 1955 that to have a summit by no means would guarantee a positive result. "To have a conference at an ill-chosen moment, or in unfavourable circumstances, would only raise false hopes and probably finish by leaving things worse than before."[21] There is a right and a wrong time to meet "at the highest levels."

"Appease the weak, defy the strong." Churchill understood diplomacy and appeasement quite differently than former Prime Minister Neville Chamberlain, who chose to kneel before Hitler at a time when Britain lacked the power and influence to direct or confidently address events on the European continent. "Appeasement in itself may be good or bad according to the circumstances," he believed. "Appeasement from weakness and fear is alike futile and fatal. Appeasement from strength is magnanimous and noble and might be the surest and perhaps the only path to world peace."[22] Elsewhere Churchill admonished that in times of crisis and tension, statesmen must "allow no appeasement of tyranny and wrong-doing in any form."[23]

Churchill's estimation of the value of his personal involvement in the settlement negotiations constituted a third element. During the early postwar years, Churchill felt that a special connection between himself and Stalin continued to exist as a product of the wartime alliance.[24] Even after this connection had dissolved, however, Churchill continued to believe that he alone could represent the West best in future negotiations. He clearly believed that the efforts by Labour between 1945 and 1951 were deficient and that only after his reelection would peace be attained.[25] After Churchill's reelection to the premiership in 1951, John Colville indicated that this very feeling circulated throughout Britain. Churchill's return to the premiership, he wrote, seemed "to presage the recovery of hopes tarnished by the dismal aftermath of the war. . . . Churchill is Back."[26] Churchill, in fact, admitted that the hopes of a high-level summit was the predominant reason for his wishing to become again prime minister.[27] He confessed similar motives in 1953 to Lord Moran, his personal physician: "I don't like being kicked out [of office] till I've had a shot at settling this Russian business." He repeated his goal to Moran, "the easement of the world, perhaps peace over the world—without of course giving up proper means of defense." "I can do something with the Russians which no one else can do," he again told Moran. "That is the only reason why I am clinging to office."[28]

The quest for justice, the fourth element, presented yet another motive for reconciliation with the Soviet Union as quickly as possible. Great Britain entered the war against Hitler to defend the integrity of a Central European state. Throughout the postwar era Churchill returned to the tragic fate of Poland and the other occupied lands when providing a rationale for his policies. The liberation of all of Europe remained a significant policy objective. "We cannot rest content with the division of Europe into two parts—the free and the unfree."[29] The Russification of Eastern and Central Europe meant that a quick solution was needed. Delay meant time for the Soviet consolidation of power, time for the further "liquidation" of "obnoxious" elements, and that the chances were fleeting for the occupied countries to develop closer associations among one another.[30]

A fifth, very important element was Churchill's recognition that, absent common bonds and objectives, the appeal to Soviet interests would be the crux of any agreement. Said Churchill: "it is impossible to prophesy what they [the Soviet leaders] will do, or when, or how they will do it. One can only judge these matters by estimating what is their interest." Interest itself is not, he acknowledged, always reliable. "[I]t does not include accident, passion, folly or madness, madness which may arise from some error, some blunder, or from the results of some internal convulsions."[31] Nonetheless, lacking all other commonalties, attention to interest promised be the key, and Churchill would attempt to exploit this to the utmost.

A final, but no less important, element is that successful diplomacy and negotiations demanded strength in support. "The only way to deal with Communist Russia," he noted in 1950, "is by having superior strength in one form or another, and then acting with reason and fairness."[32] Commenting on the creation of the North Atlantic Treaty Organization in May of 1949, Churchill related the following:

He would be a bold, and, I think, an imprudent man who embarked upon detailed prophesies about what will be the future course of events. But it is absolutely certain that the strengthening by every means in our power of the growing ties which unite the signatories of the Atlantic Pact, of the Brussels Treaty, and the signatories of the Statute of the Council of Europe . . . is our surest guarantee of peace and safety.[33]

There is no contradiction between defensive preparations on the one hand and reconciliation on the other. This was especially true for the East-West relationship. Indeed, Churchill had hoped for a lasting settlement with Russia before the West pulled out of Central and Eastern Europe after the war.[34] Balance and prudence in these matters involving military strength, however, were ever present in Churchill's policies. "While preserving at great sacrifice and cost in building our military strength, we must never lose sight of the importance of a peaceful and friendly settlement of our differences with Russia."[35]

Churchill believed his diplomatic approach most appropriate, especially in light of the confrontation in Korea. The Communists only understood a hard bargain, he believed, and Churchill considered President Truman's decision to resist in Korea to be a "turning point."[36] He knew that the West not only had to convince the Soviet government that it had superior force but that it was not restrained by any moral consideration about using force. That was the greatest chance of peace.[37] Victory here was likely to have many positive diplomatic results. For one, it sent a message of resolve from the centers of liberal democracy to the citadel of communism that the West would not surrender the ground rules for normal diplomatic relations among states—that there would be no unopposed revolution in international affairs. It also placed the focus back on the virtues of diplomacy while emphasizing the futility of aggression.

It was the ultimate weapon of war, the atomic bomb, that Churchill relied upon to coerce the Soviets into striking a meaningful deal with the West. For this reason, Churchill strongly advocated the continued improvement of these weapons and their acquisition for military use by the United States. He did not change his views upon the invention of the hydrogen bomb.[38] Churchill wrote to Truman in April 1949 to report that he was "deeply impressed" by Truman's statement "about not fearing to use the atomic bomb if the need arose." This would "do more than anything else to ward off the catastrophe of a third world war."[39] Churchill also insisted that Britain's own nuclear arsenal was essential to her political and military influence as a world power. A new form of warfare had begun to manifest itself, particularly after the Soviet acquisition of thermonuclear bombs. He believed that "the advance of the hydrogen bomb has fundamentally altered the entire problem of defence."[40] "There could be no more certain way," he stressed, "of bringing about the destruction of civilization than that we should drift on helplessly until the Soviets are fully equipped with the atomic bomb."[41]

All of these developments were vital to the achievement of a final settlement between East and West. "The Western Powers," Churchill explained, "will be far more likely to reach a lasting settlement, without bloodshed, if they formulate their just demands while they have the atomic power and before the Russian Communists have got it."[42] And although conditions worsened after the Soviets obtained the bomb, the West, the United States, still retained significant superiority. While a nuclear balance would do an admirable job to maintain the peace, Churchill recognized the deficiencies of the "sturdy balance of terror." The achievement of a settlement would make for a more honorable and sure peace. "It is my earnest hope, he said, that we may find our way to some more exalted and august foundation for our safety than this grim and sombre balancing power of the bomb. We must not, however, cast away our only shield of safety unless we can find something better and surer and more likely to last."[43]

THE MAY 11, 1953 INITIATIVE

Thus it was on May 11, 1953 that Churchill delivered yet another speech that caught the breath of the nation and the world. The Foreign Secretary, Anthony Eden, could not perform his obligation before the House to deliver a speech on the state of foreign affairs due to yet another illness. Prime Minister Churchill, believing his grasp of foreign affairs and official experience more than adequate, took it upon himself to assume the duties of the Foreign Secretary, with the assistance of Lord Salisbury, until Eden returned rather than appoint someone else temporarily. (There is little speculation that Churchill needed his arm twisted in order to assume these additional duties.) He therefore requested that the House give his thoughts on the subjects he addressed their due consideration.

In the speech he discussed the most important issues relating to British foreign policy, namely, the Korean truce, rising troubles in Indo-China, Egypt and British interests in the Suez Canal, the German question, and the new changes that had taken place in the Soviet Union. Stalin, of course, had died earlier that year, and the new leaders, who appeared to operate less antagonistically than Stalin, were taking their seats at the top.

This initiative was, in fact, long awaited by many of his colleagues in the House. Conservatives won a majority in October 1951. Many of them, Churchill in particular, ran on a platform advocating a bolder diplomacy to achieve a reconciliation with the Soviet Union. After he was elected by his party to become prime minister, much time had elapsed without any new foreign policy initiatives, and many in the party opposite accused Churchill of having been opportunistic and disingenuous about his true intentions to negotiate with Stalin. The following exchange among members of the Commons during the question and answer period on the April 7, 1952 is representative of the debate.

Mr. Dodds: Will the right hon. Gentleman state if he is as enthusiastic now about the meeting as he was before the Elections in 1950 and 1951? Does he not appreciate that the vast majority of the people would rather that he tried and failed than that he should not try at all?
The Prime Minister: It is not a question of enthusiasm, but of earnestness, and that is in no way diminished.
Mr. Shinwell: What has caused the right hon. Gentleman to change his mind?
The Prime Minister: No, I have not changed my mind at all, but apparently the right hon. Gentleman has changed his since he and his party in 1951 called my observation a stunt.
Mr. Shinwell: Are we to understand that the right hon. Gentleman's reluctance to take up the point is that he now regards it as a stunt himself?
The Prime Minister: I have no reluctance at all. If the circumstances and situation were favourable, I would welcome the occasion.[44]

Churchill frequently referred his accusers back to a statement he made in November 1951: "There are at present no plans for negotiations on general problems with the Soviet Union, but the possibility of a high-level meeting should not be excluded if circumstances are favourable."[45] The consequences of pushing rashly for peace could generate mistakes that ultimately would be detrimental to diplomacy.[46]

While Churchill consistently championed high-level meetings between East and West since the end of the war (recall the Fulton speech), he chose May 1953 to offer a bold new approach and to rekindle interest in the proposal. Churchill expressed a sense of urgency. Tensions abounded in the international system, and both the United States and the Soviet Union were beginning to invest rather heavily in nuclear weapons.

A second reason for his new initiative may have been that, during the Soviet Union's thirty-six year history, the Soviet people had recognized only two leaders, Lenin and Stalin—and most of those years they knew only the tyrant Stalin.

By 1953, many probably had assumed that the Soviet tyranny was very nearly a personal tyranny, and that when Stalin had left the scene, new avenues would be presented to the Soviet people and to future statesmen interested in far-reaching diplomacy.[47] Before Stalin's death, the personality of Stalin, and his numerous erratic, ideological, and barbarous policies, could hardly have been conducive to traditional diplomacy and compromise. This attitude could not be joined easily with any policy of friendliness or collaboration with the West.[48]

Stalin's death appeared to open up a rare opportunity to achieve a meaningful settlement, especially to a man such as Churchill who displayed inordinate confidence in his own abilities as a statesman.[49] Even before Stalin's death, however (perhaps in anticipation of it), Churchill kept close watch on events in the Soviet Union, as he indicated in a January 17, 1952 speech to the U.S. Congress: "We must not lose patience, and we must not lose hope. It may be that presently a new mood will reign behind the Iron Curtain. If so it will be easy for them to show it, but the democracies must be on their guard against being deceived by a false dawn."[50] Harold Macmillan noted in his diary the arguments Churchill gave for continuing in office later in his life (August 1954): Churchill would be able "to steer through the complications of Foreign Policy and international problems. He had a unique position. He could talk to anybody, on either side of the Iron Curtain, either by personal message or face to face."[51]

Churchill referred in his May 11 speech to the sudden change in leadership and attitude in the Soviet Union as "the supreme event."[52] "It is the policy of Her Majesty's Government," he continued, "to avoid by every means in their power doing anything or saying anything which could check any favourable reaction that may be taking place." He was encouraged by the apparent reconsideration of the new leaders of past policy, "of leaving off doing things which we have not been doing to them," although he acknowledged that there have been no specific cases of actions taken by the new leaders that warranted praise from the West. Then he addressed the possibility of a settlement.

> It would, I think, be a mistake to assume that nothing can be settled with Soviet Russia unless or until everything is settled. A settlement of two or three of our difficulties would be an important gain to every peace-loving country. For instance, peace in Korea, the conclusion of an Austrian Treaty—these might lead to an easement in our relations for the next few years, which might in itself open new prospects to the security and prosperity of all nations and every continent.

He then cautioned against trying to chart a detailed map for the course of the new negotiations and to resist any attempt to reach a comprehensive agreement in one stroke. The nature of the business at hand and the existence of fundamental differences did not lend themselves to abstract and hurried solutions. "Piecemeal solutions of individual problems should not be disdained or improvidently put aside." Most curiously, he followed these points with a message of apparently greater importance than a settlement. "Above all, it would be a pity if the natural desire to reach a general settlement of international policy were to impede any spontaneous and healthy evolution which may be taking place inside Russia." Manifestations of internal change, of beneficent developments within that country, had long-term consequences. These grand internal changes of public policy, after all, would provide a much more solid foundation for world peace than a simple negotiated settlement that may be breached by any of the parties at any time.

He then recognized that the Russian people deserved a "high place in world affairs" and that any anxieties they felt for their own security was a legitimate concern, one that the West needed to take into account. "I do not believe that the immense problem of reconciling the security of Russia with the freedom and safety of Western Europe is insoluble." In an effort to bring a new approach to find a solution to these persistent problems, Churchill suggested to the Commons that the West look back to the Locarno Treaty of 1925 as a possible example. Churchill described it as a simple collective security agreement. "It was based on the simple provision that if Germany attacked France we should stand with the French, and if France attacked Germany we should stand with the Germans."

The original Locarno agreement, at bottom, was intended to provide stability in Europe by having Germany pledge to observe the frontiers with France and Belgium, while Great Britain and Italy promised to preserve militarily the status quo. Germany was also to be reinstated as a major power. The eastern frontiers of Germany were left out of the agreement and placed under the dubious protection guaranteed by members under Article 16 of the League of Nations Covenant. The arrangements alleviated Russian fears that Germany would become a partner in a coalition against the Soviet Union under its League of Nations obligations. The treaty was a defeat for Moscow's diplomacy. Germany could now play the Soviet Union off against the West.[53]

This sort of international agreement, modified to befit the postwar circumstances, would provide security for the Soviet Union while also tending to Germany's aspirations to participate on equal terms with the rest of the civilized world. This was vital, Churchill stressed, if it was the ambition of European statesmen to "consolidate the peace of Europe as the key to the peace of mankind." "Russia," he finished, "has a right to feel assured that as far as human arrangements can run the terrible events of the Hitler invasion will never be repeated, and that Poland will remain a friendly Power and a buffer, though not, I trust, a puppet State." He then closed with a message about the importance of not delaying a summit, and how the conference itself should not be weighed down by rigid agendas, technical details, and hoards of "experts," and that the smallest number of powers and persons possible should be in attendance. These conditions, it would seem, would be ideal for someone like Churchill, who had ambition, stature, and a method for dealing with such weighty international issues.

Churchill also raised the attention of the House to the importance of Germany and the British attitude toward the EDC. Germany was considered the dominant problem in Europe, in part created by the untimely American withdrawal of her troops at the end of the last war from the eastern portions of Germany. This territory should not have been ceded until a general settlement with Russia had been reached. In the end, though, irrespective of Allied decisions, Soviet ambition was responsible for the succession of tragic and remorseful events in the heart of Europe.

In his speech, Churchill reminded the Commons of "the new and remarkable relationship" the western democracies had fashioned with the West Germans; and Churchill advised most strongly that the West adhere to any agreements made with the government of Konrad Adenauer. He continued with high praise for the impressive leader of West Germany. He said that Dr. Adenauer "may well be deemed the wisest German statesman since the days of Bismarck." Churchill greatly admired "the perseverance, courage, composure, and skill with which he ha[d] faced the complex, changing, uncertain, and unpredictable situations with which he has been ceaselessly confronted." Then, most importantly, he publicly committed himself to the protection of this new German state, even at the cost of a general settlement with the Soviet leaders. In no way, he promised Adenauer, would West Germany be "sacrificed" in any future negotiations. "[W]e are resolved not in any way to fail in the obligations to which we have committed ourselves about Western Germany."

Germany ought to be allowed to function within the united European community and, he said to the surprise of some of his co-Parliamentarians, within the EDC. Churchill believed EDC to be important to European security, but that Great Britain nonetheless should refrain from joining these European federal systems. She had a Commonwealth and Empire, and belonged to collective defense organizations such as NATO. The Europeans, he concluded, ought not to fear that West Germany would exercise a preponderate influence in the EDC.

Churchill made his speech against the advice of the British Foreign Office.[54] Recall he took over the platform momentarily on account of Eden's protracted sickness. According to John Colville, the Foreign Office believed that Churchill diplomatic initiative would hinder the unification process then currently underway in Western Europe. Others, he noted, thought Churchill's initiative to be statesmanlike and offered their enthusiastic support, the Minister of State, Selwyn Lloyd, being one of those supporters.[55]

Churchill received support for his new initiative from all sides, from Labourites, Liberals, and Conservatives alike. The leader of the Liberal Party, Clement Davies, believed that the Prime Minister's speech was "one of the greatest that he has ever delivered" and that it spoke directly to the question of "how can we best and most quickly put an end to the cold war."[56] Among the first speakers to react in the House was Philip Noel-Baker of the opposition Labour Party. Mr. Noel-Baker observed that "[s]ome people may say there are risks in such a conference, but there are risks in our situation now which require brave action, and we welcome the general tone of the Prime Minister's speech today and many of the things that he said."[57]

There was general approval for Churchill's speech within the Conservative Party as well, along with a measure of skepticism and caution. Sir Victor

Raikes, while acknowledging the need for lasting peace and settlement of differences, nonetheless cautioned the House that Russia's "game" is as yet unclear, and that Britain should oppose any attempt to sign another Yalta Treaty which could lead to the dismemberment of Europe. "The danger," he said, "is always that of wishful thinking," and that Western statesmen must look past gestures and look for evidence of communist sincerity.[58] Hugh Fraser acknowledged that Churchill "delivered himself of a great speech, based on solid grounds of hope and upon the determination that while negotiations continue, however magnanimous this country may be, we must retain the armed strength on which all parties in the House are determined."[59] Others, like C.E. Mott-Radclyffe, noted that the Soviets had changed tactics in the past, and that statesmen naturally ought to expect such behavior in the future, that is unless Moscow can pass a test of sincerity—such as a satisfactory treaty regarding Austria.[60] Still others, like Godfrey Nicholson, lauded the new direction of British foreign policy for the independence from the United States it gave the country in the realm of foreign affairs.[61]

There were, of course, varieties of backhanded praise by those generally opposed to Churchill's ideas and policies. Mr. R.H.S. Crossman of Labour noted (wrongly) that the speech "read so very differently from another famous speech—the Fulton speech—which was the proclamation of cold war. . . . This speech was a proclamation of the hope of ending the cold war."[62] Churchill's position at Fulton was defended in the House at this time by the Joint Under-Secretary of State for Foreign Affairs, Mr. Anthony Nutting.

I thought he [meaning Crossman] did less than justice to the efforts of the propagandists for the Soviet Union in the Communist Party. . . . The Fulton speech was the reply to those who had already started the cold war. Yesterday's speech by the Prime Minister was the response to what we hope is a new breeze blowing upon the world.[63]

One of the strongest criticisms of Churchill's initiative came from the socialist Michael Foot. He noted first (after chiding the Conservative half of the Commons for not being more enthusiastic about their party leader's new approach) that the Prime Minister had broken new ground with his speech, and he praised him for that. However, he regretted the lack of detail about the proposed negotiations. Mostly, he deplored the failure by Churchill to translate his principles into a practical negotiating position that included Germany, as anyone knew that a general settlement had to include that divided state.

In particular, Foot criticized Churchill for not seeing, from the Soviet point of view, how critical an unarmed Germany, one not too closely associated with its bellicose past, was for a settlement. Foot, therefore, found much room to criticize Churchill for heaping praise on Adenauer and comparing him to the founder of the modern German state, Bismarck. German involvement in the EDC, and Adenauer's insistence that West Germany remain aligned with the western powers and within the western security system, would lace the negotiations with the Russians with irresolvable contradictions. These contradictions in Churchill's approach would have "a crippling effect on bringing about a four-Power conference."[64] Neither would this sort of talk, Foot remarked, help to endear the German nation to the French. He concluded by stating that "recognizing that if we are to take full advantage of the changes that have taken place in Russia we shall also have to make some changes in our policy," otherwise the prime minister "will have missed one of the greatest opportunities in history."

Foot's points were seconded by several other members. Many came down hard in favor of an essentially neutral or disarmed (perhaps unified) Germany. Mr. Crossman understood Churchill's talk of a new Locarno agreement to mean that "we should say to the Russians that we would guarantee them the Oder-Neisse line if we could get a unified Germany (this despite the fact that there was no mention of German reunification in Churchill's speech). He also interjected that he was confused about the attempt to rearm West Germany under Adenauer. He saw Dr. Adenauer as "a profiteer of the cold war." The only chance for free elections, Crossman believed, was to "postpone the re-armament of Western Germany in exchange for the disarmament of Eastern Germany and free elections in a disarmed Germany."[65] Others, like Mr. John Hynd of the opposition, championed similar solutions regarding Germany and a general settlement. A settlement of the German question by the major powers may then help to facilitate an Austrian treaty, he believed, and that this approach should be considered "even if it merely means establishing for a long period something a little less than a free, independent and united Germany."[66]

Some members voiced the Soviet concern about an armed and reunified Germany (although, again, talk of reunification never entered into the Prime Minister's proposals). Mr. F. J. Bellenger linked practically the entire Soviet "fear complex" and subsequent expansionism to Germany's aggressive actions. "The pushing out of the Soviet boundaries westward into Europe . . . are themselves all due to the fear which Russia has, particularly of Germany."[67] Mr. A.J. Irvine expressed in equally vivid language his understanding of Soviet fears. "The first objective of the German people is the recovery of the lost provinces, and the best prospect for them of the recovery of the lost provinces is for a fearful conflict to break out between the Soviet Union and the West."[68] Germany was not to be trusted by either side, and this, of course, was contrary to the spirit Churchill had attempted to engender.

Churchill believed, and his speech on May 11, 1953 made it clear, West Germany's participation in the western security union was vital to lasting peace in Europe. Unlike his critics, Churchill saw little justification for the hysteria on the part of the Commons members against the creation of a strong German state.[69] Unlike his critics, Churchill was prepared to stand by the German nation, even at the price of losing a general settlement with the Soviet Union. He did not believe that the two positions were necessarily contradictory as many of the members of the Commons argued. He believed that the solution could be found in what he referred to as a new Locarno Agreement.

There were moral reasons for Churchill's stubborn support of Adenauer and the fledgling German Republic. The German people, he believed, were part of the human family. Churchill always was careful to make the distinction between those who ruled tyrannically and those who were ruled and had little complicity with the atrocious policies of the government. "People who let themselves fall into the grip of dictatorship and totalitarian tyranny cannot escape the consequences of their carelessness and folly and heavily have the Germans suffered for them." Quoting Burke in a speech given almost a year and a half after his call for a new initiative, he once again censured those who would condemn the entire German nation: "I do not know the method of drawing up an indictment against a whole people."[70] He warned that "terrible would be the accountability of those in any country who, for petty, narrow, or selfish ends, weakened the common cause by stirring bygone passions, hates and tragedies."[71]

On moral grounds (and for reasons involving the future security of Germany), Churchill argued strongly against Stalin's proposal to begin mass executions of the German military leadership after the war.[72] In the same spirit and out of concern for future peace in Europe, Churchill earnestly hoped that there would be no pariah nations after the guilty had been punished.[73]

For security reasons, Churchill eschewed any proposals that called for German reunification. For one, at this point in time, such an achievement probably would have entailed the neutralization of the unified German state, removing a central pillar from Churchill's proposed alliance structure—namely, Europe united and working with the Commonwealth and the United States to secure prosperity and peace in the world.[74] Churchill's commitment was not just to the new German state but to its leader as well. In February 1954 Churchill boldly restated his long-standing support for the man and the state. Adenauer had "staked his political existence upon the cause of Germany in Europe. That we should desert him now would be not only an unfair blow to him, but it might react upon the whole future mind of the German people to an extent to which no one can set limits."[75]

Churchill believed that western efforts to overcome the 1948-1949 Berlin blockade had demonstrated that "the future of Germany lies with the European family and with the glory and civilization of the West, to which the German race has still a measureless contribution to make."[76] The stakes in that confrontation with the Soviet Union in Berlin over the character of the new German state were high. "If we were to yield upon this grave issue," he warned at that time, "we should, in my opinion, destroy the best chance, which is now open to us, of escaping a third world war."[77] For this reason alone he resisted a neutral but unified Germany. Without Germany there could be no force in the West that could hold the balance with Soviet military power.[78]

Other reasons for his defense of Germany and Adenauer were diplomatic in character. To ask that Germany be armed and reunited, and that a general settlement with the Soviet Union be reached, was quixotic.[79] There also was the problem of France and the understandable fear of the French people in a unified Germany. France, Churchill frequently emphasized, was vital to peace in Europe and that, therefore, it was both critical and natural that she be on working terms with the new German state. It would be "a merciful and glorious forward step towards the revival of Europe and the peace of the world."[80] There were those who believed that the EDC was "too small a cage" to contain safely a rearmed Germany (meaning that some larger alliance system—such as NATO—would be more appropriate), a situation in which France would be left as the sole guarantor of an effective balance in Europe.[81] Whatever the French decided regarding the EDC and the status of West Germany, Churchill was resolved to have Germany participate in the future security arrangements.[82]

It was clear that the German problem had to be taken up if there was to be a general settlement between East and West. Germany was important for the West for the foundation of stability it could provide in Europe. On the other side, despite their militarily enhanced position along forward frontiers, the Soviet Union expressed real fears about a German revival. Churchill wrote that Stalin believed that within fifteen to twenty years after the war, aggressive German nationalism would once again bring war to Europe.[83] After the war, fears of "rollback" by forces directed by the United States and Great Britain haunted Soviet leaders.[84]

The extent to which the Kremlin viewed Germany's position within Europe to be militarily significant can be judged by the timing of the formation of the Warsaw Treaty Organization, formed only after Germany was admitted to NATO. Without German involvement, NATO evidently was not the same threat. The Soviet Union, it seemed, would have paid a very high price to keep Germany demilitarized between the years 1950 to 1954.[85] By 1954, the Soviet leaders had relinquished the objective of German reunification-neutralization and directed their efforts toward the isolation of West Germany. Their hope was to isolate Germany from Western Europe as a means of strengthening the communist regime in East Germany and extending it through the country as a whole.[86]

Thus, it was left to Churchill's Locarno suggestion to ease Soviet fears about the military reemergence of the German nation. The plan was not, as some of his critics suggested, a sellout of Germany; it was the solution to future negotiations with Soviet Russia, that is if Moscow could be convinced of the plan's viability. The plan also would enable Western Germany to remain free, independent, and armed, ready to contribute to the prosperity and security of a new Europe. The Soviet leaders, Churchill believed, were entitled to this reassurance arrangement. He told the conference at Bermuda, where the U.S., Britain, and France gathered on the fourth of December 4, 1953 to discuss the opportunities for novel diplomatic approaches to the Soviet Union: "We wish them [the Soviet leaders] no harm and would feel it our duty to help them if they were maltreated or assaulted, that we would instantly play our part on their side as intended if they were right."[87] The essence of the proposal was a collective security agreement, supported by the United States, France, and Great Britain—to rescue the Soviet Union in the event of renewed German aggression. Of course, the original Locarno Agreement did not prevent war, but Churchill then looked to the great advantage presented by the active involvement of the United States in the peacekeeping process.

The May 11 initiative was the prelude to a three-power conference in Bermuda to have been held in July 1953. Churchill's failure to attend the conference with the United States and France was due only to a massive stroke he suffered in June. Miraculously, Churchill was well on his way to recovery within a month's time, and he once again picked up on the idea of a summit conference.[88] Churchill's optimism demonstrated his tireless spirit in the face of great physical adversity.

During his recovery, Churchill continued to receive news of American doubt surrounding the idea of a conference. Eisenhower wrote to him on July 21 and expressed his understanding that it was dangerous "to talk generalities to the Russians unless and until their proposals for Germany and Austria show that we can depend on them. I like to keep talks informal with those I can trust as friends." Eisenhower was fearful of entrapment and embarrassment at the hands of the Russians.[89]

Churchill continued to believe that it was possible that significant changes could take place in the Soviet Union. He reportedly stated to Lord Moran, his physician, "I want to satisfy my conscience and my honour that the Russians are not just play-acting. I believe they do mean something."[90] Indeed, his plans for a visit with Malenkov sustained him throughout his struggle.[91]

Feeling compelled to stay in office, Churchill fought suggestions that he resign because he believed he could still have an influence. Some of Churchill's colleagues did not share his enthusiasm. Eden did not think the four-power conference would be as fruitful as Churchill did, and he dreaded approaching the Russians to discuss weighty matters of state without an agenda. Eden apparently was depressed with the direction in which events were leading the government.[92] Churchill persisted on his course of action, to which his speech of October 9, 1953 at Margate attested.

I asked for very little [on May 11, 1953]. I held out no glittering or exciting hopes about Russia. I thought that friendly, informal, personal talks between the leading figures in the countries mainly involved might do good and could not easily do much harm, and that one good thing might lead to another as I have just said. . . . [L]et us try to see whether there is not something better for us all than tearing and blasting each other to pieces, which we can certainly do.[93]

Churchill's hopes for a rapid four-power conference were diminished by a negative Soviet response to a meeting of the Foreign Ministers. This only compelled Churchill to attempt yet another three-power conference at Bermuda with Britain, the United States, and France in order to take stock of the situation with Russia and discuss other issues, including the EDC and Egypt. With minor reservations, Eisenhower accepted Churchill proposal, and the date of December 4 was chosen for the meeting.

This time the conference went on as scheduled in Bermuda, but the lack of collective enthusiasm for easing relations with the Soviet Union at the conference's end upset Churchill. Eden himself did not see much hope for improving the message of the conference communique. Churchill had additional problems with the American Secretary of State, John Foster Dulles, who was unlikely to change his mind about the benefits of a more positive approach to the Soviet Union. Churchill referred to him as "a terrible handicap."[94] In all of his efforts to persuade his own countrymen and allies, Churchill staunchly held to his view that reassuring the Russians "was a minor thing compared to the need of maintaining our unity and self-defense."[95] Churchill, however, did not want to miss an opportunity if one were presented.

The disappointment at Bermuda was not a major setback for Churchill and his plans. He insisted that the government's foreign policy in general be cognizant of the opportunity presented by the changes in Russia. He also pushed hard for trade, which he thought "would mean, not only assistance to our exports, but greater possibilities for infiltration behind the Iron Curtain."[96] These were proposals that the United States, again, could not wholeheartedly accept. Churchill, nonetheless, continued to argue that there was no contradiction between a policy of military preparedness in the free world (in particular the build up of NATO forces) and trying at the same time "to create conditions under which Russia may dwell easily and peacefully side by side with us all."[97]

Not until June 1954 was President Eisenhower finally receptive to Churchill's proposal for a summit, under the conditions that the meeting not take place anywhere under Soviet rule, that normal diplomatic channels be used (to hold down public expectations), and that France be included. Not too long after these agreements, however, events were to turn negatively on Churchill—in his own cabinet no less.

Members of his Cabinet were furious at Churchill's proposed informal head-to-head meeting with Malenkov, wherein he would look to arrange a meeting of the heads of government of the United States, Great Britain, and the Soviet Union. Lord Salisbury's vehement opposition to the plan (he threatened to resign if the meeting went ahead) led to the classification of the minutes as secret. Should Lord Salisbury resign, the whole idea of a summit would have become a political hot potato in both Great Britain and the United States, where anti-communist sentiment was especially strong. To lend a bit of irony to the situation, in the middle of this growing firestorm, Churchill's hopes for a summit were enhanced by a telegram he received from Foreign Minister Molotov. Molotov told Churchill that his personal contact initiative would be favorably received in Moscow.[98]

Churchill was criticized sharply by his colleagues for not consulting them before embarking on his foreign policy adventure. He expected that he would have the confidence of his cabinet when he dealt with other heads of state. Lord Salisbury and others, however, did not take so charitable a view. Lord Salisbury argued that the prime minister could determine policy, but if he "took a decision of policy which involved the collective responsibility of the whole Government without prior consultation with his Cabinet," any "who dissented from the decision might thereby be forced to the remedy of resignation." He viewed the message Churchill sent to Molotov as an important act of policy. Harry Crankshank concurred with Lord Salisbury that the message "was bound to commit the Government to some extent to the view that this was an opportune moment for a meeting of the kind suggested."[99]

Churchill underestimated the reaction of his colleagues and took a more apologetic defense of his action, stating that furthering the cause of world peace was urgent and that delay should be avoided. Eisenhower himself was supportive of the efforts Churchill made toward enhancing world peace. It had been agreed that the parties would meet on the basis of full equality, that the Soviets should give proof of their sincerity in deed and word, and that the ratification of an Austrian treaty was a good beginning.[100] Despite these reassurances from across the Atlantic, the appearance was growing that a breach had been created in Anglo-American relations.

On July 23, 1954, the cabinet debate reached its climax. Churchill was prepared once again to state his case for a meeting with the Russians. He insisted that the cabinet decide immediately whether there should be any further communications with Molotov and was prepared to send a telegram he had drafted with Eden that called for a summit in September between Britain and the Soviet Union. Churchill insisted also that he be allowed to continue his career-long practice of conducting personal correspondence with heads of state and that such conduct was not constitutionally improper. The cabinet, however, insisted that the contents of the telegram be consistent with the cabinet's views as a whole.

After a discussion of the threats the Soviet Union posed to world peace, the importance of unity within the alliance and between the United States and Great Britain, and the probability that any substantive agreement could be reached with the Soviet people, Churchill decided to withdraw his proposal to Malenkov for a personal meeting. According to Martin Gilbert, "nobody pressed Churchill to continue with his Malenkov plan. Churchill's last great foreign policy initiative was at an end."[101]

CHURCHILL'S SETTLEMENT OBJECTIVES

What were the motives behind Churchill's settlement initiative? Clearly he envisioned a peace of sorts, but what were its limits? What was the basis or foundation for this new peace? The remainder of this chapter will focus on these questions and examine the possibility that Churchill intended much more to happen with his proposal for East-West peace than the simple resumption of normal diplomatic ties. It may be argued that Churchill held out some hope for the possibility that his actions and the eventual reintroduction of the Soviet Union back into the international community would cause significant changes in the political makeup of that country. In other words, he may have desired to build a foundation for the new peace that would endure the upheavals and uncertainties of international politics. Through statesmanship, he sought what he often referred to as a lasting settlement. The nature of this kind of statesmanship will be explored below. We shall examine here the degree to which words and public diplomacy may affect political orders and the shape of the world Churchill yearned for and believed he could help bring about.

It is necessary to recognize that there are limits to statesmanship—that sometimes fortune and human nature will not respond favorably to human design. I would argue that Churchill operated at the very edge and that his chances for significantly influencing political events in the Soviet Union and Soviet foreign policy probably were very remote. Nonetheless, Churchill believed confidently in his own abilities as a statesman. As shall be demonstrated, he evidently desired more than just a paper agreement with the Soviet leaders.

One can only speculate as to why Churchill believed he could fashion a more acceptable world. Clearly he was a man with a sense of duty to his country. While campaigning for his reelection in 1950 and 1951, Churchill told of his heart-felt obligation to lead Britain on the path to greater prosperity and peace—he still believed Britain had a diminished but yet major role to play in world affairs. "We in this small Island have to make a supreme effort to keep our place and station to which our underlying genius entitles us."[102] He lamented the decline of Britain's influence to shape world events, but believed her leaders nonetheless had the obligation to press forward with their ideas if for no other reason than that the world needed the input of a good and decent people.[103]

There was also a need to show that his statesmanship could be as brilliant in peace as it had been in war. He believed that a golden opportunity had been wrested from him when he lost his 1945 reelection bid. He passed along these reflections in March 1959. "I was astonished at the result of the 1945 election. I thought it would be much more beneficial to the country to allow the Government that won the war to win the peace. I have never felt more sure of this than I do now."[104] The best opportunity for him had been lost perhaps, yet he was convinced that there still would be others. The best of those opportunities for winning the peace, he believed, came when Stalin died.[105]

The question that Churchill wrestled with since the end of the war was how to effect change in Moscow. His interest in change did not blind him to the intransigence of the Soviet problem; time may have even strengthened his appreciation for the persistence and solidity of the Soviet regime. This being the case, other provisions had to be in place to secure what peace there was.

Ideological realities forced Churchill to search beyond the clash between Marxism-Leninism and democratic liberalism. Clearly, normal diplomatic approaches and appeals to reason would fail. Perhaps the key lay in what Churchill referred to as "Russian interests." "It is idle to reason or argue with the Communists," he believed. On the level of doctrine and political conviction, a reasonable accommodation was virtually impossible. It was, however, possible to deal with the Communists "on a fair, realistic basis, and, in my experience, they will keep their bargains as long as it is in their interest to do so, which might . . . be a long time, once things were settled."[106] (This thought is not as naive as it may look upon first reading. That any party will keep a bargain as long as it is in their interest, assuming rational behavior, is as sure a bet as one could make in international politics.) Churchill tried to measure Russian interests at that moment in history. This was the key to successful diplomacy.[107] "My hope," Churchill declared in May 1953, "is that it is their self-interest which will bring about an easier state of affairs."[108]

This appeal to interest would be all the more successful if it were done while the West had military superiority (a factor no doubt very significant to Soviet calculations of interest). To strike a bargain with the Soviets, he believed, favorable conditions were vitally important. If you wish for peace, he said in 1949, "it is absolutely necessary that you should be stronger" and that you "stop at nothing that honour allows."[109]

Aside from military weakness, Churchill recognized that an appeal to interest could be limited by other factors as well. Interest "is, at any rate, the only guide—and it does not include accident, passion, folly or madness, madness which may arise from some error, some blunder, or from the results of some internal convulsion."[110]

Interest also was limited by the nature of the governments involved and the quality of the leaders that were to be dealt with. Churchill clearly realized the task before him was monumental if only because he was dealing with a political order that operated on principles diametrically opposed to those he believed in. On the other hand, the regime also was set up so that decisions were taken only "by a handful of able men."[111] While a situation such as this was inimical to good government, it did provide for the quick implementation of policy once a few men were persuaded as to a more advantageous course. The influence of a few could change a lot. Churchill no doubt had this in mind whenever he insisted that negotiations proceed through personal contacts, in isolation from diplomatic constraints and bureaucracy. He knew that he was appealing to men who had the ability to make major changes and influence the future course of events. Stalin, he believed, had within him the capacity for statesmanship and "the sovereign remedial functions."[112] Malenkov, of course, had the advantage of appearing on the scene at the most propitious time for a change in policy as Stalin's successor. Interest, despite these limitations, was the only leverage available to Churchill to effect change and he had resolved to use it.

What was it that Churchill believed was in the Russian national interest? The Fulton speech gives us some indication of his estimation of these interests. Churchill hinted that this new world would be one where the spread of destructive revolutionary propaganda by the Communists would be halted in return for recognition and normal diplomatic ties with the rest of the world. Oppression in overrun countries would be thrust aside by the people. Trade would be allowed to flourish and Soviet ships would be welcomed on the high seas.[113] At Fulton, Churchill, aside from warning the West about the growing dangers, attempted to explain the benefits to be derived from peaceful interaction and friendship between countries that were once comrades in arms. Before the major powers embroiled themselves in the second world war, Churchill was equally candid about his hopes that the Soviet Union would one day join the international community. The conditions he envisioned back in November 1936 were as follows:

Negotiation and Persuasion 151

Now surely the time has come when Russia should choose once and for all her path to safety. Stalin, with the chiefs of the Russian army and the leaders of Russian foreign policy, should disperse and eradicate the Comintern. They should present themselves to Europe as a Soviet Socialist state strongly armed to maintain its national independence, and absolutely divorced form any idea of spreading its doctrines abroad otherwise than by example.

Such a step, taken now, and proved to the satisfaction of every country which desires to preserve peace and bears goodwill to the Russian people, would enormously reduce world tension and increase the prospects of Russian safety.[114]

These words written by Churchill easily could have been placed within his speeches of the early 1950s, once again testimony to his remarkable consistency. These benefits he believed were entirely within Soviet self-interest and in the interest of the world. Churchill explained to Eisenhower in July 1954 that he believed the Soviets would be "attracted by the idea of a peaceful period of domestic prosperity and external contacts. This is certainly my view of what is in their self-interest."[115]

The appeal to Russian self-interest did not mean that other countries would not benefit from the newly established peace. On the contrary, a lasting settlement was intended to multiply prosperity and plenty throughout the world. Trade, without question, so long as it was friendly, would be welcomed by all.

When there is so much prosperity for everybody round the corner and within our reach it cannot do anything but good to interchange merchandise and services on an increasing scale. The more the two great divisions of the world mingle in the healthy and fertile activities of commerce the greater is the counterpoise to purely military calculations. Other thoughts take up their place in the minds of men. Friendly infiltration can do nothing but good. We have no reason to fear it and if Communist Russia does not fear it, that, in itself, is a good sign.[116]

It would be a mistake, however, to associate Churchill too closely with the interdependence theorists of today. Churchill recognized that political factors ultimately determined relationships, and international trade was but one avenue of influence. Trade was not expected to lead the world inexorably to peace.[117]

Churchill believed that the realities that confronted the world were "numerous, adverse, and stubborn." However, he warned that emotions could sometimes get the best of people and cause unhealthy policy swings, and that therefore a steady and measured course needed to be set so that all involved could benefit. "[T]he creation of a new atmosphere and climate of thought, and of a revived relationship and sense of human comradeship," he maintained, "would be an enormous gain to all nations."[118] The duties and interests of East and West were such that both sides should strive to outlive their differences. Should this come about, the self-destruction that science has enabled men to accomplish could be used to create instead a "vision of plenty and comfort," comfort "of which masses of no race have ever known or even dreamed."[119] Satisfying the needs and interests of the major countries, Churchill reasoned, could be the start of lasting stability and peace in Europe and the world.

Human comradeship, or friendship, was the vehicle Churchill chose on his journey to establish a more stable peace. Malice would not serve his purpose. Churchill's earlier views on communism would seem to belie such an approach. After all, he did express in June 1919 the following opinions on the Bolsheviks.

> Theirs is a war against civilised society which can never end. They seek as the first condition of their being the overthrow and destruction of all existing institutions and of every State and Government now standing in the world. They too aim at a worldwide and international league, but a league of the failures, the criminals, the unfit, the mutinous, the morbid, the deranged, and the distraught in every land; and between them and such order of civilisation as we have been able to build up since the dawn of history there can, as Lenin rightly proclaims, be neither truce nor pact.[120]

The rise of the Soviet Union to the status of a major power, the comradeship developed between East and West in the defeat of Nazism, and the urgent task to found a more lasting peace in an age of nuclear weapons all conspired to change the parameters Churchill used to view the communist regime.

Since before the end of the war, Churchill had been obsessed with the unpleasant prospect that the world would be divided into two warring camps. Such a condition, he wrote to Stalin in April 1945 (and recited to the Commons in February 1950), "would be a disaster hampering the great developments of world prosperity for the masses which are attainable only by our trinity."[121] Churchill's immediate concern was to fashion a relationship that would not lead to conflict and cause horrible dislocations in the world. He emphasized that governments were made for men and not men for governments; but "if the Soviets really like being governed by officials in a sealed pattern, *and so long as they do not endanger the safety or freedom of others*, that is a matter for them to decide themselves for themselves."[122] This meant that the West had to be resolved to maintain its unity and self-defense to guard against the times when Moscow did "behave badly."[123] The idea, Churchill confided to his cabinet in January 1952, was to get the Soviet leaders to "fear our enmity more than our friendship" so that they would seek the friendship of the West.[124]

Even back as far as 1918, however, despite his belief that "no real harmony [was] possible between Bolshevism and present civilization," he urged his countrymen to "trust for better or for worse to peaceful influences to bring about the disappearance of this awful tyranny and peril."[125] This realization did not prevent him from preparing the West for war, if necessary, against communist aggression. His efforts in both these directions intensified only after the formation of the Grand Alliance with Stalin. He assured Stalin near the war's end that arrangements for a better friendship would be made upon the condition that Europe be permitted to begin her recovery. He wrote that in these matters there would be no secrets, as long as Stalin kept Great Britain and the United States equally informed of what he needed. Friendship, he recognized, had to work both ways.[126]

Established friendship among states was the greatest assurance that a third disastrous war would be avoided.[127] The division of Europe into two warring parts was not Churchill's aim; he sought, rather, Europe's transformation and eventual reunification. "Let there be sunshine on both sides of the Iron Curtain; and if ever the sunshine should be equal on both sides, the Curtain will be no more."[128] Anyone could join the Club of Europe as long as they were sincerely attracted by its principles.[129] For this reason, he persistently advocated that a door be left open to the Soviet leaders. He repeated these sentiments in February 1950.

At least I feel that Christian men should not close the door upon any hope of finding a new foundation for the life of the self-tormented human race. What prizes lie before us; peace, food, happiness, leisure, wealth for the masses never known or dreamed of; the glorious advance into a period of rest and safety for all.[130]

These reflection also help to explain the moral of Churchill's World War II memoirs: In War: Resolution; In Defeat: Defiance; In Victory: Magnanimity; In Peace: *Goodwill*.

After the war, Churchill attempted to bring civility back into international relations; he sought to renew respect for lawful international conduct. Nothing short of both physical and moral strength would suffice in support of these objectives and prevent the drift into war. His attempts to cultivate friendship with Soviet Russia meant the removal of oppression from the heart of Europe. "There will never be a settled peace in Europe while Asiatic Imperialism and Communist domination rule over the whole of Central and Eastern Europe."[131] The West should at least be strong enough to hold out for the opportunity (the sort of opportunity, for example, that Russian leader Boris Yeltsin presented to the world following the August 1991 coup in the Soviet Union and the subsequent dissolution of that empire) when the winds of change in Moscow will blow in the West's favor. Contrary to what one might be led to think, Churchill was wary of Malenkov and Khrushchev. He asked that vigilance not be relaxed and that strength not be left to dwindle, "to await developments in hopeful and, I trust, a helpful mood."[132]

The peace that rested on the establishment of a Western military alliance and the possession of the atomic bomb was sound, but it left international conditions in a state conducive to war. In other words, it was Churchill's hope to "find our way to some more exalted and august foundation for our safety than this grim and sombre balancing power of the bomb."[133] The beginning of such a peace had to be based on the manifest interests of all sides to form new and routine relationships, to form what Churchill referred to as a "workaday understanding" with the Soviet people and government.[134] As relations developed through these channels, the possibilities that more fundamental agreements may be reached would increase. Churchill never viewed such an approach in isolation from other political realities, but viewed it as one of the (few) possible steps available that promised to reach beyond the threshold.

Increasing contact and trade alone would not build a new world. The new interactions would have to lead to an easing of relations and then to agreements on principle and political purposes. All of this would be done in the interest of "peace and plenty."[135] By interesting the Soviet leaders in the objectives of peace and plenty, Churchill not only sought closer contacts with the Soviet people and government for the people and governments of the West. He also recognized that the efficient production of prosperity meant the adoption, or approximation, of a free-market economy. Churchill's view of what constituted a stable, healthy, prosperous domestic economy reminds one very strongly of those ideas expressed by Adam Smith, the father of modern-day capitalism.[136]

Churchill's political economy also stressed the need for governments to reorganize themselves to institutionalize the economy so that it would be inclined to growth and the creation of wealth for the whole society.

It is not nature which has failed mankind. It is Governments, which, misled and steeped in folly or perversity, have rejected and squandered the fruits of nature, endeavoring to prevent the normal working of its processes, even though those fruits are presented by the ever-more efficient servitors of an ever-widening science.[137]

By making prosperity a goal of the Soviet leaders, Churchill no doubt hoped to effect real changes in the mechanics of the Soviet government. A society more inclined toward the creation of wealth and concerned for the material well-being of its citizenry would be less inclined to have a foreign policy favoring aggrandizement and more inclined to work for peaceful international relations. Trade, after all, is a mutually beneficial activity.

Churchill believed in the possibilities of this approach because he perceived a "deep underlying demand on the part of the Russian people to enjoy a better life, particularly after suffering oppression for more than fifty years."[138] Science, he repeatedly stated, was better harnessed by man in the interest of his prosperity and well-being and not for the instruments of destruction it could offer. Twentieth century science could permit governments to achieve that which was considered impossible in all previous centuries—the relief of the lot of the masses.[139] He said to the House on October 9, 1954 that ever since Stalin's death,

I have cherished the hope that there is a new outlook in Russia, a new hope of peaceful co-existence with the Russian nation and that it is our duty, patiently and daringly, to make sure whether there is such a change or not. It is certainly the interest of the Russian people, who have experienced a terrible half-century of war, revolution, and famine, it is certainly in their interest--and interest is always a thing we should consider in estimating the conduct of foreign countries—it is certainly in their interest to have an easier and more prosperous generation with more food, more fun, and more friends.[140]

Previously it was stated that Churchill did not mind what form of government the Soviet people desired for themselves, "so long as they do not endanger the safety and freedom of others." This did not mean Churchill was indifferent to the form of that government. It may be argued that Churchill never lost faith that the nature of the Soviet regime would change to the benefit of the common man and that he believed himself capable, through a subversive diplomacy, of effecting that change. Churchill attempted to rid the world of the communist menace through the vehicle of friendship and increasing ties. If this failed, he saw to it that the West should have the strength to make sure that communism did not expand. The peace could be kept by either approach, only Churchill considered the product of peace secured through negotiation and persuasion more "exalted and august."

The best publicity for the Soviet Union, Churchill believed, "would be the happiness and well being of her people."[141] The hope, in the end, was for a confident easing of relations among the major states, or peaceful international relations.

The Soviets hope that the doctrine of Karl Marx may eventually prevail. *We on our side trust and believe that as the mild and ameliorating influence of prosperity begins at last to uplift the Communist world, so they will be more inclined to live at ease with their neighbors.* This is our hope. We must not be rigid in our expression of it; we must make allowance for justifiable Russian fears; we must be patient and firm.[142]

International organizations also would assist significantly in the transformation of behavior that Churchill clearly believed was possible. For this reason he talked of a "real" United Nations, one "with Russia working with the rest for the good of Europe," and, it could be added, for the good of the world.[143] Churchill left the London audience attending his speech of November 9, 1954 with the following message of hope: "I look forward to the time when . . . having brought about a stability and a common purpose in the West, we shall have established the essential basis on which we can seek an understanding with the East. Thus we may by patience, courage, and in orderly progression reach the shelter of a calmer and kindlier age."[144]

NOTES

1. Churchill, *The Gathering Storm*, pp. 376-377.

2. Churchill, *Complete Speeches*, p. 8,604. Churchill believed that a unified Europe was a blessing regardless of the existence of the Soviet menace. "It would be quite fair to ask me whether I should have welcomed this event even if there were no such thing as this Russian menace, or the Soviet Government or the Communist movement in many lands. I should say, 'Yes, certainly'" (Churchill, *Complete Speeches*, p. 8,023).

3. Churchill, *Complete Speeches*, p. 8,132.

4. Churchill, *Complete Speeches*, pp. 8,072 and 7,952. See also Gilbert, *Never Despair*, p. 279.

5. See for example Churchill's masterful essay "The Scaffolding of Rhetoric" in Randolph S. Churchill, *Winston S. Churchill: Companion Volume 1; Part 2 1896-*

1900 (London: Heinemann 1967), pp. 816-821, and L. P. Arnn, "Principles and Phrases: The Place of Rhetoric in the Statesmanship of Winston Churchill," *Rhetoric and American Statesmanship*, ed. Glen Thurow and Jeffrey D. Wallin (Durham, NC: Carolina Academic Press and The Claremont Institute for the Study of Statesmanship and Political Philosophy, 1984), pp. 123-151.

6. Churchill, *Complete Speeches*, p. 7,484.

7. Kenneth Thompson observed, *Churchill's World View*, p. 302, that "Churchill's avowed objective was that the major powers not rule the whole world but that they prevent the nations from tearing themselves to pieces."

8. Churchill, "Consistency in Politics," *Thoughts and Adventures*, p. 24.

9. Gilbert, *Never Despair*, p. 239.

10. Churchill, *Complete Speeches*, p. 7,242.

11. Cited by Gilbert, *Never Despair*, pp. 24-25.

12. Churchill, *Complete Speeches*, p. 7,985.

13. Gilbert, *Never Despair*, pp. 691-692.

14. Churchill, *Complete Speeches*, p. 7,708. In that same speech (p. 7,709) he stressed that "while patience should be practiced to the utmost limits which our safety allows, we should not delude ourselves with the vain expectation of a change of heart in the ruling forces of Communist Russia."

15. Thompson, *Churchill's World View*, p. 7.

16. Churchill, *Complete Speeches*, p. 7,770.

17. See Gilbert, *Never Despair*, p. 1,080.

18. Churchill, *Step By Step*, p. 152.

19. See Churchill, *Triumph and Tragedy*, p. 575.

20. Gilbert, *Never Despair*, p. 690.

21. Churchill, *Complete Speeches*, p. 8,640.

22. Churchill, *Complete Speeches*, p. 8,143. See also Gilbert, *Never Despair*, p. 529. See also *Triumph and Tragedy*, p. 326.

23. Gilbert, *Never Despair*, p. 467.

24. Ulam, *Expansion and Coexistence*, pp. 408-409.

25. See for example Churchill, *Complete Speeches*, p. 7,401, and *Their Finest Hour*, p. 134. See also Anthony Adamthwaite, "Overstretched and Overstrung: Eden, the Foreign Office and the Making of Policy, 1951-5," *International Affairs* (UK), Spring 1988, p. 251.

26. Colville, *The Fringes of Power*, p. 633.

27. Gilbert, *Never Despair*, p. 869.

28. See Moran, *The Struggle for Survival*, pp. 473, 481. The importance of the personal and informal approach in diplomacy was emphasized by Churchill in his *Marlborough*, bk. 2, p. 500. "It is often inevitable that the first overtures of peace should be made by secret and informal means."

29. Churchill, *Complete Speeches*, p. 7,794.

30. Churchill, *Complete Speeches*, p. 7,351.

31. Churchill, *Complete Speeches*, p. 8,131.

32. Gilbert, *Never Despair*, p. 533.

33. Churchill, *Complete Speeches*, p. 7,817. See also pp. 7,726-7,727, (the A-bomb and U.S. commitment to Europe "alone . . . prevents the rebarbarization and enslavement of Europe by the Communist forces directed from the Kremlin"), 7,246, 7,978, 7,984, 8,006, 8,050, 8,063, 8,573.

34. Churchill remarked that a final settlement was necessary for peace, for he could not rid his mind of the fear that the victorious armies of democracy would soon disperse (Churchill, *Triumph and Tragedy*, p. 570).

35. Churchill, *Complete Speeches*, p. 8,574.

36. Gilbert, *Never Despair*, p. 680. "It is of vital consequence to these hopes of world peace that what the Communists have begun in Korea should not end in their triumph. If that were to happen a third world war, under conditions even more deadly than now exist, would certainly be forced upon us." (Churchill, *Complete Speeches*, p. 8,033).

37. Gilbert, *Never Despair*, p. 464.

38. See for example Churchill, *Complete Speeches*, pp. 7,206, 7,709, 7,806, 8,039, 8,064, 8,549-8,550, 8,629.

39. Gilbert, *Never Despair*, p. 468. See also p. 575, where Churchill deplored the adoption of a "no first use" policy. See also Churchill, *Complete Speeches*, p. 8,143.

40. Churchill, *Complete Speeches*, 8,620. See also pp. 8,629-8,631. Reflecting new attitudes about defense, Churchill insisted that the western powers "must put themselves in a position to ensure that no surprise attack, however large, could wholly destroy their power of effective retaliation" (Gilbert, *Never Despair*, p. 1,019). He also noted that certain factors, such as "superiority," would lose much of their meaning once a great quantity of nuclear weapons were produced together with novel (i.e., faster and more accurate) forms of delivery. He was also convinced that a "powerful incentive to achieve surprise would be given to the weaker," in effect casting this novel form of warfare in terms that would find their place in the defense jargon of the United States from the early 1960s to the present (Thomas Schelling being among the first of the defense intellectuals to speak in these terms in *The Strategy of Conflict*, 1960). (See Gilbert, *Never Despair*, p. 959.)

41 Churchill, *Complete Speeches*, p. 8,039. See also pp. 7,709, 8,064, 8,629. The new nuclear relationship led to Churchill's famous appraisal of the foundation of present-day peace. "[I]t may well be that we shall by a process of sublime irony have reached a stage in this story where safety will be the sturdy child of terror, and survival the twin brother of annihilation" (Churchill, *Complete Speeches*, p. 8,629). See also Colville, *The Fringes of Power*, pp. 675-676.

42. Churchill, *Complete Speeches*, 7,710. See also p. 8,038 and Gilbert, *Never Despair*, p. 440.

43. Cited by Gilbert, *Never Despair*, p. 510.

44. *Hansard*, vol. 498, c. 2279.

45. Statement of November 12, 1951, *Hansard*, vol. 493, c. 644.

46. See statement of Winston Churchill of June 16, 1952, *Hansard*, vol. 502, c. 777.

47. The other side to this view also at various times was presented by Churchill. For one, his personal relationship with Stalin, cultivated during the war years, always led Churchill to believe that he had an inside opportunity that no other statesman in the world could take advantage of. Another reason that Churchill may have desired to deal with Stalin rather than his successors was revealed by Colville in *The Fringes of Power*, p. 650: "He [Churchill] told me that if Eisenhower were elected President, he would have another shot at making peace by means of a meeting of the Big Three. . . . He thought that while Stalin lived we were safer from attack than if he died and his

lieutenants started scrambling for the succession." See also *Complete Speeches*, p. 8,598.

48. Ulam, *Expansion and Coexistence*, p. 402.

49. Churchill, like Eisenhower, immediately upon the death of Stalin was alert to any change in Soviet behavior or mood. See Gilbert, *Never Despair*, p. 818. See also p. 806, pp. 812-813 and Moran, *The Struggle for Survival*, p. 429.

50. See Churchill, *Complete Speeches*, p. 8,329.

51. Cited by Gilbert, *Never Despair*, pp. 1,047-1,048.

52. Churchill, *Complete Speeches*, p. 8,483. The speech can be found on pp. 8,475-8,485.

53. Ulam, *Expansion and Coexistence*, p. 159.

54. According to Anthony Adamthwaite, "Overstretched and Overgrowing," pp. 251-252, Churchill was frequently at odds with his own Foreign Secretary, Anthony Eden, over issues of foreign policy. Eden, in fact, had some reservations about Churchill's summit initiative.

55. Colville, *The Fringes of Power*, p. 667.

56. Speech of May 12, 1953, *Hansard*, vol. 515, c. 974.

57. Speech of May 11, 1953, *Hansard*, vol. 515, c. 898 and 899.

58. Speech of May 11, 1953, *Hansard*, vol. 515, c. 923.

59. Speech of May 11, 1953, *Hansard*, vol. 515, c. 934.

60. Speech of May 11, 1953, *Hansard*, vol. 515, c. 958 and 959.

61. Speech of May 12, 1953, *Hansard*, vol. 515, c. 1154.

62. Speech of May 12, 1953, *Hansard*, vol. 515, c. 1115.

63. Speech of May 12, 1953, *Hansard*, vol. 515, c. 1176.

64. Speech of May 11, 1953, *Hansard*, vol. 515, c. 953-954.

65. Speech of May 12, 1953, *Hansard*, vol. 515, c. 1120-1121.

66. Speech of May 11, 1953, *Hansard*, vol. 515, c. 932. Hynd, incidentally, ardently opposed Churchill's plans for a united and militarily strong Europe.

67. Speech of May 12, 1953, *Hansard*, vol. 515, c. 1103.

68. Speech of May 12, 1953, *Hansard*, vol. 515, c. 1141.

69. Emotional reactions to an armed German state were prevalent in Britain. Not until December 1950, after it was evident that the Conservatives were making a comeback (they narrowly missed achieving a majority in the House in elections held earlier that year), that Prime Minister Clement Attlee committed Great Britain to German rearmament. See Gilbert, *Never Despair*, p. 575.

70. Churchill, *Complete Speeches*, pp. 8,598-8,599.

71. Cited in Gilbert, *Never Despair*, p. 774. In the same speech delivered in November 1952, Churchill praised the work of Konrad Adenauer and Robert Schuman in unifying Europe and also declared that "there can be no effective defense of European culture and freedom unless a new Germany, resolved to set itself free from the ghastly crimes of Hitlerism, plays a strong and effective part in our system." In February 1954 he explained to the Commons why Germany should be considered part of the European family: "My deep feeling to-day is that the horrors of war have sunk deep into the German mind, and still deeper is the fear and hatred of Soviet domination" (Churchill, *Complete Speeches*, p. 8,536).

72. Churchill, *Closing the Ring*, p. 374. In order for Germany to make a meaningful contribution to the common defense, Churchill would later call for the release of the German admirals and generals from prison so that Germany might draw upon the invaluable military experience and leadership these men could provide (Gilbert,

Never Despair, p. 637). See also *Complete Speeches*, p. 8,611, where Churchill argued with House members in favor of using German troops to beat back Soviet advancing forces in the event of war.

73. Churchill, *Complete Speeches*, p. 7,302.

74. Well before the Americans conceded the point, Churchill urged the allies to include West Germany within the NATO alliance and argued against the suggestions that the United States move to peripheral positions on the continent, effectively creating a power vacuum in the heart of Europe. See Colville, *The Fringes of Power*, p. 687.

75. Churchill, *Complete Speeches*, p. 8,537.

76. Churchill, *Complete Speeches*, p.7,711. The Berlin Blockade was, in part, an early attempt by the Soviet Union to weaken the Western commitment to West Germany before it developed into a viable republic. Churchill thought of the confrontation as a battle for "the soul of Germany." See, for example, Gilbert, *Never Despair*, p. 432.

77. Churchill, *Complete Speeches*, p. 7,681.

78. Gilbert, *Never Despair*, p. 279, 842.

79. Colville, *The Fringes of Power*, p. 686.

80. Churchill, *Complete Speeches*, p. 8,023.

81. See Mr. Gordon Walker's speech of November 5, 1953, *Hansard*, c. 339.

82. Churchill, *Complete Speeches*, pp. 8,495-8,496. "If the European Defense Community should not be adopted by the French, we shall have no choice in prudence but to fall in with some new arrangement which will join the strength of Germany to the Western allies through some rearrangement of what is called NATO. You [the House] must not mind my putting these things plainly to you because I have had a life of experience in the matter and I am bound to say that I feel that every word that I am now saying gives us the best chance of securing the peaceful development of the world."

83. Churchill, *Closing the Ring*, pp. 359-360.

84. See Ulam, *Expansion and Coexistence*, pp. 449-451.

85. Ulam, *Expansion and Coexistence*, p. 508.

86. Speech of Anthony Eden, February 24, 1954, *Hansard*, c. 409. He also reiterated Britain's persistent position that "a policy of permanent disarmament and neutralization of Germany is not a practical proposition and it abounds in the gravest danger."

87. Gilbert, *Never Despair*, p. 935. Lord Moran reported these words of Churchill: "The Germans are taking my line. They want a Locarno. America must be ready to attack Germany if she should attack Russia, while if Russia is the aggressor America would declare war on her" (Moran, *The Struggle for Survival*, p. 473).

88. Gilbert, *Never Despair*, p. 863.

89. Gilbert, *Never Despair*, p. 865.

90. Moran, *The Struggle for Survival*, p. 475.

91. Moran, *The Struggle for Survival*, p. 483.

92. Gilbert, *Never Despair*, pp. 893-94.

93. Cited by Gilbert, *Never Despair*, p. 895.

94. Cited by Gilbert, *Never Despair*, p. 936.

95. Cited by Gilbert, *Never Despair*, p. 935.

96. Cited by Gilbert, *Never Despair*, p. 944.

97. Cited by Gilbert, *Never Despair*, p. 955.

98. Gilbert, *Never Despair*, p. 1,020-1,021.
99. Cited by Gilbert, *Never Despair*, p. 1,024.
100. Gilbert, *Never Despair*, pp. 1,030-1,031.
101. Gilbert, *Never Despair*, p. 1,036. For greater details on Churchill's problems with the cabinet, see pp. 1,018-1,041.
102. Churchill spoke these words in a speech to the boys at Harrow, his old school. Cited by Gilbert, *Never Despair*, p. 773. See also p. 896.
103. Cited in Gilbert, *Never Despair*, p. 643.
104. Churchill, *Complete Speeches*, p. 8,691.
105. Even after his May 11, 1953 initiative perished, he was convinced that his plan rested on a solid foundation. See Gilbert, *Never Despair*, p. 1,070.
106. Churchill, *Complete Speeches*, p. 7,589. As early as October 1939, Churchill believed that Russia was "a riddle wrapped in a mystery inside an enigma." But he also thought, "perhaps there is a key. That key is Russian national interest" (Churchill, *Triumph and Tragedy*, p. 449). See also p. 7,799: "It's no good trying to convert a communist, or persuade him."
107. Churchill, *Complete Speeches* (December 1954), p. 8,619. See also p. 8,504: The best guide to Soviet behavior—"What are their interests?"
108. Cited by Gilbert, *Never Despair*, p. 828.
109. Churchill, *Complete Speeches*, p. 7,799.
110. Churchill, *Complete Speeches*, p. 8,131.
111. See, for example, Churchill, *Complete Speeches*, p. 7,300.
112. See Smith, "Winston Churchill and the Rise of Totalitarianism," p. 18. See also Churchill, *Step By Step*, pp. 66-67.
113. Churchill wrote in his *Closing the Ring* (p. 382) that he was entirely responsive to the Soviet desire for warm-water ports in the postwar world. "I wished to meet the Russian grievance, because the government of the world must be entrusted to satisfy nations, who wished nothing more for themselves than what they had."
114. Churchill, *Step By Step*, pp. 66-67.
115. See Gilbert, *Never Despair*, p. 1,027.
116. Churchill, *Complete Speeches*, p. 8,536. See also p. 7,474: "We earnestly hope that all the peoples of Russia may be safe, prosperous and happy under whatever form of Government they may choose or may accept. We wish them well and will welcome every possibility of increasing trade and intercourse between our countries in order to give each a better understanding of the other."
117. In volume four of his *A History of the English Speaking Peoples*, p. 67, Churchill poked some criticism at a few mid-nineteenth century interdependence theorists. British industry "would be international, proclaiming the benefits of free trade between nations and looking forward to the universal peace which it was then supposed must inevitably result from the unhampered traffic in goods. Few people foresaw the war with Russia that was soon to break out." For further reading on modern-day interdependence theory, see James E. Dougherty and Robert L Pfaltzgraff, *Contending Theories of International Relations: A Comprehensive Study* (New York: Harper & Row, Publishers, 1981), chapter 10, pp. 417-467.
118. See Gilbert, *Never Despair*, p. 660.
119. Gilbert, *Never Despair*, p. 992.
120. Gilbert, *The Stricken World*, p. 903. See also p. 440: "The policy I will always advocate is the overthrow and destruction of that criminal regime."
121. Churchill, *Complete Speeches*, p. 7,944.

122. Churchill, *Complete Speeches*, p. 8,603. Emphasis added.
123. Gilbert, *Never Despair*, p. 927.
124. Gilbert, *Never Despair*, p. 678. See also Acheson, *Present at the Creation*, p. 599.
125. Gilbert, *Churchill's Political Philosophy*, p. 80.
126. Churchill, *Triumph and Tragedy*, p. 255.
127. Churchill, *Complete Speeches*, p. 7,322: "The more closely the largest Powers of to-day are bound together in bonds of faith and friendship the more effective will be the safeguards against war and the higher the security of all other states and nations."
128. Churchill, *Complete Speeches*, p. 7,509. Many of Churchill's words and reflections on the plight of Europe and his own hopes for her recovery are reminiscent of President Lincoln's objective of healing the wounds of a republic divided. He spoke these words at his second inauguration: "With malice toward none; with charity for all; with firmness in the right, as God gives us to see the right, let us strive on to finish the work we are in; to bind up the nation's wounds; to care for him who shall have borne the battle, and for his widow, and his orphan—to do all which may achieve and cherish a just and lasting peace among ourselves, and with all nations." Churchill ended his speech, cited above, "with malice to none and with hope for all."
129. Churchill, *Complete Speeches*, p. 7,508-7,509. See also pp. 7,901 and 8,052.
130. Churchill, *Complete Speeches*, p. 7,944. See also p. 8,633: "The day may dawn when fair play, love for one's fellow-men, respect for justice and freedom, will enable tormented generations to march forth serene and triumphant from the hideous epoch in which we have to dwell. Meanwhile, never flinch, never weary, never despair."
131. Cited by Gilbert, *Never Despair*, p. 400. See also Churchill, *Triumph and Tragedy*, pp. 579-580.
132. Churchill, *Complete Speeches*, p. 8,503.
133. Churchill, *Complete Speeches*, p. 7,943. This approach, he often stressed, should "not lead to appeasement that compels any nation to submit to foreign domination" (pp. 8,584-85).
134. Churchill, *Complete Speeches*, p. 8,535.
135. Churchill, *Complete Speeches*, p. 8,619.
136. See, for example, Churchill, *Complete Speeches*, p. 7,218: "The production of new wealth must precede common wealth, otherwise there will only be common poverty." (The creation of new wealth tends to have a multiplier effect throughout the rest of the society.) See also, pp. 7,263-7,264 and 7,544-7,545.
137. Churchill, *Complete Speeches*, p. 7,545.
138. Cited by Gilbert, *Never Despair*, p. 998.
139. See, for example, Colville, *The Fringes of Power*, p. 673.
140. Churchill, *Complete Speeches*, p. 8,599. See also p. 8,574: The Russian people "would dearly love the easement and the leisure, the comfort and the diversions, which could be theirs should those who rule them so decide."
141. Cited by Gilbert, *Never Despair*, p. 77.
142. Churchill, *Complete Speeches*, p. 8,694. Emphasis added.
143. Moran, *The Struggle for Survival*, p. 456.
144. Churchill, *Complete Speeches*, p. 8,604.

Chapter 7

Conclusion

I only remain in politics because I think it my duty to try to prevent the great position we won in the war being cast away by folly, and worse than folly, on the morrow of our victory.

—Winston Churchill
December 6, 1945
House of Commons

Churchill attempted to use the magnificent victory fashioned by the Grand Alliance to fix upon the world a lasting peace, or perhaps more accurate yet, a peace that rested upon a solid foundation, one that could not be easily overturned by folly or design. He did not place his greatest faith, we have seen, in the protection offered by the balancing power of the bomb. Rock-solid peace could come only when the major military and economic powers had "a workaday understanding" with one another. Churchill took up this task with relish, for it meant that he could play a great role in the salvation of his own country and perhaps even the world. "We ought to rejoice at the responsibilities with which destiny has honored us," he said in April 1953, "and be proud that we are the guardians of our country in an age when her life is at stake."[1]

War, as Churchill understood it, was one of the few constants in international politics. International conflicts are natural to the world, a manifestation of intense national disagreement caused by opposing ambitions and ideological competition. These facts do not mean, however, that wars are inevitable. There are many factors that figure into the causes of war, including that of statesmanship. Churchill, as he consistently demonstrated throughout his career, possessed seemingly limitless faith in his own abilities to shape the world around him. It was the duty of statesmen, he believed, to educate themselves in the ways of the world, to recognize the actions that may lead to international hostilities and to make a tolerable peace their aim. The responsibilities of the statesman are great, for his decisions affect the lives of many millions. He also must aim, therefore, at justice. He that managed to achieve both peace and justice would be worthy of many honors.

We also have emphasized the tragic side of politics and the limits of statesmanship. Politics operates in the realm of human choice. Tragedy, itself a product of human choices, naturally finds its way into man's political activities. Churchill recognized that the follies that lead states into life-and-death struggles with other states are exhibitions of tragedy that are not all that uncommon to human experience. Despite the desire for peace in the 1930s, the states of Europe nonetheless behaved in such a manner that soon made war inevitable. With a little foresight and the right policies, Churchill believed, the nations of Europe might have retained their peace. The tragedy resulting from the second world war could be found in the nature of the peace that followed. After their shining victory, the allied countries were faced with yet more years of struggle and uncertainty as to their well-being and safety.

Tragedy is almost too strong a description of what occurred during and after the war (in as far as tragedy results from human choice rather than simple misfortune), as there was very little that could have been done by any western leader during the war to stem the growth of Soviet influence on the Continent. Nonetheless, Churchill accepted these realities perhaps more easily than others, for he believed that it was possible for western statesmen to improve the conditions at home and repair their position vis-á-vis the East.

Churchill's understanding of international politics went far beyond balance-of-power notions. What he saw was a colorful mosaic, a world of many states, each of which had distinctive institutions, political objectives, and moral qualities. He saw states as "heaving, thrusting, pulsating organisms which think and act with purpose." Balance-of-power diplomacy had been an integral part of successful British foreign policy for many decades,[2] and Churchill by no means intended to do away with a helpful tool for keeping the peace in the twentieth century. But Churchill, believing that the outcome of the second world war concerned not "mere matters of the balance of power," refused to abstract from questions of right and wrong in international politics. The "salvation" of the world relied upon recognizing the benefits available to the vast number of nations when countries gave their discriminating support to "liberal nations with free parliamentary institutions"—nations that were, in his view, inherently peaceful.[3]

To abstract from regime characteristics, as some "systems theorists" are wont to do,[4] entails a gross form of reductionism, that is, the reduction of state motivations to their lowest common denominator—that of survival and "power" considerations. In this way, all states can be treated as "like units." While survival is a prerequisite for all states, states also act and shape foreign policies to satisfy other ambitions (to promote democratic principles, secure markets, promote national liberations, acquire land, spread the revolution, etc.) and they do so often while jeopardizing their survival and national interests. Indeed, there would be no such phenomenon as war if states were unwilling to risk their survival. According to Raymond Aron, "all great states have jeopardized their survival to gain ulterior objectives.... It would be useless to define the objectives of states by exclusive reference to power, to security, or to both. What life does not serve a higher goal? What good is security accompanied by mediocrity."[5] To conclude that Churchill understood international life otherwise would be to misinterpret him radically. Estimations and assessments of state behavior according to mere balance-of-power notions were essential for the conduct of his affairs, but at the same time these theories clearly were deficient.

Churchill distinguished among political orders according to the degree to which they permitted liberty to flourish internally. He cherished the liberal democratic regimes in the West for their establishment of law, their acknowledgement that political men are the servants of the people, and the institutional protections they offer to individuals. He despised the communist regimes, for they operated on principles that were in every way the opposite of those he valued. According to Churchill, "[t]hose that dwell under totalitarian dictatorships are gripped by an all-pervading apparatus of propaganda and compulsion which welds them into a State machine primarily adapted to war."[6] Decent political orders, he believed, had to recognize first the dangers of a radically heterogeneous international order and then take the necessary defensive and diplomatic measures to preserve what they had. The chances for a true peace, therefore, rested on the hope that the liberal democracies would hold the upper hand in any contest of power. This thought was the cornerstone of his campaign for peace after the second world war.

The problems facing the Grand Alliance in World War II were fundamental, rooted in the nature of the states that comprised it. The coalition, and hence the foundation for postwar cooperation, had been ill-grounded; for the unity that was inspired by the collective hatred of Nazi Germany disintegrated at the moment of victory. Churchill eagerly embraced his new Soviet ally when Hitler turned his forces against the East, forgiving practically all that had been said and done in the past. The first order of business was to survive and to beat down the aggressors. It was during these war years that Churchill warmed to the idea of an international order wherein all the major powers settled their disputes peaceably and cooperated on all major problems. Such conditions, he believed, would offer the best chance of avoiding a third world war.

Throughout the war, Churchill demonstrated his attachment to the principles of liberty, political sovereignty, honor, and safety. His principles led him to dispute Stalin on several matters. The sovereignty of Poland and the eventual lifting of the oppression from the remaining occupied countries of Eastern and Central Europe were first upon his mind. On these questions he often collided with Stalin. For this reason, the Yalta Agreement is perhaps most illuminating for the light it shed on the fundamental differences on both sides.

Despite Churchill's efforts to give the western democracies more of a say in the postwar negotiations through the achievement of an advantageous military position in Europe (his Balkans campaign being just one example of his efforts), none of the western allied forces were in a position to prevent the colonization of Eastern Europe. The only remedy that remained, short of another war, was negotiation and the acceptance, on faith, that sovereignty and liberty would be respected by the Soviet leaders. Churchill's acceptance of the Yalta accords was, therefore, not a sign that he had lost his convictions or that Stalin had been dealing with a gullible man. It meant only that he was playing from a very poor hand.

Much of Churchill's good-natured rhetoric toward Stalin during the war was intended to keep the disintegrating Alliance together. But the war vastly changed the correlation of forces in the international system; the Soviet Union was the new land power in Eurasia and its leaders had an agenda quite different from Churchill's. Despite his hatred of communism, he believed that tremendous efforts had to be made by political men in all countries to overcome political differences as best they could, or at least to find common ground upon which outstanding questions might be addressed. He believed the circumstances that forced the Alliance into being could have laid the ground for the development of easier international relations. Interest in peace and security brought East and West together to fight a war. Could it not also give shape to a viable union during peacetime?

Churchill's actions and thoughts, as they have come down to us through his written and spoken words, teach us about one of man's most noble activities: statesmanship. Statesmanship at its highest point of excellence is governing according to sound principles and for the benefit and improvement of the political community. The end of politics is the good of man, and therefore statesmanship also is concerned about the well-being and improvement of like-minded states. After all, the decisions of the statesman may affect many millions, and so his responsibilities, his burdens, and his awards can be immense. Thus, according to Aristotle,

even if the good [achieved by politics] is the same for the individual and the state, the good of the state clearly is the greater and more perfect thing to attain and to safeguard. The attainment of the good for one man alone is, to be sure, a source of satisfaction, yet to secure it for a nation and for states is nobler and more divine.[7]

The activity of the statesman entails the application of universal principles (such as liberty, individual security, or the security of the liberty-loving states) to particular circumstances. Churchill's postwar activities, perhaps best encapsulated and expressed in his Fulton address, were directed to attaining the highest good for the western democracies: security in the face of a growing threat from the East; the protection of liberty and the nurturing of the conditions of freedom in lands where liberty was threatened or did not exist; and fraternity among the English-speaking peoples—a supreme action that would further the cause of safety as well as liberty.

In Fulton on March 5, 1946, Churchill announced the existence of some very disheartening facts to the free world's new leading defender, the United States, and sought to persuade his American audience to adopt a new strategy in response to the increasingly gloomy developments in Europe. On the one hand he pressed upon his audience the need for unity and strength in the face of the growing Soviet menace. Collective strength could best be fashioned by the establishment of a fraternal association between the United States and Great Britain, two countries that shared common principles and heritage. The establishment of other international institutions and collectivities, such as a world organization and the unification of Europe, also would have served as the basis of a new collective alliance to protect liberty and promote the virtues of democracy.

On the other hand, Churchill also called for negotiations with Britain's former ally, the Soviet Union. A settlement of some of the major differences would lead to an easing of relations, Churchill emphasized, and perhaps to the reintroduction of the Soviet Union back into the "community of nations." Churchill desired to establish peace on a firmer foundation, one that would allow western ideals to flourish, one that would protect the liberty and property of the common man and his family.

Churchill's postwar career was dedicated to "winning the peace," the fullest opportunity for which was denied him when the British electorate voted his Party out of the leadership in July 1945. The paradoxical strategy he developed entailed military preparedness and openness to diplomatic opportunity—prudent confrontation and confident cooperation.

Churchill feared that the free countries would find themselves without a persistent and coherent foreign policy. He often lectured his allies and his countrymen that it was the obligation of all western leaders to arm their countries either to deter or to meet the eventuality of war. For this reason, Churchill embraced Truman's containment strategy as essential to the safety and prosperity of the West. The containment policy and the Marshall Plan signaled to the world that the United States had assumed the major share of the responsibility for maintaining international order, thereby lifting a tremendous burden from the shoulders of an impoverished and weakened Great Britain.

New threats were ranged against the West and the stakes in the postwar contest never seemed greater in these early years. Ambitious attempts were made by Moscow to divide the fledgling and still developing western military alliance. The Red Army stood at Europe's doorstep; indeed, they stood inside the threshold. Without unity and military strength, Churchill knew, the liberal democracies would be in no position to either fend off communist incursions into the West or bargain with the Soviet Union. Without such leverage, the chances that a more lasting peace could be achieved were slim.

Churchill's policy to remedy the Cold War seemingly operated on contradictory exertions.[8] But once the "essential basis" for peace had been established, once the liberal political orders had put themselves onto an equal or superior military footing vis-á-vis their enemies, he believed new inroads could be made on the diplomatic side. Churchill knew there were moral imperatives to make every effort to explore this route since his diplomacy may have meant the difference between war and peace. He was convinced that the solution lay in the discovery of what was in the Russian national interest.

Churchill not only desired to ease international relations with his appeal to Soviet interest through trade inducements, the enticement of normal relations with their neighbors, and greater prosperity for their people. Churchill also desired to change the composition of the Soviet Union with his foreign policy. He was, on one level, an advocate for better relations with the Soviet Union as it existed and, on another level, a subversive of that same order. If he could persuade the Soviet leaders to believe that new economic and foreign policies were in their best interest, there was then the *likelihood* that the new Soviet behavior would change gradually the character of the regime to one that was less interested in worldwide revolution. Why, after all, would Moscow want to overturn the very international system that was providing the Soviet people with a better standard of living than they had ever known? If they could accept the status quo, there would be no need to act disruptively. This was the surest method, Churchill believed, for introducing the world to a calmer and kindlier age.

If Churchill is to be criticized for his diplomatic initiative, it would be for his failure to acknowledge that statesmanship does have its limitations. That is, perhaps the appeal to Russian interest did not move deeply enough to affect the mainsprings of the communist system. Clearly, the achievement of "peace and plenty" would be desired by the Soviet people and possibly even the Soviet leadership. However, perhaps peace and plenty were not their ruling motivations?

In April 1953, Churchill noted that at the end of the war, he "could not understand why Soviet Russia did not join with the western Allies in seeking a just and lasting treaty of peace."[9] Instead, he observed, they exhibited a "measureless ambition" to expand their doctrine and power. It is indeed possible that Churchill had been confused by his own limitless desire for peace and prosperity in the world, and that given the apparent desperate conditions that the Soviet people lived under, he attributed ideals to the Soviet leaders that did not exist. It was very unlikely, especially during Stalin's reign, that a settlement, once agreed to, would have affected significantly the power base of the Communist Party, or induced a people still imbued with the ideals of communism, still ruled by "the man of steel," to embrace their enemies. Indeed, the exhibition of measureless ambition could be said to be at the very center of the communist soul; for revolution was the Communist's goal, and not the maintenance of the status quo. In an international system where the main reasons for the conflict could be sought in the very character of the regimes that dominated that world, how could it be expected that these two opposing parties could coexist in a mutually beneficial give-and-take relationship? Experience has shown, to the contrary, the willingness of the Soviet leadership to sacrifice internal prosperity and cozy relations with their neighbors for the fruits of aggression and the support of revolutions and "national liberation movements" around the world. Political or ideological goals, in other words, account for much when one is searching for an understanding of state behavior.

Churchill also may be criticized for the value he placed on negotiations. He once said that "[i]t is not easy to see how things could be worsened by a parley at the summit, if such things were possible."[10] In the debate over his May 11,

Conclusion

1953 initiative recounted above, some members of the Commons voiced their concern that such talks could have led to the further undermining of Great Britain's security position in the world; for the Soviet negotiators were known to be rather adept at their practice. In other words, it is not so much the actual "parley" that worried his colleagues, but rather the consequences of those talks. The ultimate outcome could have made for a more dangerous situation than the Cold War situation that existed previously.

The above criticisms alone, while significant for the light they shed on the nature of communism and the problems with which statesmen are confronted in their dealings with communist regimes, cannot provide a proper assessment of Winston Churchill's own statesmanship. Churchill decided after the war to confront the imperatives of ideology with the imperatives of peace and the new international situation. He believed that it was wrong to "take an over-sanguine view of the [settlement] position whatever efforts [were] made." He declared, however, that it was "our Christian duty to try our best."[11] Clearly he did recognize that statesmanship had its limits. However, he also recognized that his limitations were less than those that restrained average political men.

Churchill had his own principles to guide him, as has been demonstrated throughout this book. Many of those he summed up in the following passage from his *Marlborough: His Life and Times*: "It is not given to princes, statesmen, and captains to pierce the mysteries of the future.... One rule of conduct alone survives as a guide to men in their wanderings: fidelity to covenants, the honour of soldiers, and the hatred of causing human woe."[12] This gentleman's code of conduct, admirable for its simplicity and the self-evident truths it conveys, is an adequate guide, in general, for statesmen. It conveys the decent objectives of good men everywhere. However, like any code of ethics, even the firmest principles may be subject to modification if the situation warrants it. If more good can be done by breaking a covenant, then there could be plausible and even honorable grounds for doing so.[13] Therefore, a worthy measure of a statesman is his ability to apply his principles judiciously, according to the circumstances, for the benefit of the people he governs. Such strictures as those listed above are but rough guides and hardly the last word on human conduct in the international sphere.

Churchill's judgment and actions during and after the war demonstrated that he had such a complex understanding of political ethics. Churchill argued against adhering to what he called the "lawyer's agreement" made in Quebec between Great Britain and the United States regarding the Allied invasion of Europe. It was an agreement made in advance of the circumstances, one that he believed ought to have been amended to fit new conditions and to integrate new military strategies (such as his Balkan strategy). Similarly, Churchill deplored the American withdrawal from Central Europe simply on the reasoning that it was agreed upon at an earlier date. Wrote Churchill in his *Triumph and Tragedy*:

It is not permitted to those charged with dealing with events in times of war or crisis to confine themselves purely to the statement of broad general principles on which good people agree. They have to take definite decisions from day to day. They have to adopt postures which must be solidly maintained, otherwise how can any combinations for action be maintained?[14]

The world to Churchill was complex and manifested competing moral claims. He believed that there were two factors that had to be employed prudently by statesmen in order to account properly for that complexity. "One—Time—Do not throw away time. There are lots of things that seem impossible but it can be worked out given time; and two—Vigilance—Eternal vigilance that is needed to guard the freedom of the world against the intolerable philosophy of Communism."[15] Time is important because circumstances change. Changes in the make-up or attitude of the communist bloc, or changes in the attitude or military position of the liberal democracies, could have created opportunities to fashion a new peace. For the first time in forty-five years, the world in 1990 could envision an end to the Cold War and a new era in international relations. There is little doubt that the hopes nourished by Churchill in 1953 were based on such an understanding of time and change. But Churchill was not reckless either. He constantly warned the free states to keep up their guard. His past experience and the lessons taught to him by history informed him that decent states easily can fall prey to the more aggressive states. Time and vigilance, as significant factors in a state's foreign policy, came together for Churchill in a coherent strategy, a two-pincer strategy to meet the novel threats of the twentieth century.

It is therefore unfair to write that "[i]t seems that neither Churchill nor FDR had given sufficient attention to the precarious nature of their relationship with the calculating Stalin."[16] As was demonstrated in Chapter three, Churchill was fully aware of the precarious position of the Grand Alliance and that he strove to place the western allies on a better footing by the end of the war in order to facilitate negotiations. The principle of "peace through strength" was his guide throughout the postwar period precisely because he recognized the exploitative, Machiavellian character of the Soviet leaders and the character of the struggle facing the West.

Churchill's moderation as a statesman was demonstrated by his recognition of the differences between East and West as essentially unbridgeable. The Soviet attitude toward their people disturbed him.[17] Thus, he recognized that an appeal made to the Soviet leaders in the interest of the Soviet people probably would be of limited value. Churchill admitted in his postwar memoirs, after all, that he did not fully understand the Soviet regime, that it was "a riddle wrapped in a mystery inside an enigma."

He did not find this justification enough, however, to cease all diplomatic efforts to fashion an acceptable peace. It did not mean that men should lose faith and that attitudes could not change. Russian interest, he believed, may have been the key to exploit the new opportunities manifested after Stalin's death. It may have been the key to the reconciliation of Soviet security interests and freedom. As long as moderation was one element in western diplomacy, as long as a proper perspective of the stakes involved was kept in the forefront of any

Conclusion

diplomatic initiative, Churchill did not believe that efforts to bridge the gap between East and West would come to any harm. As he often stressed, "we must not place undue hopes upon the success of any negotiations which may be undertaken." It was, however, the "duty" of all involved to make every effort for "the cause of peace."[18] Hardly one to believe in the inevitability of a peace between East and West, Churchill confessed that a permanent peace was in many ways (although not entirely) out of the control of men, and that men ought to "pray for it."[19]

Recognizing that politics and statesmanship have their natural limits (limits that are not always perceptible), must we not also recognize the limits of ideology? The experience of Soviet leader Mikhail Gorbachev, a legendary reformer in his own time (though perhaps not as radical a reformer as his successors), is a lesson to all who believed in the immutability of Marxist-Leninist ideology. Indeed, the final years leading to the August 1991 coup and the December 1991 dissolution of the USSR exhibited a gradual deterioration in the forces sustaining the ideology. The historic and revolutionary events of the early 1990s were evidence of Churchill's deep insight into fundamental problems of government organized on the despotic principles of communism. Change within these gloomy political orders proved possible; statesmen of the present and the future, therefore, must not lose their patience or their vigilance. Churchill's advice to political men, not to succumb to despair, holds much more meaning today than it did when he attempted to fashion a new peace out of the paltry materials available to him in the 1940s and 1950s.

As events played themselves out over the decades, it is not difficult to conclude that many of Churchill's insights into the nature of state relations and the chances for peace between East and West were fairly accurate. The world historic events centering around the collapse of communism are testimony to the most successful peacetime military alliance between free states in the history of man. International institutions like NATO and the UN organization and those that encouraged western unity were championed by Churchill as essential components of a more ordered international system. His dream was to "contrive a system and practice to resolve [international] disputes and settle them peacefully."[20] The Western alliance succeeded, by and large, in containing communism to where it already existed in the hope that it would one day die out of its own accord. It also succeeded in preventing the catastrophic third world war about which Churchill frequently warned.

The collapse of the Soviet system of government also helps to shed some light on the origins of the Cold War. Throughout the history of the Cold War, the chance for a principled reconciliation between East and West was practically nonexistent. Many in the West, including Churchill, knew that the relationship would improve only following a change in the character of the Soviet regime. With the collapse of the Soviet Union, failure of communism, and the concomitant rise of political men sensitive to *Russian* national interests, relations between the capitals of the western democracies and Moscow have improved beyond all expectations. These cheery events indicate quite emphatically that measureless Soviet ambitions, rather than western intransigence (allegedly anchored by Churchill's Fulton speech), rightly may be held accountable for the chilly atmosphere of the postwar years.

In the end, Churchill, did not compromise the security of the West with his diplomatic initiatives. He did not transgress political limits to the point were the free states were endangered or would have been endangered by his activities. For him, negotiations and diplomacy were not a substitute for the peace and freedom won by the liberal democracies in the last war. It was the folly of his countrymen that Churchill consistently warned of and fought against. Thus, it would be difficult to argue convincingly that he was unable to grasp the serious consequences of reckless behavior, or to argue that he did not have a sense of the limits of such behavior.

Churchill's postwar statesmanship attempted to add justice to the peace that was won by the triumph over despotism in 1945. He sought to utilize the interests and sense of honor of the Soviet leaders to accomplish this feat. Churchill once made the remark in a conversation about human mortality and man's short time on earth: "We are all worms. But I do believe that I am a glowworm." Despite his failure to achieve a lasting settlement, it may be said that only a man of Churchill's confidence, competence, common sense, and sense of history could have embarked on such a mission.[21]

Winston Churchill believed that democratic statesmen ought to exhibit an unyielding confidence in their purpose and dedication to their duties. Such a bearing was vital to the existence and prosperity of democracy itself. "[T]he democracies of the West must be constantly convinced that those who lead them do not despair of peace if they are to take even the measures which self-preservation demands in case the worst should come to the worst."[22] For this, Churchill's political career after the war deserves the sort of praise and appreciation he received before that time from people the world around.

NOTES

1. Churchill, *Complete Speeches*, p. 8,473.
2. See Churchill, *The Age of Revolution*, p. 286.
3. See Churchill, *The Gathering Storm*, pp. 208 and 275, and Gilbert, *Never Despair*, p. 25.
4. See Kenneth Waltz, for example, *Theory of International Politics* (Reading, MA: Addison-Wesley Publishing Company, 1979). Waltz attempted to discredit any approach to understanding state behavior that gave heavy consideration to regime characteristics (i.e., liberal or illiberal, moderate or revolutionary, democratic or tyrannical) because "systems-level [i.e., the level of the international system where analysts interpret the balance of power] causes become entangled with unit-level [state-level] causes and the latter tend to dominate" (p. 45). By remaining at the level of the system in attempting to understand international politics, Waltz rendered himself incapable of explaining the twentieth century. This century has witnessed the age of ideology (a factor that is only to be found at the state level). "Traditional

diplomacy" also did not characterize the twentieth century. While there is persistence in the international system, there is also a wealth of state activity and other international forces that supplement and affect those activities caused by the international structure itself.

5. Aron, *Peace and War*, p. 598. Churchill once said that a "nation without a conscience is a nation without a soul. A nation without a soul is a nation that cannot live" (*London Times*, September 17, 1951, p. 4).

6. Churchill, *Step By Step* (December 1937), p. 167.

7. Aristotle, *Nichomachean Ethics*, pp. 4 and 5. See also p. 153: Statesmen, men of practical wisdom, "have the capacity of seeing what is good for themselves and for mankind, and these are . . . the qualities of men capable of managing . . . states."

8. Churchill often addressed the charge that he was an inconsistent politician with the observation that he who stood behind his principles, even though he may change policies or parties to address a particular problem, was a man who demonstrated true consistency. He also had this observation: "I think a statesman in responsible office shows courage rather than inconsistency in changing his mind if he is convinced that his country's safety and freedom are involved" (Churchill, *Complete Speeches*, p. 8,605). He also believed that "it is better to be both right and consistent. But if you have to choose—you must choose to be right" (Churchill, *Complete Speeches*, p. 8,414).

9. Churchill, *Complete Speeches*, p. 8,470.

10. Churchill, *Complete Speeches*, p. 7,949.

11. Churchill, *Complete Speeches*, p. 7,985.

12. Churchill, *Marlborough*, bk. 2, p. 996.

13. While the first principle in this list may lend itself to violation once in a rare while, the remaining two, faithful adherence to honor and hatred of causing human misery appear to be inviolable. I can think of no circumstances in which a statesman would profit by acting dishonorably or behaving sadistically on a grand scale.

14. Churchill, *Triumph and Tragedy*, p. 402.

15. Cited by Gilbert, *Never Despair*, p. 1,004. The fact that Churchill considered the communist philosophy "intolerable" demonstrated his belief that mankind had an obligation to confront it always and to alter or destroy it wherever possible.

16. Morton Frisch argued that Churchill's overweening desire to secure a peaceful agreement immediately after the war led him to be hoodwinked by Stalin at Yalta; he argued that Churchill placed too much confidence in the strength of covenants and treaties. Frisch, "The Diplomacy and Statecraft of Roosevelt and Churchill," p. 238.

17. See, for example, Churchill, *Complete Speeches*, p. 8,138.

18. Churchill, *Complete Speeches*, p. 8,143.

19. Churchill, *Complete Speeches*, p. 8,625.

20. Churchill, *Complete Speeches*, p. 8,683.

21. Churchill was a man who respected the judgment of history and, therefore, strove to leave a good name to history. He once wrote the same of his famous ancestor, the Duke of Marlborough: "There is no doubt that the desire for posthumous fame, to 'leave a good name to history', to be remembered long generations after he passed away, was in these years his strongest passion" (Churchill, *Marlborough*, bk. 2, p. 754).

22. Churchill, *Complete Speeches*, p. 7,985.

Bibliography

WORKS BY WINSTON S. CHURCHILL

Churchill, Winston S. *The Aftermath being a sequel to The World Crisis.* London: Macmillan & Co. Ltd., 1941.
_____. *Blood, Sweat, and Tears.* New York: G.P. Putnam's Sons, 1941.
_____. *The Collected Essays of Sir Winston Churchill.* 4 vols. Edited By Michael Wolff. vol. 1: *Churchill and War.* vol. 2: *Churchill and Politics.* vol. 3: *Churchill and People.* vol. 4: *Churchill At Large.* Bristol, England: Library of Imperial History, 1976.
_____. *Great Contemporaries.* London: Thornton Butterworth Ltd., 1937.
_____. *A History of the English Speaking Peoples: The Birth of Britain.* vol. 1. New York: Dodd, Mead & Company, 1966.
_____. *A History of the English Speaking Peoples: The New World.* vol. 2. New York: Dodd, Mead & Company, 1966.
_____. *A History of the English Speaking Peoples: The Age of Revolution.* vol. 3. New York: Dodd, Mead & Company, 1967.
_____. *A History of the English Speaking Peoples: The Great Democracies.* vol. 4. New York: Dodd, Mead & Company, 1966.
_____. *Marlborough: His Life and Times.* 4 vols. in 2 bks. London: George G. Harrap & Co. Ltd., 1958.
_____. *Savrola: A Tale of The Revolution in Laurania.* New York: Random House, 1956.
_____. *The Second World War: The Gathering Storm.* vol. 1. Boston: Houghton Mifflin Company, 1948.
_____. *The Second World War: Their Finest Hour.* vol. 2. Boston: Houghton Mifflin Company, 1949.
_____. *The Second World War: The Grand Alliance.* vol. 3. Boston: Houghton Mifflin Company, 1950.
_____. *The Second World War: The Hinge of Fate.* vol. 4. Boston: Houghton Mifflin Company, 1950.
_____. *The Second World War: Closing The Ring.* vol. 5. Boston: Houghton Mifflin Company, 1951.

_____. *The Second World War: Triumph and Tragedy*. vol. 6. Boston: Houghton Mifflin Company. 1953.
_____. *Step By Step: 1936-1939*. New York: G.P. Putnam's Sons, 1939
_____. *The Story of My Life: A Roving Commission*. New York: Charles Scribner's Sons, 1941.
_____. *Thoughts and Adventures*. Long Acre, London: Odhams Press Limited, 1949.
_____. *Winston S. Churchill: Companion Volume 1; Part 2: 1896-1900*. Edited by Randolph S. Churchill. London: Heinemann, 1967.
_____. *Winston S. Churchill: His Complete Speeches*. 8 vols. Edited by Robert Rhodes James. New York: Chelsea House Publishers in association with R.R. Bowker Company, 1974.

WORKS ON WINSTON S. CHURCHILL

Ben-Moshe, Tuvia. *Churchill: Strategy and History*. Boulder, CO: Lynne Rienner Publishers, 1992.
Broad, Lewis. *Winston Churchill: The Years of Achievement*. New York: Hawthorne Books, Inc., 1963.
Cohen, Eliot A. "Churchill At War." *Commentary*, May 1987, pp. 40-49.
Colville, John. *The Fringes of Power: 10 Downing Street Diaries; 1939-1955*. New York: W.W. Norton & Company, 1985.
_____. *Winston Churchill and His Inner Circle*. New York. Wyndham Books, 1981.
Eade, Charles, ed. *Churchill by His Contemporaries*. New York: Simon and Schuster, 1954.
Fainsod, Merle. *How Russia is Ruled*. Cambridge, MA: Harvard University Press, 1963.
Frisch, Morton J. "The Diplomacy and Statecraft of Roosevelt and Churchill." *Power, Principles & Interests: A Reader in World Politics*. Edited by Jeffrey Salmon, James P. O'Leary, Richard Shultz. Lexington, MA: Ginn Press, 1985, pp. 229-240.
Gilbert, Martin. *Churchill's Political Philosophy*. Oxford: Oxford University Press, 1981.
_____. *Winston S. Churchill: The Stricken World; 1916-1922*, vol. 4. Boston: Houghton Mifflin Company, 1975.
_____. *Winston S. Churchill: Finest Hour; 1939-1941*, vol. 6. Boston: Houghton Mifflin Company, 1983.
_____. *Winston S. Churchill: Road To Victory; 1941-1945*, vol. 7. Boston: Houghton Mifflin Company, 1986.
_____. *Winston S. Churchill: Never Despair; 1945-1965*, vol. 8. Boston: Houghton Mifflin Company, 1988.
_____. *Winston Churchill: The Wilderness Years*. Boston: Houghton Mifflin Company, 1982.
Harbutt, Fraser J. *The Iron Curtain: Churchill, America, and the Origins of the Cold War*. New York: Oxford University Press, 1986.
Lord Moran. *Churchill: Taken from the Diaries of Lord Moran; The Struggle for Survival 1940-1965*. Boston: Houghton Mifflin Company, 1966.

Loewenheim, Francis L., Harold D. Langley, and Manfred Jonas, ed. *Roosevelt and Churchill: Their Secret Wartime Correspondence*. New York: Saturday Review Press/E.P. Dutton & Co., Inc., 1975.
Manchester, William. *The Last Lion: Winston Spencer Churchill; Alone: 1932-1940*. Boston: Little, Brown and Company, 1988.
Nixon, Richard. *Leaders*. Chapter 2: "Winston Churchill: The Largest Human Being of Our Time." New York: Warner Books, 1982.
Smith, Charles Roger. "Winston Churchill and the Rise of Totalitarianism: Statesmanship and the Challenge of Modern Tyranny." Ph.D. dissertation, The Catholic University of America, Washington, DC, 1982.
Stansky, Peter., ed. *Churchill: A Profile*. New York: Hill and Wang, 1973.
Taylor, A.J.P., Robert Rhodes James, J.H. Plumb, Basil Liddell Hart and Anthony Storr. *Churchill Revisited: A Critical Assessment*. New York: The Dial Press, Inc., 1969.
Thompson, Kenneth W. *Winston Churchill's World View: Statesmanship and Power*. Baton Rouge, LA: Louisiana State University Press, 1983.
Young, Kenneth. *Churchill & Beaverbrook: A Study in Friendship and Politics*. London: Eyre & Spottiswoode, 1966.

OTHER SOURCES

Acheson, Dean. *Present At The Creation*. New York: W.W. Norton & Company, 1969.
Adamthwaite, Anthony. "Overstretched and Overstrung: Eden, the Foreign Office and the Making of Policy, 1951-5." *International Affairs* (UK), Spring 1988, pp. 241-259.
Aristotle. *The Nicomachean Ethics*. Translated by Martin Oswald. Indianapolis: Bobbs-Merrill Educational Publishing, 1979.
_____. *The Politics*. Translated by Carnes Lord. Chicago: The University of Chicago Press, 1984.
_____. *Rhetoric and Poetics*. Translated by W. Rhys Roberts and Ingram Bywater. New York: The Modern Library, 1954.
Aron, Raymond. *The Century of Total War*. Garden City, NY: Doubleday & Company, Inc., 1954.
_____. *The Committed Observer: Interviews with Jean-Louis Missika and Dominique Wolton*. Translated by James and Marie McIntosh. Chicago: Regnery Gateway, 1983.
_____. *Peace and War: A Theory of International Relations*. Translated by Richard Howard and Annette Baker Fox. Garden City, NY: Doubleday & Company, Inc., 1966.
Barzini, Luigi. *The Europeans*. New York: Simon and Shuster, 1983.
Beloff, Nora. *Tito's Flawed Legacy: Yugoslavia and the West; 1939 to 1984*. London: Victor Gollancz Ltd., 1985.
Berlin, Isaiah. "Political Ideas in the Twentieth Century." *Foreign Affairs*. vol. 28, no. 3. April 1950, pp. 351-385.
Birch, A.H. *The British System of Government*. New York: Frederick A. Praeger, 1967.
Brodie, Bernard. *War and Politics*. New York: MacMillan Publishing Co., Inc., 1973.

Bullock, Alan. *Ernest Bevin: Foreign Secretary.* New York: W.W. Norton & Company, 1983.
Burke, Edmund. *Reflections on the Revolution in France and The Rights of Man by Thomas Paine.* Garden City, NY: Doubleday & Company, 1961.
_____. *Selected Writings and Speeches.* Edited by Peter J. Stanlis. Chicago: Regnery Gateway, 1963.
Charlton, Michael. *The Eagle and the Small Birds: Crisis in the Soviet Empire; from Yalta to Solidarity.* Chicago: The University of Chicago Press, 1984.
Clausewitz, Carl von. *On War.* Edited and Translated by Michael Howard and Peter Paret. Princeton, NJ: Princeton University Press, 1976.
Djilas, Milovan. *Conversations with Stalin.* New York: Harcourt Brace Jovanovich, 1962.
Dougherty, James E. and Robert L. Pfaltzgraff. *Contending Theories of International Relations: A Comprehensive Study.* New York: Harper & Row, Publishers, 1981.
Eden, Anthony. *Full Circle.* Taipei, Taiwan: Cave Books Co., 1959.
Eisenhower, Dwight D. *Crusade in Europe.* Garden City, NY: Doubleday & Company, Inc., 1948.
Feis, Herbert. *Churchill, Roosevelt, Stalin.* Princeton, NJ: Princeton University Press, 1957.
Hamilton, Alexander, James Madison and John Jay. *The Federalist Papers.* Edited by Clinton Rossiter. NY: The New American Library, Inc., 1961.
Heller, Mikhail and Alexander Nekrich. *Utopia in Power. A History of the Soviet Union from 1917 to the Present.* Translated by Phyllis B. Carlos. NY: Summit Books, 1986.
Johnson, Paul. *Modern Times: The World from the Twenties to the Eighties.* New York: Harper & Row, 1983.
Kissinger, Henry A. *A World Restored: Metternich, Castlereagh and the Problem of Peace; 1812-1822.* Boston: Houghton Mifflin Company, Sentry Edition 1979.
_____. *American Foreign Policy.* New York: W.W. Norton & Company, 1977.
Lincoln, Abraham. *The Collected Works of Abraham Lincoln.* vols. 4 and 5. Edited by Roy P. Basler. New Brunswick, NJ: Rutgers University Press, 1953.
Lippmann, Walter. *U.S. Foreign Policy: Shield of the Republic.* Boston: Little, Brown and Company, 1943, p. 164.
Locke, John. *Two Treatises of Government and Robert Filmer Patriarcha.* Edited by Thomas I. Cook. New York: Hafner Publishing Company, 1966.
Lord, Carnes. "American Strategic Culture." *Comparative Strategy.* vol. 5, no. 3. pp. 269-293.
Montesquieu, Baron de. *The Spirit of the Laws.* Translated by Thomas Nugent. New York: Hafner Publishing Company, 1949.
Morgenthau, Hans J. *Politics Among Nations: The Struggle for Power and Peace.* New York: Alfred A. Knopf, 1978.
Nathan, James A. and James K. Oliver. *United States Foreign Policy and World Order.* 2nd edition. Boston: Little, Brown and Company, 1981.
Neumann, William L. *After Victory: Churchill, Roosevelt, Stalin and the Making of the Peace.* New York: Harper & Row, Publishers, 1967.
Nisbet, Robert. *Roosevelt and Stalin: The Failed Courtship.* Washington, DC: Regnery Gateway, 1988.

Nye, Joseph S., Jr., Graham T. Allison and Albert Carnesale. *Fateful Visions: Avoiding Nuclear War.* Cambridge, MA: Ballinger Publishing Company, 1988.
Parliamentary Debates. *Hansard.* vols. 420, 423, 427, 446, 459, 464, 473, 477, 482, 493, 495, 498, 502, 505, 515, 520, 522, 524, 526, 530. London: Her Majesty's Stationery Office.
Pipes, Richard. *Survival Is Not Enough: Soviet Realities and America's Future.* New York: Simon and Schuster, 1984.
Plato. *The Republic.* Translated by Allan Bloom. New York: Basic Books Inc., 1968.
Ponomaryov, B., A. Gromyko and V. Khostov., ed. *History of Soviet Foreign Policy: 1945-1970.* Translated by David Shirvsky. Moscow: Progress Publishers, 1974.
Solzhenitsyn, Alexander. *The Gulag Archipelago: 1918-1956; An Experiment in Literary Investigation.* vol. 1. Translated by Thomas P. Whitney. New York: Harper & Row, Publishers, 1974.
Solzhenitsyn, Alexander. *The Mortal Danger: How Misconceptions About Russia Imperil America.* New York: Harper & Row, Publishers, 1981.
Sowell, Thomas. "Visions of War & Peace." *Encounter.* December 1987, pp. 40-49.
Strauss, Leo and Joseph Cropsey., ed. *History of Political Philosophy.* Chicago: The University of Chicago Press, 1987.
Thurow, Glen E. and Jeffrey D. Wallin. ed. *Rhetoric and American Statesmanship.* Durham, NC: Carolina Academic Press and The Claremont Institute for the Study of Statesmanship and Political Philosophy, 1984.
Tocqueville, Alexis de. *Democracy in America.* 2 volumes in 1. Edited by J.P. Mayer and Max Lerner. Translated by George Lawrence. New York: Harper & Row, Publishers, 1966.
Tolstoy, Nikolai. *The Secret Betrayal: 1944-1947.* New York: Charles Scribner's Sons, 1977.
_____. *Stalin's Secret War.* NY: Holt, Rinehart and Winston, 1981.
Treadgold, Donald W. *Twentieth Century Russia.* Chicago: Rand McNally & Company, 1964.
Ulam, Adam. *Expansion and Coexistence: Soviet Foreign Policy, 1917-73.* 2nd edition. New York: Holt, Rinehart and Winston, Inc., 1974.
Urban, George R., ed. *Stalinism: Its Impact on Russia and the World.* Cambridge, MA: Harvard University Press, 1986.
Waltz, Kenneth N. *Man, the State and War: A Theoretical Analysis.* NY: Columbia University Press, 1959.
_____. *Theory of International Relations.* Reading, MA: Addison-Wesley Publishing Company, 1979.
Wilmot, Chester. *The Struggle for Europe.* St. James Place, London: Collins, 1952.
Woodhouse, C.M. *British Foreign Policy Since The Second World War.* London: Hutchinson & Co., 1961.

Index

Abysinnia, 34
Adenauer, Konrad, 141-144, 158n
Agadir crisis, 112, 113
alliance, as a tool of statesmanship, 10, 11, 35, 42
Anglo-Soviet relationship, 52, 57, 133
Aristotle, 10, 12, 13, 166; on fortune, 107n; *Nichomachean Ethics*, 10; *The Politics*, 13, 16; *The Rhetoric*, 12; on tyranny, 16, 28n, 105n, 106n, 128n
Aron, Raymond, 9, 17, 72, 73, 164
Atlantic Charter, 39, 44, 52, 59, 65, 133
Attlee, Clement, 112, 118, 122, 128n
Austria, 55, 61, 146
Austrian Treaty, 139, 143, 148

Baldwin, Stanley, 36, 37
Balkans, 38, 48-58
Baltic countries, 39, 61
battle of Stalingrad, 42, 64
Bellenger, F.J., 143
Beloff, Nora, 53
Berlin blockade, 117, 123, 144, 159n
Bermuda Conference, 145-147
Bessarabia, 39

Bolshevism, 3, 17, 19, 20, 22, 152. *See also* Churchill, Winston S., on communism; communism
Bulgaria, 48, 51, 52, 53, 55, 56, 61, 66
Burke, Edmund, 7, 76n, 88, 104n, 128n, 142

Casablanca, 58
Chamberlain, Neville, 36, 135
China, 117, 123, 124, 128n
Christianity, 13, 21, 94, 95, 106n, 116, 127n,
Churchill, John (Duke of Marlborough), 2, 12, 35, 114, 125, 132, 169, 173n
Churchill, Randolph, 53
Churchill, Winston S.: and 1945 election, 72; on A-bomb, 100, 101, 109, 137, 153, 157n, 163; and alliance with Moscow, 34, 36, 37, 40-42, 57, 68; on appeasement, 135, 161n; on balance of power, 12, 93, 99, 133, 164; Balkan strategy, 49, 50, 56; and belief in natural selection, 5n; on civilization, 57; on communism, 18-26, 30n, 40, 107n, 152; combining thought and action, 7; on cross-

channel invasion, 48, 50; on democracy, 54; on despotic regimes, 19, 28n, 29n, 91, 93; on disarmament, 81n; on division of Germany, 60; on duty of good men, 83n; economic philosophy, 21, 154, 161n; on efficient government, 14, 16, 28n; embrace of Germany, 119, 122, 144, 145, 158n, 159n; failure in Yugoslavia, 53-54; on fortune, 100, 101; and fraternal association with US, 70, 92-95, 96, 97, 109, 117-119, 122, 126n, 166; on free elections, 65; on freedom, 57; on friendship, 153; and Fulton speech, 85-104; German policy, 144; on good government, 14, 17, 18, 89, 90, 94, 148, 150, 152, 154, 165; and Greece, 54, 55; growing mistrust of Stalin, 66; in history, 2; hopes for Russia, 23, 160n; on human nature, 19, 29n; on importance of Germany, 62; interest versus principle, 37, 39; on intervention, 22, 23, 30n, 90; on justice, 76n, 135; on liberal and despotic political orders, 12-18; May 11, 1953 speech, 134, 137, 143, 146-148, 150; on military strength, 112, 114, 116, 117-125; on morality and politics, 19; on nature of settlement, 99; and negotiation from strength, 12, 24, 46, 57, 66, 69, 111, 125, 131, 136, 147, 150, 167; nonrecognition of Soviet state, 22, 33; opinion of *The God That Failed*, 30n; opposition to unconditional surrender, 59; and percentage agreement, 50, 52, 53, 70; on personal approach to diplomacy, 157n; Polish policy, 45, 46, 69, 78n; political consistency of, 2, 69, 111, 132, 133, 134, 151, 173n; and political failure, 15, 109, 112, 172; political understanding, 2; on postwar international order, 34; postwar statesmanship, 2, 3, 4, 7, 8, 33, 34, 45, 70, 85, 109, 111, 112, 115, 116, 118, 124, 131, 132, 137, 148, 149, 166, 167, 169, 170, 172; and Providence, 100; on purpose of UN, 68, 95, 96, 97, 106n, 128n; and recognition of Soviet grand strategy, 59; relationship with Stalin, 49, 73; on resistance to tyranny, 18, 24, 25, 111, 121; and rhetoric, 132; self-understanding, 10; and settlement with Moscow, 20, 70, 88, 91, 97, 99, 103, 109, 110, 114, 117, 131, 132, 134, 136, 137, 148, 160n, 161n, 163, 167, 168; settlement objectives, 148-155; on Soviet threat, 69, 72, 111, 116, 117, 157n; statesmanship, 25, 26, 70; on strength of Fulton speech, 110; and strategic vision, 70, 71; support for Germany, 144, 145; "The Dream," 28n; on U.S. retreat from eastern Germany, 61, 63, 66, 67, 117; understanding of morality and politics, 133, 134; on unity in Europe, 120-123, 155n; on unity of Grand Alliance, 77n; on war, 8-12, 26n; wartime objectives, 37; wartime statesmanship, 34, 41, 44, 48, 52, 53, 73, 74; as "warmonger," 85, 86, 104n, 128n; on world government, 128n, 129n; youth, 8

Clausewitz, Carl von, 106n
Cohen, Eliot, 65
Cold War, 2, 5, 17, 48, 85, 98, 103, 110, 112, 115, 116, 118, 124, 134, 142, 143, 167, 170, 171
collective security, 5, 11, 35
Colville, John, 40, 42, 64, 135, 141
communism, 1, 4, 5, 20, 103, 112, 133, 150, 153, 155, 165, 170, 171; and despotism, 16; excesses of, 25; and falsification, 19; nature of, 38; philosophy of, 21; similarities to Nazism, 40
Communist Manifesto, 116
constitutional government, 14, 15, 18
containment, 4, 48, 57, 58, 103, 111, 112, 115, 116, 171

Index

Crossman, R.H.S., 142, 143
Czechoslovakia, 48, 55, 61, 121

Dardenelles, 52, 57
Declaration of Liberated Europe, 44, 63, 65, 66
DeGualle, Charles, 47
democracy, 3; and foreign policy, 18; meaning of, 43; and need for vigilance, 4, 10, 91, 93, 171; and passion for law, 105n; principles of, 4, 149, 164; strength of, 35; weakness of, 93
Denikin, A.I., 23, 24
despotic regimes: definition of, 13; ends of, 15; nature of, 16, 38; and persecution of minorities, 16; and unlimited powers, 14
deterrence, 107n, 115, 135, 156n, 165; and "no first use" policy, 157n
disarmament, 9, 10, 11, 81n
Djilas, Milovan, 62, 74
Dulles, John Foster, 118, 147

East-West relationship, 33, 34, 42, 47, 48, 55, 64, 68, 74, 85, 110, 114, 116, 124, 133, 152, 170. *See also* Cold War
Eden, Anthony, 38, 40, 57, 60, 62, 63, 64, 65, 68, 71, 80n, 122, 133, 137, 146, 148
Egypt, 146
Eisenhower, Dwight, 50, 118, 123, 146, 147, 148, 151
Europe: balance of power in, 35, 38; division of, 59, 68
European Coal and Steel Community, 122
European Defense Community (EDC), 122, 140, 141, 142, 145, 146, 159n

Foot, Michael, 142, 143
France, 35, 36, 47, 49, 50, 64, 88, 119, 122, 132, 140, 147
Fraser, Hugh, 142

freedom, 3, 13; conditions of, 5, 9, 14, 47, 90, 92, 166; principles of, 90
Frisch, Morton, 172n
Fulton speech, 2, 4, 85-103, 110, 111, 117, 118, 123, 138, 142, 150, 166, 172; and action and honor, 100-103; and control of A-bomb, 87; and danger of tyranny, 87, 89; and danger of war, 87, 89, 92; and fraternal association with US, 87; and freedom, 90; and iron curtain, 87; and need for action, 93; and postwar foreign policy, 86; and postwar US role, 88; and Soviet threat, 87, 98, 99, 103, 167; and three elements of peace, 88, 95; as a call for action, 86; purpose of, 86-88, 103; resistance to in United States, 107n; importance of western unity, 88

George, Lloyd, 21-24 *passim*, 33
Germany, 3, 8, 15, 34, 35, 119, 140-143 *passim*; disarmament of, 59, 143; division of, 58, 59, 60, 61, 62; invasion of the Soviet Union, 35, 40; military character of, 80n; military power of, 11; pastoralization of, 61; postwar importance of, 61; Weimar Germany, 16, 21; West Germany, 111, 145; and World War II, 58-67
Gilbert, Martin, 9, 121, 134, 148
Gorbachev, Mikhail, 171
Grand Alliance, 3, 4, 16, 33, 36, 37, 39, 42, 46, 48, 57, 58, 60, 71, 87, 152, 163, 165, 170; Balkan aims, 56; and division of purpose, 40, 60, 71, 73, 77n, 97, 98, 110, 165
Great Britain, 2, 3, 11, 51; alliance with Moscow, 35, 41; and appeasement of Germany, 37; central European allies, 38; foreign policy, 19, 21, 22, 23,

30n, 33-40 *passim*, 46, 82n; geopolitical decline of, 70, 92, 104, 109, 114, 125-126n, 149; role in the world, 34, 64, 65, 67, 137; war aims, 35, 36, 42, 46, 51; wartime principles, 41
Greece, 48, 50, 51, 52, 53, 54, 56, 57, 79n, 87

Hague speech, 121
Harriman, Averell, 72
Hitler, Adolph: 1, 4, 8, 10, 11, 16, 34-42 *passim*, 50, 52, 58, 135, 140, 165; military objectives of, 35; reflections on Grand Alliance, 67
Hungary, 48, 51, 55, 61, 66
Hynd, John, 143

ideology, 1, 5, 8, 17, 105n, 149; limits of, 171
international relations theory, 13, 17, 27n, 28-29n, 151, 160n, 164, 172n
iron curtain, 70, 98, 103, 134, 139, 147, 153
Irvine, A.J., 143
Italy, 49, 50, 55, 56, 58, 87

Japan, 56, 57, 58, 63, 66, 71
Johnson, Paul, 118

Kennan, George, 115, 116
Khrushchev, Nikita, 153
Kissinger, Henry, 28n
Kolchak, A.V., 23
Korean war, 123, 126n, 128n, 136, 157n

law: and democracy, 12, 13, 25, 111, 165; and political order, 10; source of, 13, 27n, 28n
League of Nations, 11, 21, 22, 95, 98, 140
Lenin, V.I., 1, 16, 19-26 *passim*, 42, 138; "The Grand Repudiator," 20; as a tool of the Germans, 22

liberal regimes: and tolerance, 13; definition of, 13
liberalism, 105n
Lincoln, Abraham, 14, 37, 103
Lippmann, Walter, 3
Litvinov, M., 36, 37
Locarno Treaty, 140, 143, 145
Locke, John, 14, 89, 105n
London Naval Treaties, 67
Louis XIV, 12, 35, 39, 114

Malenkov, Georgy, 146, 147, 148, 150, 153
Marshall Plan, 118, 167
Marshall, George, 118
Marx, Karl, 20, 155
Marxism-Leninism, 149, 171
Mikolajczyk, Stanislas, 44, 64
Molotov, Vyacheslav, 37, 39, 48, 147, 148
Montesquieu, Baron de, 14, 89
Moran, 1st Baron (formerly Sir Charles Wilson), 135, 146
Morgenthau, Henry, 61
Mott-Radclyffe, C.E., 142
Mussolini, Benito, 34

Nazism, 38; and despotism, 16
Nicholson, Godfrey, 142
Noel-Baker, Philip, 141
nonaggression pact (1939), 38, 39, 44, 50
North Atlantic Treaty Organization (NATO), 5, 103, 116, 120, 122, 126n, 136, 141, 145, 147, 157n, 158n, 171
nuclear weapons, 4, 5, 100, 101, 109, 137, 153, 157n, 163
Nutting, Anthony, 142

Oder-Neisse line, 43, 143
"Overlord," 49, 50, 56

peace: elusive nature of, 12, 29n; nature of, 1, 2, 4, 8, 91, 114
Persia (Iran), 69, 87, 117, 123
Plato, 128n

Index

Pokrovsky, Mikhail, 19
Poland, 10, 22, 24, 35, 38, 39, 49, 53, 54, 57, 58, 63, 64, 65, 66, 69, 70, 73, 75, 124, 135, 140, 165; border dispute, 43, 44; Curzon line, 43, 45, 46; elections, 45-47; London Poles, 43-45, 64; loss of territory, 78n; Lublin government, 43-47, 64, 65; as "Red Bridge", 42; Soviet occupation of, 48; as "test case," 43, 46, 47, 69; Warsaw tragedy, 74, 83n; during World War II, 42-48
politics: ends of, 166; and experience, 10; and tragedy, 12, 164; unpredictability of, 9, 10
Potsdam Conference, 69

Quebec Conference, 50

Raikes, Victor, 141
Ribbentrop, Joachim von, 35
Roosevelt, Franklin D., 16, 35, 42, 45, 49, 50, 51, 56, 57, 58, 61, 62, 63, 65, 66, 79n, 170; on communism, 72; on relationship with Churchill, 72; on Soviet threat, 71; and United Nations, 68
Rumania, 48, 51, 53, 54, 55, 61, 66
Russia: 1917 revolution, 33; aggressive past of, 77n; and democracy, 20; and Peter the Great, 20; and the Asiatic despotism, 20; Czarist Russia, 20, 22; provisional government, 22; tragedy of, 20. *See also* Soviet Union

Salisbury, 5th Marquess of ('Bobbety'), 147
Savinkov, Boris, 19
science, perils of, 89, 90, 91, 105n, 151
Shaw, George Bernard, 21
Shuman Plan, 122

Shuman, Robert, 158n
Sikorski, Wladyslaw, 44
slavery, 11
Smith, Adam, 154
Solzhenitsyn, Alexander, 20, 105n
Soviet Union, 1, 3, 4, 8, 25, 26, 35, 37; alliance with, 3; ambitions of, 168; and traditional Russian goals, 43; influence in Balkans, 55; influence in Europe, 37, 42, 51, 53, 55, 56, 57, 59, 60, 63, 64, 65, 66, 71, 80n, 98, 114, 121, 125n, 164, 166, 167, 171; capture of Berlin, 60; collapse of, 153, 171; growth in military capability of, 117, 123; interest in the Balkans, 52; occupation of East Europe, 48; occupation of Poland, 44; origins of, 19; reform, 1; rising power of, 70, 126n, 127n; settlement with, 4, 34, 44, 46
Stalin, 1, 4, 5, 16, 33-52 *passim*, 138, 150, 165, 168; and Greece, 55; and second front, 48, 49, 58; and strategic vision, 71; and United Nations, 68; at Yalta, 45; death of, 139, 154, 170; intransigence on Poland, 45; ignores warning of Nazi invasion, 77n; mistrust of Germany, 62, 144, 145; on alliance with London, 41; on Cold War, 110; on Polish border, 43; opposition to Balkan strategy, 49, 50
state: behavior of, 2, 8, 9, 12, 165; inclination to peace or war, 11, 17; nature of, 13, 164. *See also* international relations theory
statesmanship, 1-11 *passim*, 19, 25, 101, 114, 116, 163, 166, 169; limits of, 8, 21, 149, 164, 168, 169, 171; potentiality of, 12

Taylor, A.J.P., 69
Tehran Conference, 43, 57, 59, 60, 73

The Federalist Papers, 14, 90
Thompson, Kenneth, 134
Tibet, 117
Tito, Josip Broz, 53
Tocqueville, Alexis de, 82n
"Torch," 49
totalitarianism, 1, 4, 17, 91, 133
Treaty of Rapallo, 38
Trotsky, Leon, 1, 19, 20, 23
Truman Doctrine, 111, 115
Truman, Harry, 69, 85, 86, 111, 115, 119, 134, 136, 137, 167
Turkey, 48, 49, 50, 56, 57, 69, 87
twentieth century politics, 8, 11, 17, 89, 105n
tyranny, 3, 10, 12, 15, 16, 18, 19, 20, 35, 39; and foreign policy, 16; objectives of, 105n

Ukraine, 49, 64
Ulam, Adam, 42, 45, 48, 71
unconditional surrender, 36, 58, 59. *See also* Casablanca
United Nations, 11, 42, 56, 60, 62, 63, 68, 76n, 87, 88, 95, 96, 99, 101, 110, 122, 123, 128n, 155, 171; purpose of, 106n, 123, 124, 128n, 129n
United States, 11, 36; affinity for USSR, 72; and isolationism, 92; as a great power, 10; Civil War, 11; Declaration of Independence, 12, 37, 117; foreign policy, 3, 30-31n, 102; geopolitical understanding of, 51, 56, 63; postwar strategy, 48; role in Europe, 64; role in the world, 70, 92, 99, 102, 120; threats to, 102; war aims, 66
Urban, George, 72

Versailles treaty, 63, 67, 98
Vietnam, 116

Wallace, Henry, 118
Waltz, Kenneth N., 27n, 172n

war: and human nature, 97; can be avoided, 2, 91, 100, 127n, 129n, 163, 164; causes of, 2, 4, 163; definition of, 12; liberal view of, 93; nature of, 8, 25; origins of, 11; total war, 91
Warsaw Treaty Organization, 145
Washington Conference on Naval Disarmament, 67
weapons, as a tool of statesmanship, 10
Wilmot, Chester, 52, 56, 60
World War I, 9, 11, 16, 21, 22, 61, 96
World War II, 2, 4, 12, 24, 99, 113, 150, 153, 164, 165; origins of, 10

Yalta Accord, 4, 46, 114, 117, 142, 165
Yalta Conference, 45, 46, 57, 63, 65, 69, 73, 118, 173n
Yeltsin, Boris, 153
Yugoslavia, 48, 50, 51, 52, 55, 61

Zurich speech, 118-120, 122

About the Author

STEVEN JAMES LAMBAKIS is Analyst at the National Institute for Public Policy with a Ph.D. in world politics from The Catholic University of America.